Triangulations

CRITICAL AMERICAN STUDIES SERIES

George Lipsitz, University of California–Santa Barbara, Series Editor

Triangulations

Narrative Strategies for Navigating Latino Identity

David J. Vázquez

University of Minnesota Press
Minneapolis
London

An earlier version of chapter 1 was published as "Jesús Colón and the Development of Insurgent Consciousness," *Centro Journal* 21, no. 1 (Spring 2009): 79–99. Published by Centro de Estudios Puertorriqueños. An earlier version of chapter 4 was published as "I Can't Be Me without My People: Julia Alvarez and the Postmodern Personal Narrative," *Latino Studies* 1, no. 3 (November 2003): 383–402.

Copyright 2011 by the Regents of the University of Minnesota

All rights reserved. No part of this publication may be reproduced, stored in a retrieval system, or transmitted, in any form or by any means, electronic, mechanical, photocopying, recording, or otherwise, without the prior written permission of the publisher.

Published by the University of Minnesota Press
111 Third Avenue South, Suite 290
Minneapolis, MN 55401-2520
http://www.upress.umn.edu

Library of Congress Cataloging-in-Publication Data

Vázquez, David J.
Triangulations : narrative strategies for navigating latino identity / David J. Vázquez.
    p. cm. — (Critical American Studies)
Includes bibliographical references and index.
ISBN 978-0-8166-7326-1 (acid-free paper)
ISBN 978-0-8166-7327-8 (pbk. : acid-free paper)
    1. American literature—Hispanic American authors—History and criticism. 2. Narration (Rhetoric)—History. 3. Identity (Psychology) in literature. 4. Hispanic Americans—Ethnic identity. 5. National characteristics, Latin American. 6. Transnationalism in literature. I. Title.
    PS153.H56V39 2011
    810.9'868073—dc22
                                                                        2010049974

The University of Minnesota is an equal-opportunity educator and employer.

Contents

Introduction. Notes on Triangulation: Navigating Latina/o Identity	1
1. Zigzagging through History: Ernesto Galarza, Jesús Colón, and the Development of Insurgent Consciousness	29
2. Crazy for the Nation: Piri Thomas, Oscar "Zeta" Acosta, and the Urban Outlaw	61
3. Remaking the Insurgent Vision: John Rechy, Judith Ortiz Cofer, and the Limits of Nationalist Morality	101
4. I Can't Be Me without My People: Triangulating Historical Trauma in the Work of Julia Alvarez	135
Conclusion. New Millennial Triangulations	171
Acknowledgments	191
Notes	195
Bibliography	217
Index	231

Introduction

Notes on Triangulation

Navigating Latina/o Identity

> *What we [authors] do might be done in solitude and with great desperation, but it tends to produce exactly the opposite. It tends to produce community and in many people hope and joy.*
>
> —Junot Díaz, *Bostonist Interview*

> *Hegemony has so constructed the ideas of method and theory that often we cannot recognize anything that is different from what the dominant discourse constructs. As a consequence, we have to look in nontraditional places for our theories: in the prefaces to anthologies, in the interstices of autobiographies, in our cultural artifacts (the cuentos).*
>
> —Sonia Saldívar-Hull, *Feminism on the Border*

Triangulating Identity in the Latina/o First-Person Personal Narrative

In Piri Thomas's 1967 autobiography *Down These Mean Streets*, the protagonist cites a curious exchange he has with Brew, his African American comrade. As a dark-skinned Puerto Rican, Piri's phenotypic similarities with Brew would indicate a likely affiliation.[1] Yet a perplexing conflict arises, setting up a fascinating negotiation of the meaning of Piri's racial identity:

> I [Piri] looked at Brew, who was as black as God is supposed to be white. "Man, Brew," I said, "you sure an ugly spook."
> Brew smiled. "Dig this Negro calling out 'spook,'" he said.
> I smiled and said, "I'm a Porty Rican."
> "Ah only sees another Negro in fron' of me," said Brew.
> This was the "dozens," a game of insults . . . (121)

While the disturbing deployment of racial stereotypes and Piri's transparent attempt to preserve privilege through their deployment betray the narrator's uneasiness with black identity, Brew's hail of Piri as a fellow Negro and Piri's deployment of "the dozens" emphasize a strategic alignment of himself and his community with African Americans.[2] At the same time, Piri rejects these terms in his assertion that he is "Porty Rican," calling attention to his inability to identify with African Americans in the ways that Brew imagines (namely in terms of the one-drop rule of racial admixture). The corrupt "Porty Rican" subjectivity to which Piri clings is also lacking, as his experience as a colonized subject living in the United States alienates him from a comfortable national identification with the island.[3] Consequently, the Puerto Rican identity Piri narrates is both African American and Puerto Rican, but neither. By counterpoising the insufficiencies of both categories, Thomas attempts to navigate a position that might be more accurately termed "Nuyorican."

While this difference may seem academic, Thomas's narrative strategies attempt to posit a Nuyorican subjectivity that has important political implications for mainland Puerto Ricans. By strategically aligning himself with African Americans, he leverages oppositional traditions that emerge out of slavery, emancipation, the civil rights movement, and black nationalism. As a figure who shares phenotypic and cultural similarities with African Americans, it is logical that Thomas would use these aspects of his racial identity to contest white supremacy. At the same time, because of the history of colonization and racialization specific to Puerto Ricans on the mainland, Piri's uneasy alliance with African American identity demands reconfiguration within a colonial context. When viewed from these perspectives, Thomas's navigation between blackness and island-based Puerto Rican nationality constitutes an attempt to locate a Nuyorican subject that accounts for *all* aspects of his racial, class, and national identities.

Thomas's case is not isolated. In fact, many Latina/o authors of the late twentieth century employ similar narrative strategies in their first-person personal narratives—a continuum of literary forms that includes memoir, autobiography, *testimonio*, autobiographical fiction, and other forms of life writing. *Triangulations* examines these narrative strategies to comprehend how Latina/o authors use existing identity categories to navigate the troubled racial waters of the United States. One of this book's central premises is that Latina/o authors engage in these triangulations to contest liberal individualist notions of identity and their accompanying racial formations.

As the title of this book indicates, the navigational technique of triangulation offers a metaphor for understanding how Latina/o authors negotiate complex identities. Mariners use mathematical triangulation to calculate physical positions and chart courses. Navigators relate an unknown position to the known location of two others by mapping an imaginary triangle. The triangle then yields coordinates for the unknown position based on the distance from and angle of the other two. It is critical that triangulation emphasizes the mathematical relationships between *all three* points of a triangle, since without all the constituent points, it is impossible to navigate. Triangulation is a dynamic technique that engages multiple way points, distances, and recalculations in the process of navigation.

While the operations employed by mariners are strictly mathematical, the relationships between two known identities (the meaning of black and white racial identities in the United States, for example) and an "unknown" one (the meaning of Puerto Rican, Chicana/o, or Latina/o subjectivities) are analogous to the processes that take place in navigational triangulation.[4] Consequently, many of the Latina/o first-person personal narrativists included in this study locate their own subject positions through an analogous triangulation of identity—often in terms of serial and progressive negation (not "this," not "that," but something other). As the example from *Down These Mean Streets* that opens this book demonstrates, the triangulations that Latina/o authors employ often contrast the complexity of their own subject positions with static conceptions of identity operative in mainstream culture.

Another aspect of my understanding of Latina/o triangulation emerges from the field of semiotics. Along with Ferdinand de Saussure and Charles Morris, Charles Sanders Peirce was a founder of semiotic theory. Where Saussure and Morris focus on general theories of sign relations, Peirce's notion of the triad deals specifically with representing relations. For Peirce, representing relations occur within a tripartite process: a "thing" (the object) is represented by another thing (the representamen) to a third thing (the interpretant). The thing (or object) is signified by the representamen so that the interpretant is subsequently determined to be another representamen of the object to another interpretant. That is, the interpretant stands in relation to the original object such that it represents it to another interpretant. The sign's sense is thus conveyed by translating meaning from one interpretant to another.

This focus on representing relations facilitates a concern with social factors in signifying processes. As a result, meaning arises out of the *relation* between a thing, a symbol, and an interpretant in the signifying process. Peirce stresses the irreducibility of the triadic nature of the sign by arguing that each component gets its sense *only* through its interrelation with the other components. Any relations that are reducible to a chain of dyadic causes and effects are not true signs. Moreover, since the sign's power to represent rests equally on each component, meaning is not "fixed" within a static position. The process of translation from one interpretant to another links semiotic relations in what might be conceived as a network of signs. Peirce argues that meaning also arises out of the dynamism *between* the constituent components, as well as the sign's relation with other signs. The process of translating meaning from one sign to another is thus at the heart of the signification process.

While this book is not based on semiotic analysis, Peirce's theory of the triad informs my understanding of Latina/o triangulations. Rather than understanding identity as fixed, I show how the self that is revealed in Latina/o first-person personal narratives emerges from relations *between* the insufficiencies of traditional identity categories. These authors attempt to navigate identity in the movement between the three points. *Triangulations* maps processes through which Latina/o subjectivity emerges in these texts from the excess of binary (self and other for example) identity positions in the United States.

The representations I consider also engage other aspects of history and culture to create an alternative concept of the self. As the quote from Thomas's autobiography that opens this introduction indicates, we cannot ignore the fact that Piri's presence in the United States is determined in part by the colonial relationship between the United States and Puerto Rico. Policies like Operation Bootstrap, the projects of Puerto Rican nationalists like Pedro Albizu-Campos, as well as the burgeoning Puerto Rican movement taking place during the period when Thomas wrote *Down These Mean Streets* in the mid-1960s, are part of the historical and cultural backdrop of the scene.[5] Unlike other hermeneutic modes that obscure these underpinnings, reading Thomas's triangulations allows us to focus on how these resonances inform his narrative strategies.

Flowing from these observations, *Triangulations* is motivated by a series of basic questions: Why do many late twentieth-century Latina/o authors use first-person personal narratives? Why does this historical period and its attendant racial ideologies require and produce first-person personal narratives? Finally, what does the first-person personal narrative illuminate or occlude? Ranging from the memoirs of Ernesto Galarza and Jesús Colón to the autobiographical fiction of Oscar "Zeta" Acosta, John Rechy, and Judith Ortiz Cofer to the historical fiction interlaced with memory and autobiography of contemporary authors like Julia Alvarez, Latina/os continue to write first-person personal narratives.[6]

In noting these dynamics it is important not to conflate the differences between texts produced during the insurgent nationalist period of the 1960s and 1970s and those written during the 1980s and beyond. Indeed, texts produced during the last two decades of the twentieth century are often oriented around a different set of cultural, social, and historical imperatives. Raphael Dalleo and Elena Machado Sáez (2005) describe differences between the literature of the 1960s and what they call "post-sixties literature" (2)—texts marked by both market success and mainstream literary acceptance. Their work evidences a desire to quantify Latina/o literature at a "crossroads," a "moment of consolidation and institutionalization for a field that has historically thought of itself as marginal and oppositional" (1). Dalleo and Machado Sáez further argue that 1960s writers are often depicted as "progressive and confrontational because of their rejection of the market and alignment with the ghetto, while the newer writers are seen as apolitical or even conservative" (2) due in part to their market success. They attempt to recuperate postsixties Latina/o literature by pointing out that "recent Latino/a literature imagines creative ways to rethink the relationship between a politics of social justice and market popularity—a combination that the critical reception denies by either rejecting one of these elements or articulating them as binary opposites" (3).

I concur with Dalleo and Machado Sáez by arguing that postsixties Latina/o literature is often motivated by political perspectives that creatively rearticulate 1960s oppositional paradigms. Rather than uncritically embracing the literary and political concerns of the insurgent nationalist period, authors like Julia Alvarez, Judith Ortiz Cofer, and Sandra Cisneros reconfigure their opposition to complicate—and at times exceed—1960s politics. This is not to uncritically embrace postsixties texts. As Dalleo and Machado Sáez acknowledge, and critics like Lisa Sánchez González (2001) more forcefully point out, postsixties texts often reinscribe hegemonic values—often in terms of class bias or "tales of upward mobility" (Dalleo and Machado Sáez, 2).[7] My position is that critics who categorically problematize postsixties texts miss some of the larger political dynamics these books encounter. While they are still influenced by and evidence the residue of the insurgent nationalist period, postsixties texts attempt to constitute opposition in the contradictory space of contemporary U.S. culture—and in particular the highly contested realm of global capital.

Moreover, where Dalleo and Machado Sáez focus primarily on establishing a contemporary canon of Latina/o literature that includes postsixties texts, my analysis centers on how these first-person personal narratives constitute identity within the shifting waters of late twentieth-century U.S. society. Accordingly, this book explores form and content as related social and political phenomena. It is my contention that the first-person personal narrative forms employed by the authors I examine are intimately connected with projects of community efficacy. They represent the self as inextricably linked with larger social structures like community and national identity.

Narrating a Matrixed Subject

Reading Latina/o autobiographies as polyvocal and socially embedded reveals a rich continuum of narrative techniques that offer multilevel critiques of individual subjectivity, community formation, and national belonging. While the idea of socially embedded autobiographical writing is not new, I argue that the authors included in this study use their first-person personal narratives to imagine completely different spaces of belonging. As Sidonie Smith and Julia Watson (2001) observe in relation to postcolonial autobiographies, aggrieved subjects often use their life narratives to explore "the decolonization of subjectivity forged in the aftermath of colonial oppression" (10). In particular, Smith and Watson note that such aggrieved subjects often represent the self as distinct from the autonomous individual typically represented in the genre of autobiography. Similarly, Susan Stanford Friedman (1998) points out that "the emphasis on individualism as the necessary precondition for autobiography" advocated by critics like Georges Gusdorf and James Olney "is thus a reflection of privilege, one that excludes from the canons of autobiography those writers who have been denied by history the illusion of individualism" (75). Stanford Friedman further asserts that "instead of seeing themselves as solely unique, women often explore their sense of shared identity with other women, an aspect of identity that exists in tension with a sense of their own uniqueness" (79). While Smith and Watson and Stanford Friedman engage women's autobiography as a distinct literary formation, I extend their arguments to my analysis because I see similar dynamics in Latina/o first-person personal narratives. Rather than representing themselves as striving for freedom from obligation to others in their communities, the interdependent representations included in this study suggest mutually dependent subjectivities that challenge doctrines of liberal individualism basic to U.S. self-imagining.

Since the first-person personal narratives this book explores emerge out of polylateral dialogues, part of what they narrate are the social relations envisioned by their authors' communities. Yet as George Lipsitz reminds us, "people cannot enact new social relations unless they can envision them. But they cannot envision new social relations credibly unless they are enacted in embryonic form in their own lives. Often cultural creation bridges these needs" (2001, 182). By understanding the triangulations they construct, it is possible to comprehend how books like Jesús Colón's *A Puerto Rican in New York*, Judith Ortiz Cofer's *The Line of the Sun*, and Julia Alvarez's *¡Yo!* create imaginative spaces where new social relations are envisioned and discursively enacted.

Unlike many canonical autobiographers like Benjamin Franklin or Henry Adams, most of the authors *Triangulations* considers turn to first-person personal narrative forms in their first books rather than after a lifetime of achievement.[8] Significantly, these authors continue to deploy first-person personal narratives, even to the exclusion of other genres. Instead of passively reporting on events in their lives, they actively shape imaginative spaces of communal belonging. As Lourdes Torres (1991) suggests in relation to Latina autobiographers, these authors often "create a new discourse which seeks to incorporate the often contradictory aspects of their gender, ethnicity, class, sexuality, and feminist politics. The radicalness of their project lies in the authors' refusal to accept any one position; rather, they work to acknowledge the contradictions in their lives and to transform difference into a source of power" (278).

While Torres confines her comments to texts by Latinas like Gloria Anzaldúa, Cherríe Moraga, and Aurora Levins Morales and Rosario Morales, I expand her analysis to Latina/os more generally. I argue that Latina/o first-person personal narratives operate on a different register than mainstream narratives of the self. By representing their selves as a function of the tension between the communal and the uniqueness of the individual, the first-person personal narrativists I examine contest the myth of autonomous individualism.

Indeed, Latina/o authors frequently use the personal narrative to mark their estrangement from hegemonic (i.e., white, male, heterosexual) subjectivity. Pointing to the ways women, ethnic and racial minorities, and postcolonial authors use life-writing genres to contest liberal individualism, Linda Anderson (2001) explains that older autobiographical traditions offer "mystificatory rhetoric obscuring the ideological underpinnings of its particular version of 'selfhood'" (4). Rather than conforming to the bourgeois subject enunciated by authors like Franklin, Adams, or Ralph Waldo Emerson, Anderson asserts that women and other aggrieved subjects use life-writing genres to highlight their exclusion from white male identity. In a similar vein this book argues that many Latina/o first-person personal narratives highlight their separation from hegemonic norms by narrating a matrixed subject.

Latina/o authors matrix their lives by representing the "I" collectively, situating individual subjectivity within the multiplicity of experiences in the autobiographer's community. Writing of the traumatic disruptions to the lives of Mexican Americans and Californios after the Treaty of Guadalupe–Hidalgo in 1848, Genaro Padilla (1993) notes that when faced with the threat of historical or physical "erasure," autobiography becomes a dominant mode of discursive resistance.[9] Padilla's suggestion aids in understanding that personal narratives often engage in "a communal utterance, a collective tale, rather than merely an individual's autobiography" (8). The collective "I" substitutes for a singular narrative identity, registering resistance at the level of history and cultural remembrance.

Katherine Gatto (2000) similarly argues that Latina writers often use autobiographical forms to register collective identities. Gatto contests the idea of the atomized individual by arguing that "her [Latina's'] fictions, not always rendered through the first-person 'I' but many times through a community of women [. . .] are nevertheless the stories of her life, the interval between birth and death" (85). While Gatto essentializes Latina identity by asserting a universal subjectivity, her point resonates with Padilla's by suggesting that Latina texts frequently operate on a collective rather than individual level.

I build on Padilla's historical work and Gatto's theorization of Latina autobiography by suggesting that twentieth-century Latina/o first-person personal narratives function as culturally matrixed portals. By representing the "I" in relation to community, the authors I examine write both as individuals and as members of aggrieved groups. By representing community politics through the autobiographical "I," they both engage and reject dynamics that govern how individuals relate with their communities. Consequently, I examine the impulses these texts evidence toward the social, taking care to note the tensions many of them represent between individuality and community empowerment.

Implicit in these impulses toward the social is a desire for political empowerment for the author and his or her community. The "I" potentially serves as a portal to new, resistant political coalitions. Over three-quarters of a century ago, Antonio Gramsci (1985) suggested that the value in autobiography lies in its ability to depict exceptional identities. These identities are exceptional because of their capacity to produce large-scale political changes. Gramsci's notion of political autobiography links the representation of an exceptional self with collective social action: "Autobiography can be conceived 'politically.' One knows that one's life is similar to that of a thousand others, but through 'chance' it has had opportunities that the thousand others in reality could not or did not have. By narrating it, one creates this possibility, suggests the process, indicates the opening. Autobiography therefore replaces the 'political' or 'philosophical essay': it describes in action what otherwise is deduced logically. Autobiography certainly has a great historical value in that it shows life in action and not just as written laws or dominant moral principles say it should be" (132).

While the narrative focus of autobiography lies in the enunciation of a nonstandard life, the ideological force of Gramsci's claim emerges in relation to larger communal structures. Although the autobiographer's life is similar to his or her fellows', it is only "chance" that separates the author from the "thousand others" (132). Gramsci thereby links the representation of an individual life with people who might be described as "fellow travelers" (Saldívar 1990, 164–65). This claim suggests that subjectivity in political autobiographies is intrinsically linked with social structures.

Gramsci's concept of political autobiography emphasizes the connection between the representation of an individual life and the politics of the community to stake an ethical claim. Since only chance separates the individual from his or her fellows, autobiographers have a moral obligation to narrate exceptional identities. By narrating their lives, autobiographers "suggests a process"—a process that presumably leads to the politicization of the community. Part of the function of political autobiography is to invite readers to use the text as a road map to exceptional identities. Gramsci's theory thus proposes that new forms of political affiliation emerge in relation to discursive articulations of individual subjectivity (hence his assertion that autobiography replaces "political" or "philosophical" essays). According to this perspective, autobiography offers an entry point through which others can join the author in new, politicized communities. Yet by envisioning a coalition of progressive political actors, autobiographies also offer imaginative communal spaces that facilitate a rethinking of social relations. The autobiographical text, then, offers the potential to mobilize communities that disrupt dominant notions of citizenship and subjectivity.

There is, however, a third aspect to Gramsci's theory. Because it describes "life in action" (he repeats the phrase twice in a rather economical passage), the autobiographical project also depicts a life *of* action. Doris Sommer (2004) reminds us that when faced with the lack of an appropriate historical juncture for a workers' movement in Italy, Gramsci turned to culture to activate revolutionary potential (104–8).[10] Sommer's suggestion is helpful for situating how Latina/o authors use autobiography as a platform from which to mobilize opposition. By turning to culture to activate their modes of political expression, Latina/o first-person personal narrativists provide contemporary analogues to Gramsci's Italian workers.

Gramsci's theory of political autobiography is useful for my readings of Latina/o triangulation because it apprehends antihegemonic narratives of the self as inextricably related to the communal. In particular, Gramsci's notion of a narrative subject who discursively enacts an alternative politics is helpful in thinking about how contemporary Latina/o authors position themselves as potential models for antiracist, antihegemonic action. I extend Gramsci's analysis by foregrounding how twentieth-century Latina/o first-person personal narratives affirm communal subjectivities and alternative notions of national belonging. Where Gramsci points to a collective social function for autobiographies, the portal through which others pass is still oriented around the individual. My understanding of Latina/o triangulation, on the other hand, focuses on how these authors use narrative strategies that *simultaneously* represent individual subjects in relation to dynamic structures of community and national identity. While the self is the unit of analysis Latina/o authors employ, these selves are inextricably bound with structures of community that elaborate complex forms of collective identity. These collective identities are navigated within the space of the nation, necessitating the assertion of alternative forms of communal and social belonging. Triangulation therefore offers a metaphor for understanding how Latina/o first-person personal narratives offer matrixed, communal subjects.

Additionally, if a primary function of autobiography is the representation of a life of action capable of mobilizing political coalitions, one way to understand Gramsci's theory in relation to my readings is to consider how contemporary Latina/o first-person personal narratives respond to similar cultural and historical circumstances. Since the very notion of Latina/o identity relies on a synthetic (in terms of both artifice and fusion) political subjectivity, it is important to reflect on how authors envision these voluntary affiliations. *Triangulations* argues that first-person personal narratives provide important sites for visualizing these processes. Authors like Ernesto Galarza, John Rechy, and Judith Ortiz Cofer represent themselves in relation to a life of action that engages various aspects of community efficacy.

Another life-writing genre that documents aspects of collective identity is the Latin American *testimonio*. Commentators like John Beverly (1993, 2004), Elzbieta Sklodowska (1996), and Doris Sommer (1996), characterize the *testimonio* as a "literature of fact" (Beverly 1993, 71) that is always collaborative and oriented around the representation of a social history, and of a particular cause to which the author(s) is trying to recruit the reader. The *testimonio* is also characterized by the presence of an interlocutor who mediates the narrative, often as it is told to him or her. The classic example of the *testimonio* is the narrative collaboration between Rigoberta Menchú and Elizabeth Burgos-Debray, but there are many examples of the genre that arise from Central America, South America, and the Caribbean.[11]

As Beverly and others have suggested, the social is an essential aspect of the *testimonio*. These social aspects include the relationship between the author and interlocutor, as well as the communal history integrated with the narrator's personal story. The work of authors like Jesús Colón, John Rechy, and Julia Alvarez resonate with these aspects of *testimonio*, as the "I" frequently operates as the key to cultural and historical understanding. Colón is particularly interesting in this regard, as his narrator operates as the central interlocutor for the stories in *A Puerto Rican in New York*.[12] By positioning his work as a story designed to combat the popular image of Puerto Ricans as deficient, Colón's book also conforms to two other aspects of the *testimonio*: (1) the narrative addresses the repression of Puerto Ricans on the mainland, and (2) this account provides a more accurate version of the author's life and the history of his community. In so doing, Colón invokes his community by suggesting that many Puerto Ricans living in New York during the period lived lives that shared material and intellectual similarities with his own.

While *A Puerto Rican in New York* and many of the other books *Triangulations* considers share important similarities with classical *testimonios*, it is not accurate to characterize these works strictly as *testimonios*. As Beverly (1993) notes, one of the defining characteristics of the *testimonio* is its relationship with armed struggle. While authors like Colón, Thomas, Acosta, and Rechy espouse militant positions, it would be incorrect to consider their social and literary formations within the framework of armed struggle. From a purely formalist standpoint, their ability to represent themselves, rather than interacting with a collaborator or interlocutor, would also tend to disqualify these works from the *testimonio* tradition.

While *testimonios* and political autobiographies both aim to transform the reader through a new social awareness, the intent and potential outcomes of each genre differ sharply. In the case of *testimonios*, the writer and interlocutor attempt to raise consciousness about a social issue or struggle to enlist the reader as a potential ally and supporter. The *testimonio* addresses this change by questioning the social world of the reader (Beverly 1993, 84). Political autobiography, on the other hand, assumes continuity between reader and author, emphasizing key similarities between their social situations. In the strictest sense, political autobiography requires no interlocutor. Where *testimonio* attempts to give voice to the subaltern who cannot speak, political autobiography assumes a speaking subject who has access to both literary representation and a reading audience.

My comments are not designed to undermine the traditions of *testimonio* or political autobiography. Instead, I argue that Latina/o first-person personal narratives operate on a continuum of life writing that includes political autobiography and *testimonio*. The first-person personal narratives this book considers constitute hybrid forms that represent individual subjectivity in relation to projects of community efficacy. *Triangulations* suggests that Latina/os often reconfigure life-writing genres to more adequately represent the complexity of their lived experiences.

At the same time, *Triangulations* pays careful attention to the deployment of genre as a narrative strategy. This approach allows me to consider a range of genres including autobiography, memoir, autoethnography, *testimonio*, and autobiographical fiction. By emphasizing the critical practice as a polylateral engagement with the text, my methodology explodes older interpretive models that characterize narratives of the self as merely personal revelation, private insight, or subjective truth that ranks below nonfiction, critical essays, or even "high" literary genres like the historical novel. This book attempts to provide a perspective from which we can glimpse the aesthetic choices, politics, and social dynamics embedded in Latina/o autobiographical texts.

Consequently, *Triangulations* considers the text from the standpoint of both object *and* process. This is in part an attempt to deal with the long and conflicting critical history of "what counts" as a narrative of the self. Some critics of autobiography, like Philippe Lejeune (1989), argue that the genre is a function of the author's intent. Others, like Paul de Man (1979) suggest that autobiography is not a genre but a figure of reading and understanding that operates over a range of texts. My understanding of first-person personal narrative flows from de Man's argument about autobiography. This book suggests that narratives of the self are constituted as much by a critical practice as by characteristics of a specific genre. Yet where de Man considers the autobiography a purely discursive formulation, I argue that Latina/o first-person personal narratives also function as articulations of social values.

It is not the case that every twentieth-century Latina/o first-person personal narrative engages with progressive political communities. As authors like Richard Rodríguez (1982, 2002), Linda Chávez (1991), and others demonstrate, many Latina/o authors align themselves with doctrines of assimilation and liberal individualism. While Rodríguez's and Chávez's texts are no less "political," this book focuses on first-person personal narratives that discursively contest white supremacy as part of their project of community efficacy. Rather than asserting individuality as the goal of self-representation—as Rodríguez and Chávez do—the authors included in this study affirm the communal as a basic aspect of discursive resistance. Although most of the texts I analyze embody a tension between individual empowerment and communal affirmation, their articulations of the self tend to reject liberal individualism and its attendant racial formations.

Triangulations further suggests that narrative strategies employed by Latina/o authors are intentional and conscious attempts to disrupt racial and ethnic binaries. As philosopher Charles Mills (1997) reminds us, liberal individualism and white supremacy constitute structured and organized methods of securing privilege for whites at the expense of people of color. Viewed from this perspective, works by authors like Jesús Colón, Julia Alvarez, and Piri Thomas constitute refusals of white supremacy. These authors counter the insufficiencies of hegemonic notions of the subject in order to argue against what critical race theory scholar Leslie Espinoza (1998) calls "dichotomous categorical identity" (17). Dichotomous categorical identity is characterized by the enforcement of either/or binaries such as black/white, gay/straight, male/female, and so on. Under the terms of dichotomous categorical identity, one must choose a single aspect of identity to the exclusion of another. One is therefore black *or* white, gay *or* straight, male *or* female (17). Under dichotomous categorical identity, intersecting aspects of identity (gay, working-class Chicano, for instance) are illegible.

As the authors of the first-person personal narratives this book considers argue, binary identifications are incommensurate with the complexity of Latina/os' daily lives. As individuals and groups who exist on the margins of multiple racial, ethnic, and cultural categories, the Latina/o authors included in this study employ matrixed representations that refuse binary categories endemic to hegemonic culture.[13] In addition, rather than seeing these narrative strategies hierarchically by centering male perspectives, this book foregrounds how authors conceive of gender and sexuality to comprehend how Latina/o subjectivities evolve as complex and multifaceted phenomena.

Generative Contradictions

Although the relationships implicit in triangulation presuppose a conception of relatedness, I do not suggest that contradictions are absent from these texts. Indeed, contradictions are often the most interesting relations present in the works included in this book. It is therefore crucial to consider how contradictions serve as flashpoints that can ground other kinds of relations. For example, as scholars like Angie Chabram-Dernersesian (1992) and the Latina Feminist Group (2001) note, the misogyny of Latina/o cultural nationalist movements in the 1960s and early 1970s helped to spur the development of Chicana and Latina feminisms in the postsixties period. While these feminist movements were not facilitated or legitimated by groups like the Brown Berets or the Young Lords, Latinas' experiences of gender oppression within cultural nationalist movements constituted a relation that helped to galvanize various feminist positions.[14]

Part of the difficulty with systems of racialization is that an autonomous space outside of these ideologies is difficult, if not impossible, to imagine. Here I invoke Louis Althusser's (2001) famous theory of ideology by pointing out that nothing exists outside of ideology. While this book de-emphasizes the notion of pure, transcendent alternatives to racial ideologies, it considers the representation of the self in these texts as symptomatic of a *desire*, however incomplete, to disrupt hegemonic culture. I advocate understanding these authors and texts from the standpoint of what José Muñoz (1999) describes as "ideological contradictory elements" (12), or what we might understand as generative contradictions.

Generative contradictions disrupt ideology by interrupting the flow of power. Because they do not fit comfortably within systemic (and therefore ideological) processes, generative contradictions momentarily interrupt ideologies and clear spaces for alternative modes of being. They allow for the "reworking of those energies that do not elide the 'harmful' or contradictory components of any identity" (12). As such, generative contradictions function as aspects of oppositional practices that cannot be quantified within the logic of constituent premises. While they may be incomplete or ephemeral, these moments of interruption allow the objects of ideology perspectives that temporarily disrupt processes of racialization.

The texts I examine frequently manifest generative contradictions in their desire to oppose hegemonic culture, while reinscribing many of the ingrained racial, gender, and sexual hierarchies they aim to subvert. Among the difficulties in reading books like Acosta's *The Revolt of the Cockroach People* or Rechy's *The Sexual Outlaw* is that they don't offer transcendent subject positions. Sites like Acosta's formulation of the *vato loco* (crazy guy) or Rechy's conception of the sexual outlaw invest individual representations with public and communal aspirations.[15] In the course of using an individual form to express a collective experience, these authors link their literary personas with their imagined communities. They therefore create characters who offer momentary disruptions in ideology. Yet in writing such vexed characters, it becomes possible for these authors to deceive themselves, leading to the paradoxical reinscription of dominant hierarchies.

In addition, these authors—in fact all of the authors included in this study—use first-person personal narrative forms to express group identity and to valorize alternative imagined communities, evidencing a tension between the political desire to express group solidarity and the need for individual empowerment. Although the texts I consider counter the liberal individualism represented in canonical autobiographies, they are still informed by it and draw on the same set of literary conventions.

Discordant moments like these either cannot be quantified by my approach or complicate my conception of triangulation. For example, in chapter 2 I argue that Thomas and Acosta represent their selves as aligned with their imagined national communities. Yet while both authors engage their communities as an aspect of the self, they also assert individuality in opposition to such communal identities. These desires for individual empowerment are in part premised on alienation *from* each author's respective community of origin. Thomas's and Acosta's use of individualism contradicts my reading strategy, but it also exposes another dynamic for social empowerment. Since racialization operates on both individual and group levels, many of these authors employ multiple narrative strategies to disrupt their own marginalization and that of their groups.

These are not abstract aesthetic issues in Latina/o first-person personal narratives. Rather, they are narrative strategies that emerge from concrete historical and social circumstances. For Acosta and Rechy, the *vato loco* and sexual outlaw have to be read in light of the individualization and criminalization of poverty and political resistance, as products of brutal police repression, class exploitation, homophobia, and the radical divisiveness inherent in the lives of people of color. In the face of systemic dehumanization, it isn't easy to discern what radical rehumanization might require. This book strives to understand these texts as vexed cultural sites that evidence a desire to disrupt hegemony by reclaiming humanity for these authors—and by extension their communities.

As Stuart Hall (1996) asserts, there are no neat distinctions between hegemonic and resistant cultures. We must therefore consider both direct articulations of resistance *and* the material circumstances of opposition to understand the intricate ways that Latina/o first-person personal narrativists attempt to subvert hegemony, while continuing to embody aspects of its problematics. Rather than romanticizing how these authors imagine their communities as patriarchal or essentialist, this book provides a candid analysis that considers how generative contradictions constitute an important disruption to hegemonic culture. As a result, I examine the *impulses* in these texts rather than their results.

My analysis in *Triangulations* is thus characterized by both/and rather than either/or relations. In part, this book explores how Latina/o first-person personal narrativists use generative contradictions to contest dichotomous categorical identity. As Gloria Anzaldúa describes, "Living on borders and in margins, keeping intact one's shifting and multiple identity and integrity, is like trying to swim in a new element, an 'alien' element. There is an exhilaration in being a participant in the further evolution of humankind in being 'worked' on. I have the sense that certain 'faculties'—not just in me but in every border resident, colored or non-colored—and dormant areas of consciousness are being activated, awakened" (2007, preface).

Triangulations argues that the shifting, conflicting identities to which Anzaldúa alludes offer alternatives to dichotomous categorical notions of the self in the United States. I examine how these texts attempt to map alternative subject positions by documenting experiences that are illegible within systems of dichotomous categorical identity.

Self, Community, Nation: The Aporias of Cultural Nationalism

A secondary aspect of *Triangulations* encounters the vexed history of cultural nationalism.[16] Perhaps not surprisingly, given the prevalence of the political form during the late twentieth century, authors like Thomas, Acosta, Colón, Galarza, Rechy, Ortiz Cofer, and Alvarez often engage cultural nationalism (if only negatively) in their writings. This book complicates the tendency in both mainstream criticism and area studies to write off cultural nationalism. As scholars and writers ranging from Eric Hobsbawm (1992) to Anzaldúa have noted, nationalism is often a problematic political and social phenomenon.[17] Sonia Saldívar-Hull, for example, writes of the "dissatisfaction that so many activist *mujeres* began to feel in the face of the masculinist notions of [the Chicano movement]" (2000, 12). Carl Gutiérrez-Jones also warns against the "utopian promise held out by the Chicano movement [. . .] that] fueled a problematic collapsing of differences among Chicanos in an effort to formulate an overriding concept of *the* community" (1995, 101–2). Similarly, Chela Sandoval (2000) argues that insurgent nationalist movements have been historically unsuccessful because in their attempts to assert the validity of Latina/o identities, they became mired in identity politics and assertions of supremacy, diverting potentially liberatory impulses into hierarchies like patriarchy, essentialism, and authoritarianism.

I agree with these characterizations of nationalism as an imperfect political and social formation. Yet while some portray nationalism as irredeemably flawed, *Triangulations* suggests that these points of view overlook dynamics that explain much about how individuals and social groups conceive of opposition. Shalini Puri (2004) makes the case in a Caribbean context that the presumed demise of the nation in the face of transnationalism and globalization is premature. She argues that "differentiating amongst different nationalisms" does not necessarily represent a desire to "reinstall the nation-state or nationalism as privileged categories of cultural analysis" (6). Rather, Puri argues that transnationalism is "poorly served by denying the continuing, though discernibly declining, power of the nation-state" (6). For her, the nation offers an indispensible mode of empowerment for postcolonial and other marginalized subjects. Rather than decrying the nation or declaring its power dead, I agree with Puri in asserting that the nation continues to exert influence in the postsixties period. Accordingly, this book seeks a more nuanced critical history of the growth and transformation of cultural nationalist politics as they manifest in Latina/o first-person personal narratives.

Reconsidering insurgent nationalism also facilitates a more complete historical, cultural, and social understanding of the development of oppositional consciousness in Latina/o communities. Because the nation mediates (in part) how we experience our identities, it is possible to understand the necessity of asserting national consciousness in first-person personal narratives. As Puri further notes, the nation serves as an indispensible category for combating the homogenizing forces of globalization and discourses of celebratory hybridity: "Caribbean discourses [. . .] undo the generalized claim that hybridity and the nation-state are opposed to one another and enable a broader questioning of invocations of a 'global village' and the death of the nation-state" (6). Puri makes a useful distinction between transnationalisms, which are devoted to aspects of human societies that cannot be contained within the boundaries of a singular nation-state, and "postnationalism," which effectively argues that the nation as a political and analytical category is dead. I agree with Puri's argument that those who celebrate the triumph of the global and transnational by declaring the death of the nation overlook the important ways disempowered communities invoke the nation (as an imagined community, rather than a nation-state) as a strategy for empowerment. While this might be a risky move at a time when many theoretical currents within

Latina/o studies are oriented around the transnational, I concur with Puri that reexamining cultural nationalism through current critical and theoretical tools facilitates a better understanding of cultural nationalism as a force that was and may still be productive for aggrieved communities of color in their searches for social justice.[18]

While Puri's observations relate to the complex cultural and historical milieu of the Caribbean, I extend her analysis to U.S. Latina/os for several reasons. First—and perhaps most obviously—the history and culture of Dominicans, Puerto Ricans, and Cubans in the United States is rooted in the Caribbean. Further, as Juan Flores (2009) has recently pointed out, social and regional belonging in Caribbean, Latin American, and other diasporic communities in the United States is more accurately characterized by streams and counterstreams of migration and return rather than by discrete movements of people from the home space to the United States. Perhaps most important for my interests, Latina/os continue to deploy nationalism as a strategy for political empowerment, even in the wake of the North American Free Trade Agreement (NAFTA) and the forces of globalization that shape migration, immigration, and the flow of transnational capital. *Triangulations* thus pays careful attention to how the *rhetoric* of insurgent nationalism continues to influence how opposition is conceived during the last third of the twentieth century.

It is important to note that this study is not an attempt to recuperate Chicano, Puerto Rican, or other (male) Latino insurgent projects. On the contrary, I follow the lead of Latina feminists like Anzaldúa (2007), Chela Sandoval (2000), Asunción Horno-Delgado et al. (1989), Frances Aparicio and Susana Chávez-Silverman (1997), Norma Alarcón (1999), Paula Moya (2002), and Frances Negrón-Muntaner (2007), as well as queer studies scholars like José Muñoz (1999), Juana María Rodríguez (2003), and Roderick Ferguson (2004), who point to a major shortcoming of insurgent nationalism: the consistent reinscription of patriarchy and heteronormativity. Instead, this book attempts to understand the larger literary, historiographic, and social dynamics that contribute to insurgent nationalism as an important mode of oppositional consciousness. *Triangulations* suggests that what appears to contemporary readers as simply retrograde historically served as an *attempt* to combat white supremacy, while also validating the author's community and culture.

By considering these first-person personal narratives from the standpoint of their triangulations, it becomes possible to comprehend how the residue of cultural nationalism continues to reflect and transform how Latina/os imagine themselves and their relationships with others (both within and outside of their communities). This book grapples with both the prevalence of this residue and the transformations to nationalist discourse that Latina/os undertake to destabilize racist conceptions of identity in the United States. When viewed from this more complex perspective, we can see how authors like John Rechy, Judith Ortiz Cofer, and Julia Alvarez take up and transform the residue of insurgent nationalism.

What interests me, and what I hope will interest scholars in Chicana/o studies, Puerto Rican studies, Latina/o studies, comparative ethnic studies, and the humanities and social sciences more generally, is how these texts represent what Chela Sandoval calls a network of mobile resistance strategies. These networks include a range of narrative techniques that encompass discursive, physical, and epistemological opposition. By conceiving of opposition as relational, it becomes feasible to understand how authors triangulate their resistance to white supremacy—both in terms of and in excess of the nation. They evidence what Walter Mignolo (2000, 67) has described as "an other thinking"—a form of epistemological practice that constitutes a radical break with Eurocentricism. While it is not my claim that these authors or texts embody a transcendent break from Eurocentrism, *Triangulations* focuses on how these authors and texts evidence impulses toward an other thinking.

Latina/o Identity: Synthesizing Political Coalitions

Implicit in the previous claims is that there actually are commonalities between various Latina/o communities. Latina/o studies scholars have long pointed out that, by virtue of our various histories, languages, and circumstances of arrival to (or in the case of Chicana/os and Puerto Ricans, long-term presence in) the United States, there is no single line of Latina/o ethnicity. Earl Shorris (1992), for example, advocates that the various communities that compose a larger Hispanic or Latina/o identity are better characterized as independent ethnic groups.[19] Others, like Arlene Dávila (2001), point out that the commodification of Latina/o identity obscures the racialization of various groups with roots in Latin America. Still others, like Suzanne Oboler (1995), Juan Flores (1997), Frances Aparicio (1999), and Juan González (2000), suggest that while there is no organic connection between Latina/o groups, there is political utility in self-identifying under a collective rubric.

As astute readers have probably noticed, I use the words Latina and Latino to denote a voluntary, interethnic identity in the United States. I am interested in a disciplinary framework that encounters the diversity of Latina/o representations without losing the specificity of each group's particular relationship to power. As Frances Aparicio asks about the links between pan-Latina/o identity and Latina/o studies, "how do we reconceptualize our Chicano Studies, Puerto Rican Studies, and Latino Studies programs as sites where diverse national groups and identities are respected while forging a larger, inter-Latino space from which to produce knowledge and interact socially, culturally and politically?" (1999, 16). As a partial answer to Aparicio's question, I advocate pan-Latina/o identity as a liberatory political coalition for two reasons. First, as a voluntary association, Latina/o identity has the potential to serve as an alliance capable of unifying disparate groups for common political purposes. Second, the interethnic coalition Latina/o helps us to see how power operates on a range of racialized populations. By comparing the experiences of a Cuban American woman in Miami, Florida, with a Chicano in the West, for example, it becomes possible to understand how racialization operates across a broad spectrum of geographical, social, and political contexts.

By comparing authors and texts, this book traces the common political, social, cultural, linguistic, and aesthetic strands that travel among and between various Latina/o communities. In particular, I examine both the failures of nationalism to record the interethnic alliances that fueled many social movements (the leadership of Dominican Federíco Lora in the Puerto Rican movement group El Comité-MINP, for example), while also highlighting how many of the authors included in this study work against this impulse within insurgent social movements. While this study is not an ethnographic account that provides a definitive history of particular movement groups, it provides analyses of various interethnic (and intergender and intersexual) alliances as they are represented in literary texts. I contend that these representations often work to remedy the historical erasure of these moments in the wake of the nationalist period.

For example, Oscar "Zeta" Acosta notes the presence of Cuban American and Native American organizers as basic to the formation of various Chicana/o movement groups in Los Angeles. Similarly, John Rechy conceives of all forms of oppression as "a hungry evil" (1995, 121), suggesting that progressive actors must understand the intersecting nature of homophobia, patriarchy, and racism in order to overturn hegemony. Similarly, Piri Thomas attempts to triangulate his Nuyorican identity by leveraging the history of antiracism in African American communities. By considering the triangulations these texts construct, I argue that these authors represent moments where connection with other ethnic groups—both Latina/o and otherwise—is possible, disrupting narratives of purity inherent in many insurgent social movements.

Empire and migration provide Latin Americans with similar experiences *prior* to their arrival in the United States.[20] As Kirsten Silva Gruesz (2002) reminds us, historical commonalities between Latina/o groups in the United States reach back to the nineteenth century and beyond. Through their former (and in the case of Puerto Ricans, ongoing) colonial relations with Spain and the United States, common crops like sugar, the Spanish language, Cubans and Dominicans in Puerto Rico, migrant labor in Florida, Jamaica, and Panama, and music like salsa, merengue, and *reggaetón* that has local differences and regional similarities, these national groups carry logical affiliations. It is my contention that these resonances offer potential for organic interethnic, interracial coalitions capable of effecting larger political changes.

These claims are not intended to essentialize Latina/o identity; on the contrary, they seek to locate common—and voluntary—political associations asserted by various first-person personal narrativists. The texts included in this study offer rich insights into the political implications of nascent Latina/o consciousness. Accordingly, this book demonstrates how authors like Colón, Acosta, Rechy, and Alvarez mediate essentialist notions of identity with larger political and social coalitions. This analysis situates common themes and tactics that might serve as foundations for a variety of interethnic, interracial, and intergender coalitions that defy monolithic conceptions of Latina/o identity.

Scholars William Flores and Rina Benmayor (1997) have championed a concept they call "Latino cultural citizenship" to designate an emerging collective identity structure that links disparate groups with roots in Latin America. Latino cultural citizenship embodies an active political agenda designed to defy traditional notions of political citizenship as conferred by the state. The terms of Latino cultural citizenship are informative for my readings of Latina/o triangulation because they suggest a complete overhaul of mainstream U.S. identity. Rather than understanding these texts as narrating a subject that exceeds the bounds of a normative U.S. citizen, Latino cultural citizenship helps in envisioning a political subject that serves as the foundation for more egalitarian communities, communities that are themselves based on voluntary interethnic alliances.

Following this logic, it is important to consider that the political articulations of various Chicana/o, Puerto Rican, and Dominican authors constitutes—if not a claim to a larger sociopolitical grouping in the United States—at least a similar logic of empowerment. By examining their triangulations, it becomes possible to comprehend what seem to be incompatible social movements (the Brown Berets and the Young Lords, for example) according to what Michael M. J. Fischer (1986, 230) describes as "families of resemblance." For example, while each group imagined their community differently (reclaiming Aztlán for the Brown Berets, as opposed to the decolonization of Puerto Rico and the enfranchisement of Puerto Ricans living on the mainland for the Lords), both organizations staked claims to an essential identity that served as the basis of social affiliation. Likewise, while the Lords' official position on gender equity was more progressive than the patriarchal one articulated by the Brown Berets, in practice there was little difference between the organizations.

By examining these authors' similar responses to the insufficiencies of racialized subjectivities in the United States and national identities in Latin America, it becomes possible to locate these occluded families of resemblance. As Michael Omi and Howard Winant (1994), Orlando Patterson (1982) and others have noted, while racialization is not a phenomenon confined to life in the United States, the authors included in this study share a common commitment to countering liberal individualism as a primary aspect of their antiracist strategies. Although I am careful not to conflate the similarities and differences between ethnic groups and individual texts, *Triangulations* endeavors to understand the political utility of coalescing in an interethnic alliance like Latina/o. First-person personal narratives offer primary sites where one can glimpse how these authors navigate similar alternatives to the liberal political subject posited by Western systems of thought.

Imagining Community Efficacy in the First-Person Personal Narrative

Reading Latina/o triangulations opens the social and cultural possibilities encoded in these first-person personal narratives. Since these texts narrate socially embedded subjectivities, it follows that they also provide spaces where multilevel conversations can imaginatively take place between individuals, communities, and social movements. For example, it is well known that authors like Galarza, Colón, and Acosta had links with various social and political movements.[21] By understanding their triangulations, we can see how their texts facilitate conversations between individuals, their communities, and the views espoused by social movements.

As I have noted, one aspect of *Triangulations* is dedicated to tracing an intellectual history of oppositional consciousness in Latina/o communities during the late twentieth century. Part of this work depends on understanding the oppositional strains that operate before this period. Michael Denning (1998) observes that 1960s oppositional groups owed a debt to the Cultural Front of the 1930s. Regardless of whether activists were conscious of how Cultural Front models of activism influenced them, Denning asserts that the 1930s formed part of the collective unconscious that shaped political contestation throughout the last half of the twentieth century.

These complicated dialogues facilitate interethnic and intergenerational conversations in Latina/o first-person personal narratives—what Benedict Anderson (2005) describes as the "zigzags" of history (81). Because history does not progress according to a linear timeline, it moves in fits and starts, engaging other moments across time and space. These zigzags are in part proleptic—they anticipate, dialog with, or foreshadow certain moments in the future. It becomes possible then to read authors like Colón (1961) and Galarza (1971) as essentially speaking from, to, and about similar cultural contexts, political projects, and historical moments.

In a similar vein, *Triangulations* argues that the (sometimes) unconscious strains of political activism within Latina/o communities form part of the fabric of oppositional consciousness activists draw upon to constitute social movements. This book demonstrates how these political strains emerge out of similar logics and oppositional frameworks. For example, how does the failure of the inclusive ethnic Americanism of the Cultural Front propel figures like Galarza and Colón toward increasingly militant positions that anticipate insurgent nationalism? How do the shortcomings of mainstream feminism and the exclusive subjectivities endemic to Latina/o nationalisms of the 1960s relate to the multiple contestations of female authors like Ortiz Cofer and Alvarez? Similarly, how do the disappointments of the civil rights movement and the unfulfilled promise of the sexual revolution contribute to John Rechy's sexual outlaws?

Mapping discursive identities onto social structures in the personal narrative is not a phenomenon associated solely with Latina/o communities in the United States. Citing the function of canonical personal narratives like Franklin's *Autobiography*, Jeffrey Louis Decker (1997) argues that the representation of the self "extends the new concept of individualism to the condition of the U.S. nation." Decker's analysis underscores how Franklin's *Autobiography* is particularly evocative of this ethic, as it advocates "illustrations of the frugality and industry" that would serve as foundations for individualist subjects in the fledgling nation (xix).

The fact that Franklin's *Autobiography* employs a socially engaged representation underscores the need to analyze the complex ways that women and ethnic and racialized subjects use first-person personal narrative forms to contest individualist ideologies. As subjects who are written out of the social contract by figures like Franklin, Latina/os often assert communal identities in an attempt to reconfigure how the nation is imagined. Some of these conceptions of the nation verge on the transnational. Ranging from the articulations of the Brown Berets and the Raza Unida Party who conceived of Aztlán, the mythical homeland of the Aztecs, as a geographic space that straddles the border between the U.S. and Mexico, to the complex understandings of Puerto Rican nationality in both the United States and the island contexts enunciated by groups like the Young Lords, Latina/os often characterized their struggles for space and rights from international, if not transnational, points of view.[22] Since many authors included in this study were involved with twentieth-century social movements, these first-person personal narratives informed and were formed by the political and theoretical currents that swirl around Latina/o cultural nationalist groups. Part of the way that Latina/os were able to conceive of and enact these complex challenges was through the discursive representation of "nations" that linked disparate oppositional traditions in the United States, Latin America, and beyond.

A Few Words about Genre

Given the complex history of criticism dealing with autobiography, *testimonio*, and other life-writing genres, it is important to address the ramifications of focusing on first-person personal narrative forms. Besides quantifying the genre itself, one concern of many critics of autobiography is the tension between fact and fiction in these texts. Books like Oscar

"Zeta" Acosta's *The Revolt of the Cockroach People*, Julia Alvarez's *In the Time of the Butterflies*, or Judith Ortiz Cofer's *The Line of the Sun* invite these questions because they consciously blur the distinctions between truth and fiction. As Marta Sánchez (2005) points out about *Down These Mean Streets*, even texts that claim autobiographical truth often introduce fictional elements.

Rather than understanding the first-person personal narrative from a purely teleological or ontological standpoint, it is important to consider how Latina/o authors blend multiple genres to reveal alternative versions of history and subjectivity. Writing of what she calls "historiographic metafiction," Linda Hutcheon (1989) argues that "in granting new and emphatic value to the notion of 'experience,' feminisms have also raised an issue of great importance to postmodern representation: what constitutes a valid historical narrative? And who decides? This has led to the re-evaluation of personal or life narratives—journals, letters, confessions, biographies, autobiographies, self-portraits" (160).

Hutcheon's point centers on the idea that the "veracity" required in personal narratives is difficult to achieve for people who cannot represent themselves.[23] Because what counts as truth relies on Eurocentric, liberal individualist frameworks, collective utterances are anathema to the system of representation associated with autobiography. Hutcheon therefore urges us to consider how life-writing genres are reconfigured to represent versions of historical events that support communal affirmation.

Similarly, I argue that Latina/os often disrupt life-writing forms in order to destabilize dominant historical narratives and contest exclusive subjectivities. Because it is impossible for an author to represent every event that takes place in even a small segment of a life, it is necessary to select *representative* events to construct a coherent narrative. As literary scholar Charles T. Davis (1979) suggests, the "editing of the raw matter of life is necessary" (427) to produce meaning in autobiography. The principles behind this editing usually conform to fiction. Accordingly, I suggest that the veracity of Latina/o first-person personal narratives is less important than the historical material they represent. At the same time, because Latina/o first-person personal narratives question the epistemological foundations of meaning making for aggrieved ethnic subjects, they revise the "I," while also recording alternative versions of the history and culture of their communities.

This argument is not intended to contest the genres of autobiography, memoir, *testimonio*, or other forms of life writing. Neither is my intention to conflate the historical narrative with fiction. Instead, I concur with Hutcheon and Davis that life writing constitutes a continuum that includes a number of genres and literary forms. *Triangulations* therefore offers one interpretive strategy for uncovering the embedded politics contained in these texts. Concomitantly, the texts that follow provide a rich portrait of the challenges to liberal individualist notions of self, community, and nation mounted by Latina/os during the late twentieth century.

I argue in chapter 1, "Zigzagging through History: Ernesto Galarza, Jesús Colón and the Development of Insurgent Consciousness," that both authors' memoirs triangulate the "inclusive nationalism" of the Cultural Front of the 1930s with the militant practices of the insurgent nationalist period of the 1960s. Galarza's *Barrio Boy* and Colón's *A Puerto Rican in New York* evidence the zigzags of history by demonstrating how the material circumstances of their writing emerge in dialogue with various social movements. Ranging from the trade union activism of the United Farm Workers Union (UFW) and the Congress of Industrial Organizations (CIO) to the militant positions of groups like the Brown Berets and the Young Lords, both authors represent their history of activism in relation to the politics occurring as they write their books. I further demonstrate how the memoir must be destabilized to accommodate these imagined Latina/o nations. Accordingly, Galarza's and Colón's works constitute a fabric of oppositionality that proposes cultural sites where communal subjectivities are imagined and enacted, if only in circumscribed terms.

In chapter 2, "Crazy for the Nation: Piri Thomas, Oscar 'Zeta' Acosta, and the Urban Outlaw," I argue that Piri Thomas (1967), a Puerto Rican, and Oscar "Zeta" Acosta (1989b) Chicano, deploy the figure of the outlaw in their autobiographical texts in order to politicize their respective communities. Since both authors operate in urban settings, I suggest that the figures of the *vato loco* and urban outlaw offer liberatory models of oppositional consciousness in metropolitan spaces. Since these authors often lived within close proximity to other communities of color, *Triangulations* reconsiders the cultural nationalist movements of the period as interethnic and coalitional from their inception.

The third chapter of *Triangulations*, "Remaking the Insurgent Vision: John Rechy, Judith Ortiz Cofer, and the Limits of Nationalist Morality," also examines the outsider. But as autobiographical novels by Judith Ortiz Cofer (1989) and John Rechy (1977) demonstrate, the revolutionary subjects valorized by cultural nationalist groups were premised on patriarchy and heteronormativity. Chapter 3 demonstrates how many female and gay and lesbian Latina/os adapt first-person personal narratives to contest these exclusive subjectivities, proposing more complicated and inclusive notions of intersecting identities as alternatives for the imagined social community.

Chapter 4, "I Can't Be Me without My People: Triangulating Historical Trauma in the Work of Julia Alvarez" examines four of Alvarez's novels (1991, 1994, 1997b, 2000). I argue that Alvarez's novels complicate the stability of history, autobiography, and fiction in her literary constructions of Dominican communities on the island and in the United States. Because of the historical trauma inflicted on Dominicans in both homeland and diasporic contexts, a linear, univocal history of the nation can no longer be constructed. Alvarez superimposes her story on historical figures in her novels in order to reimagine history in a manner that resolves the dislocation of migration and exile, while also clearing a space for individual identity and feminine agency. Concomitantly, I show how Alvarez uses generic innovation to imagine interethnic and coalitional Latina/o politics at the intersections of various borders.

The conclusion to *Triangulations*, "New Millennial Triangulations," draws together the arguments in chapters 1 through 4 by considering how understanding textual triangulation allows critics to reconceptualize the political function of Latina/o first-person personal narratives. As a part of this elaboration of triangulation, I provide a brief reading of Sandra Cisneros's 2002 novel *Caramelo* that examines the transformations that take place in twenty-first-century Latina/o first-person personal narratives.

1

Zigzagging through History

Ernesto Galarza, Jesús Colón, and the Development of Insurgent Consciousness

> Personhood can be taken for granted by some, while it (and all that accompanies it) has to be fought for by others, so that the general human political project of struggling for a better society involves a different trajectory for nonwhites.
>
> —Charles Mills, *The Racial Contract*

Many Latina/o cultural nationalist movements of the late 1960s and early 1970s envisioned new social relations and alternative formulations of community. But the politics of these movements were not without predecessors. Indeed, cultural nationalism owed a debt to the leftist social movements of the 1930s, what scholar Michael Denning (1998) calls the "age of the CIO."[1] Rather than understanding the 1960s as antithetical to 1930s-style activism, this chapter argues that the age of the Congress of Industrial Organizations (CIO) constitutes part of the political logic of the cultural nationalist period. I examine Jesús Colón's *A Puerto Rican in New York* (1982) and Ernesto Galarza's *Barrio Boy* (1971) to understand how they triangulate concrete intellectual foundations for Latina/o insurgent nationalisms out of the historical shortcomings of older (although no less important) oppositional models.[2] Colón's and Galarza's navigations of older oppositional models anticipate the politics of insurgent nationalism. While neither text conforms neatly to insurgent nationalist political positions, *Barrio Boy* and *A Puerto Rican in New York* attest to the evolution of multifaceted and increasingly militant intellectual strands developing in Chicana/o and Puerto Rican communities during the twentieth century.

While Colón's *A Puerto Rican in New York* foreshadows the politics of insurgent Puerto Rican social movements at the time of its publication in 1961, Galarza's *Barrio Boy* has a more complex relationship with Chicana/o nationalisms. It is not my contention that the association between *Barrio*

Boy and Chicana/o movement groups like the Brown Berets or Raza Unida Party (some of which were virtually exhausted by 1971) is similar to the prolepsis evident in Colón's text. This temporal anomaly is accounted for in part by the way *Barrio Boy* leverages a longer, *lived* history of opposition as a foundation for contemporary Chicana/o nationalist struggles. While Galarza likely would have thought of his book as documenting a past history, it also reflects the currents of oppositional consciousness operative during the period when he drafted *Barrio Boy*. As Antonio C. Márquez points out, "autobiographies are the products of a specific historical moment and are responses to the exigencies, crises, accomplishments or failures of an individual life lived in a particular time and place" (1990, 58). When considered from this standpoint, Galarza's text engages both the past and the political urgency of its present. Consequently, *Barrio Boy* affirms the militant politics of the present via a representation of the past.

While there is no evidence that the two knew one another, this chapter also proposes an intellectual conversation between Galarza and Colón designed to encounter the similarities and differences between their literary, cultural, and intellectual trajectories.[3] When viewed from a comparative perspective, it becomes possible to understand how Galarza and Colón respond to analogous impulses in their political development—what Benedict Anderson (2005) has called the "zigzags" of history (81). These zigzags of history constitute implicit dialogues between individuals, communities, and ideas across time and space. This chapter analyzes how each author represents a parallel process of political change during the post–World War II period.

Since both authors were Popular Front activists, they witnessed the mounting disappointments of the age of the CIO. The Left's enthusiastic support of World War II, the hero worship that elevated FDR and Lincoln, and the acceptance of American exceptionalism that ultimately led to the Cold War, the red-baiting of the 1950s, racist and anti-immigrant nationalisms like the (so-called) Zoot Suit Riots of the 1940s, and exploitative state policies like Operation Bootstrap and the Bracero Initiative. These escalating disappointments pushed aggrieved subjects like Galarza and Colón to adopt positions that foreshadow insurgent nationalism. By reading their first-person personal narratives comparatively, we see how these authors employ similar narrative and political strategies to intervene in the historical and structural changes occurring within Latina/o communities.[4]

Because the exuberant multiculturalism of the culture of unity (Lipsitz 2001, 304) encouraged Latina/os to express class demands in ethnic form, during the Cold War it became necessary for raced members of the working class to take nationalist approaches. Yet this turn toward ethnic nationalism was premised on earlier oppositional models. As Lizabeth Cohen (1990) shows, the class politics of the 1930s only became possible with the demise of the dominant ethnic frame of the 1920s. The demise of the dominant ethnic frame of the 1920s left a residue of ethnic consciousness that lingered into the 1930s. During the age of the CIO, processes of racialization that were often ignored (or adopted) by the Left accentuated ethnic consciousness in Latina/o communities. These estrangements from mainstream leftist politics rendered Latina/os with few options for opposition. Subjects like Galarza and Colón were pressed to assume increasingly militant political strategies based on their ethnic identities.

The unraveling of leftist coalitions was not the only factor that propelled Latina/os away from the culture of unity. Indeed, the political culture of the Right during the postwar period also contributed to the radicalization of Latina/o communities. The anticommunism of the Cold War that characterized the gains of the New Deal and the class struggles of the 1930s and 1940s as un-American, the red baiting of Senator Joseph McCarthy, and the actions of the House Committee on Un-American Activities (HUAC) (before which Colón appeared in 1959) are a few examples of events that led to disillusionment among Latina/os and other aggrieved groups. In response, figures like Galarza and Colón increasingly adopted race-based nationalist politics that called the burgeoning U.S. empire into question.

Galarza's and Colón's texts remake the political forms of the 1930s, investing them with radical meanings in the 1960s. Their works evidence these transformations by representing an evolution from modes of resistance that emphasize ethnic unity, harmony, and accommodation, to the militant (and often more violent), separatist rhetoric of insurgent nationalism. While it is arguable that there was more violence on the picket lines of labor strikes, in the conflicts between Socialists and Communists, and in the activities of the Industrial Workers of the World (Wobblies) during the first third of the twentieth century, the rhetoric of insurgent nationalism espoused militant positions that often exceeded the ideals of the age of the CIO.

One site where it is possible to see how Galarza and Colón navigate the politics of the 1930s with insurgent nationalisms is in the residue of Popular Front activism. This residue is evident in the foregrounding of cultural production in relation to political action. As Denning observes, one of the hallmarks of Popular Front aesthetics was the representation of radical democracy in novels, poetry, plays, movies, painting, sculpture, and other cultural productions. Whether it is through the valorization of indigenous resistance in Jalcocotán in Galarza's case or a demand that the United States reconcile its colonial relationship with Puerto Rico through public art projects in Colón's, both authors link projects of radical democracy with cultural production. By carefully examining how each author represents cultural production, the growing strains of militancy emerging within Latina/o communities become visible.

Because neither author provides a linear transition from 1930s activism to the militant politics of insurgent nationalism, my reading of their triangulations helps to situate their works within a continuum of developing Latina/o insurgent consciousness. For example, Colón maintained his affiliation with the Communist Party, including staunch support for Stalinist policies, until his death in 1974. Likewise, Galarza's problematic characterization of Bracero workers as union busters and scabs undermines his larger project of empowerment for Chicana/os and Mexicana/os. Like intellectuals of any generation, these authors and their works evidence contradictions that are impossible to completely embrace or entirely reject. By examining their triangulations it is possible to understand how their texts anticipate some of the radical potential of insurgent nationalism, while also embodying many problematics. They provide a more nuanced historical account of the development of insurgent consciousness, while also partially explaining the uncritical incorporation of hegemonic norms within cultural nationalist movements.

It is critical to note that these discordant moments also complicate, revise, and work against any unifying reading practice. As individuals who formed and were formed by their historical and cultural contexts, Galarza and Colón were subject to dynamics within hegemonic culture like ideological indoctrination, racialization, poverty, and police repression. These forces undoubtedly contributed to their world views. My consideration of their triangulations is therefore not designed to render a perfect and total reading. In fact, I am equally interested in understanding the inconsistencies and contradictions between their political projects.

Rather than understanding the period of the 1960s as antithetical to projects of 1930s activism, it is crucial to consider how the age of the CIO constitutes part of the political logic of insurgent nationalism. It is therefore possible to reassess the 1960s as emerging in part from the incommensurability of inclusive ethnic Americanism with the increasing militancy of Latina/o and other communities of color in the United States.

Inclusive Nationalism and the Cultural Front

Nationalism has often been characterized as an inherently problematic mode of political expression. Ranging from the famous European, neo-Marxist critiques offered by Benedict Anderson (2007) and E. J. Hobsbawm (1992) to scholarship by Chicana and Latina feminists like Angie Chabram-Dernersesian (1992), Arlene Dávila (1997), Sonia Saldívar-Hull (2000), Lisa Sánchez González (2001), and the Latina Feminist Group (2001), critics have condemned cultural nationalisms either as truncated and incomplete or as positing a subject position that reproduces the hierarchies of hegemonic culture. Particularly relevant are the critiques mounted by Chicana and Latina feminists who point out that these social movements often used machismo as the foundation for revolutionary subjectivity.

All these critiques share a common assumption: nationalism has historically functioned as a problematic phenomenon. While invaluable in their analysis of the contradictions inherent in many social movements (especially in relation to gender and sexuality), these critiques do not always credit the complex ways nationalism is deployed by aggrieved groups. In fact, nationalism constitutes an important aspect of the development of oppositional consciousness in Latina/o communities. I justify this position in part by understanding nationalism from a different standpoint. David Lloyd (1997) argues that there is nothing organic to nationalism that determines it as a regressive political formation. For Lloyd, nationalism is particularly destructive when it is wielded by the state. This view suggests that the way ethnic and racialized subjects use the *form* of nationalism is distinct from state-sponsored nationalisms. Flowing from Lloyd's argument, I use the term "insurgent nationalism" to distinguish nationalisms practiced by Latina/os *against the state* as distinct from modes enacted in support of the state.

It is also important to recognize that nationalism does not always function according to a regressive cultural logic. The Popular Front conceived of the project of inclusive American nationalism as one that emphasized ethnic consciousness. Denning points out that there were many forms and uses to which nationalism was put during the age of the CIO:

"there emerged [during the 1930s] a paradoxical synthesis of competing nationalisms—pride in ethnic heritage and identity combined with an assertive Americanism—that might be called 'ethnic Americanism.' This dominates much of the culture of the second-generation ethnic workers, who Louis Adamic called the 'new Americans.' This combination created a potent ideological constellation, sustaining both radical 'cultural pluralism' of the left-wing Popular Front and the white ethnic nationalism that characterized the anti-communist anti-capitalism of the CIO's right wing" (1998, 9).

Rather than subscribing to a cultural pluralist or multicultural model, the age of the CIO was characterized by a reconfiguration of citizenship in the United States. The Popular Front offered spaces where subjects who were not indoctrinated within structures of citizenship in the United States were able to theorize new conceptions of American identity. Nationalism in this context was an exercise in constructing an inclusive national identity and culture. While some on the Left reduced ethnic and racial identity to a manifestation of class, other Popular Front activists saw inclusive American nationalism as a product of ethnic identity.[5] This view decouples ethnicity from assimilation, facilitating a rethinking of mainstream identity *through* ethnic identification.

While many of the ethnic subjects to which Denning refers were first-generation Americans who were subsequently incorporated into whiteness (Irish, Italian, or Polish Americans, for example), the inclusive nationalism of the age of the CIO has important implications for my analysis. Inclusive nationalism facilitated a process through which marginalized subjects could become signatories to the social contract. Since Popular Front activism placed an emphasis on ethnic coalitions, the Left required alliances between ethnic groups, trade unionists, socialists, and the Communist Party USA (CPUSA). Likewise, the strategic character of the Left often meant that ethnic subjects occupied leadership positions at the forefront of political action. Ethnic Americanism provided aggrieved subjects with opportunities to determine how and where they defined themselves as citizens of the United States. Nationalism was used in this context to rethink mainstream American identity from an ethnic standpoint.

Moreover, ethnic Americanism constituted an important form of nationalism because it contributed to the militant activism of the last third of the twentieth century. There are many examples of militant activism during the age of the CIO, including the San Francisco General Strike of

1934 and the Little Steel Strike of 1937.⁶ This militant fervor was reflected in the actions of people of color like Galarza and Colón. Ranging from the DiGiorgio strike organized by Galarza's Southern Tenant Farmers Union (STFU), to Colón's participation in anticolonial, Puerto Rican nationalist organizations, both authors saw the project of ethnic Americanism in militant terms. Their activism, and the activism of others like them, located militant politics within Latina/o communities, providing homegrown models for insurgent consciousness in the 1960s.

As two of the leading organic intellectuals of their generation, the evolution of Galarza's and Colón's views are representative of the strains of insurgent nationalist thinking developing in Latina/o communities.⁷ In fact, the unfulfilled promises of inclusive ethnic Americanism were among the factors that radicalized figures like Galarza and Colón. For example, Galarza was named in a number of lawsuits that limited his ability to participate in labor struggles after the 1950s. Similarly, Colón was summoned before the HUAC in 1959 as part of the red-baiting of the McCarthy era. These forms of hegemonic repression limited Galarza's and Colón's abilities to engage in forms of opposition based on labor organizing and trade union activism. With these ideas in mind, it is crucial to examine their autobiographical projects in order to map their evolution from inclusive ethnic Americanism to insurgent nationalism.

Galarza's *Barrio Boy*: Leveraging a Lived Revolutionary Past

A giant of twentieth-century Chicana/o culture, Ernesto Galarza was born in the town of Jalcocotán, Nayarit, in 1905. After a three-year journey with stops in Tepic and Mazatlán, he and his mother arrived in the United States in 1913. Like many Chicana/os and Mexicana/os, the Galarzas came to the United States to escape the factional violence of the Madero Revolt.⁸ As chronicled in *Barrio Boy*, the author and his family labored as migrant workers, field hands, and in other trades, engaging in *la lucha*, the daily struggle for survival, during the early twentieth century. After the death of his mother and one uncle during the influenza epidemic of 1917, another uncle made it possible for Galarza to continue his education. He entered Occidental College in 1923, where he earned a BA in 1927. Galarza received an MA in Latin American History in 1929 and a PhD from Columbia University in 1944.⁹

During and after the completion of his PhD, Galarza spent eleven years working for government agencies in Washington, DC. He served as a research associate in education, chief of the Division of Labor and Social Information at the Pan-American Union, and consultant to the Bolivian government on labor and economic conditions. The author of numerous reports and articles on labor issues related to farmworkers and Latin American immigrants throughout the 1930s and 1940s, Galarza directed his energy toward union activities in 1947. He soon became director of research and education in California for the STFU, an organization dedicated to promoting the interests of black farmers in the South and Mexican and Chicana/o workers in the Southwest.

While working for the STFU (later renamed the National Farm Labor Union [NFLU]), Galarza was a central architect of the DiGiorgio fruit strike in 1947. Lasting for nearly thirty months, the strike was one of the earliest and longest farm worker strikes in the nation. In the spring of 1950, the NFLU was forced to retreat due in part to the availability of Bracero workers. Between 1948 and 1959, Galarza and the NFLU were involved in some twenty strikes. Galarza was a primary organizer of these strikes, resulting in a number of lawsuits directed at limiting his involvement with these struggles.

During the 1960s, Galarza turned to issues affecting urban Chicana/os and Mexicana/os. He helped found the Council of La Raza in Phoenix and became chairman of the La Raza Unida Unity Conference at its organizational meeting in 1967. Around the same period, he served on the board of the Mexican American Legal Defense and Education Fund (MALDEF), while also devoting time to teaching and writing for Occidental College, San José State University, the University of California, San Diego, the University of California, Santa Cruz, and Harvard Graduate School. He is often cited as a foundational figure in contemporary Chicana/o studies—despite the fact that he spent only a small portion of his life as an academic.

Best known for *Barrio Boy*, Galarza was also the author of many books, articles, and government reports. Among his books are *Merchants of Labor* (1964), *Spiders in the House, Workers in the Field* (1970), *Farm Workers and Agri-business in California, 1947–1960* (1977a), and *Tragedy at Chualar: El crucero de las treinta y dos cruces* (1977b). In 1979, he was the first Latino nominated for the Nobel Prize in Literature. Galarza died in 1984 at his home in San José, California.

Using humor and irony to convey his sense of social justice, *Barrio*

Boy traces the author's early life in Mexico through his "acculturation" in Sacramento during the early twentieth century.[10] Unlike Colón's explicitly polemical essays, *Barrio Boy* conforms to a more linear literary and historical trajectory. But Galarza's triangulations transform the traditional narrative of the self by positing a communal subject that challenges liberal political ideology. The "I" Galarza represents in *Barrio Boy* emerges in relation to the history and culture of his people, valorizing community values over individual experience and transforming national citizenship through a narrative of subversive education. Concomitantly, Galarza's triangulations critique the insufficiencies of ethnic Americanism, propelling him toward militant positions that anticipate insurgent nationalism.

Several critics have noted transgressive dynamics in Galarza's work. Raymund Paredes (1981) explains that *Barrio Boy* presents a critical assessment of the "American Dream." For Paredes, Mexican American writers are loath to subscribe to the American Dream partially because it blames those who do not achieve success for their own fate and because of Mexico's history of poverty that makes any myth of abundance untenable. Consequently, the dangers of materialism become a major concern of Chicana/o writers during the late twentieth century. *Barrio Boy* fits within this rubric by presenting the American Dream as a positive phenomenon, but with a critical difference. While the book portrays Young Ernie's acculturation in positive terms, it stops short of vindicating the American Dream by attributing his successes to individual talent rather than systemic conditions. Ultimately, *Barrio Boy* portrays "Galarza [. . .] as one of these rare American types, like Frederick Douglass or W. E. B. DuBois, who will not be turned from their goals" (79).

Renato Rosaldo (1987) also examines *Barrio Boy* as a text that transgresses academic and ideological discourses. But where Paredes looks at the book within the context of the American Dream, Rosaldo uses *Barrio Boy* to demonstrate how Chicana/o authors critique Gilles Deleuze and Félix Guattari's (1986) conception of *minor literature*. Briefly, Deleuze and Guattari argue that minor literature is written in the colonizers' language, but "deterritorialized" through the political nature of the text, allowing minor authors to emphasize the collective and enunciative value of their work (16–17). Rosaldo shows how Galarza counters this conception by utilizing Spanish and English to produce a proto-Borderlands consciousness. This proto-Borderlands consciousness allows Galarza to transpose his experiences of injustice in Mexico to contemporary Chicana/o struggles in the United States: "When the autobiography nears its end, 'The Conflict' and the target of Galarza's political attacks come more clearly into focus. His central subject is not patriarchy but the Chicano struggle against Anglo-American domination" (Rosaldo 1987, 80).

Ramón Saldívar (1990) also considers transgression in the narrative. But where Rosaldo and Paredes focus on Anglo-American domination, Saldívar's analysis centers on the transformation of the "I" in Galarza's text. As Saldívar notes, the "motifs of transformation and identity, which might have been offered in terms of the individual, are transferred instead to the entire community within which individuals exist, by which they are created, and which they in turn dialectically transform" (164). But what is transformed in *Barrio Boy* isn't a narrative of one-way assimilation (as is the case in Richard Rodríguez's work); rather, Galarza offers an account of the "complex historical-psychological process of acculturation" unfolding "as a discursive formation in which the historically constituted possibilities for identity are complexly dispersed" (167). Galarza's autobiography therefore disrupts conceptions of discrete "private" and "public" selves. Instead, the "interior self that Galarza describes does not exist in empty space but in an organic human collective, in what he calls *la raza*" (169).

I concur with these critics that transgression and transformation are basic to *Barrio Boy*. Whether it is through the disruption of traditional discourses of identity or a critique of widely held notions of national belonging, Galarza's text is replete with references to the transformation of Young Ernie and his community.[11] In particular, I build on Saldívar's analysis by suggesting that Galarza transforms individual subjectivity and the concept of struggle as an individualist project. The "I" in *Barrio Boy* therefore signifies both community history and national belonging. It undermines the liberal political subject that serves as the foundation for state power, posing instead a multifaceted "I" that resists the narrative closure of individualism and the limits of dualism inherent in the individual–community binary. *Barrio Boy* represents more than the transformation from individual identity to a communal sense of the self; in fact, Galarza triangulates the individual and the community in relation to national structures: in this case, conceptions of social belonging in Mexico and the United States.

These transformations are visible in Galarza's description of Jalcocotán. By mapping the "I" onto the community, Galarza challenges liberal individualism, contesting the basic principles of capitalist society. Unlike later descriptions of his formative years, Jalco is represented as an Edenic socialist paradise:

> Jalcocotán and the forest had always been a part of each other. "El Monte," the old men said, "no es de nadie y es de todos"—the forest doesn't belong to anyone and it belongs to everyone. Like those of my pueblo, the men of Tecuitata and the other villages on the mountain talked vaguely of boundary lines between their portions of the *monte*. But when anyone asked how far the village timber extended, the *jalcocotecano* would answer with a sweeping wave of the hand. The gesture could mean that it all belonged to us, even the farthest ridges of the Sierra Madre, even to Jalisco. (1971, 5)

It seems that in Jalcocotán there is no individual property ownership, as evidenced by the description of the land and pueblo as belonging to each other. In contrast to the other spaces on his journey (including his barrio in Sacramento), there are no borders on El Monte.[12] Since the land "no es de nadie y es de todos" (doesn't belong to anyone, but is shared among all), Galarza contests the capitalist system that maintains land ownership as the ultimate expression of liberal individualism.[13] This is the case not only in Jalco but also in neighboring pueblos throughout the Sierra Madre.

Underscoring these ideas is the fact that the social contract in Jalco has a different epistemological foundation. This epistemological shift is signaled in the transformation from the "I" to the voice of the community. Galarza triangulates the "I" by merging individual consciousness with community and national identity. He shifts the personal revelation of details about the village to the voice of the pueblo: when "anyone" asks about village land, *any jalcocotecano* (citizen of Jalcocotán) can attest to the status of property ownership. Thus the silent "sweeping wave of the hand" and the phrase, "it all belonged to us, even the farthest ridges of the Sierra Madre."

The communal character of land in the Sierra Madre also functions as a designation of national identity. Evoking a precondition of Benedict Anderson's (2007) famous characterization of the "imagined community" (6), *jalcocotecanos* define themselves in relation to a contiguous geographical space. The "sweeping wave of the hand" signifies a shift in consciousness by implying that *all* the land belongs to the imagined community of the pueblo—and by extension the nation—as part of its inhabitants' birthright.

Another aspect of Galarza's engagement with national consciousness is signified in Young Ernie's break with capitalist modes of representation. Accordingly, the narrative challenges liberal democracy and its accompanying governmental forms in Mexico and the United States.[14] Considering that many significant political events of the period (from the Madero Revolt to Emiliano Zapata's guerrilla tactics) centered on land reform and the hacienda system, the fact that communal property is the dominant mode of land distribution in Jalco constitutes a break with the political system in Mexico. Likewise, in a time and space where the hacienda system was entrenched in Mexican life, Galarza's denial of it through the representation of Jalco as a protosocialist paradise contradicts the realities of nascent capitalism.[15] The fact that *jalcocotecanos* take only what they use from the forest further contests the system of labor exploitation and accumulation.

But this is not a prehistory that romanticizes Jalco. In fact, Jalco is politicized before the author's (literal) arrival into the community.[16] One way this politicization functions is in the backdrop of revolutionary consciousness that underpins the narrator's description of his pueblo:

> Besides providing shelter from wind and sun, the location of
> Jalcocotán was meant to give protection against outsiders. The
> old men of the pueblo told it the way it had been. And it was true,
> because they had heard it from the old men before them, and they
> in turn from the old men who had founded Jalco in the days of the
> Spaniards, perhaps even before that. The first settlers were refugees from the fertile river bottoms and the coast lands, taken from
> them by force. They had moved into the rugged mountains of the
> Sierra Madre, founding their villages where attack was difficult.
> A few hundred yards above and below Jalco, the trail squeezed
> through natural strong points, bottlenecks where rocks were
> plentiful and from which boulders could be rolled on approaching
> enemies. (1971, 5)

While the history of struggle embedded in the description of Jalco serves as a foundation for individual identity (and by extension the transformation of community and national consciousness), it also seems that the town was one of a number of mountain villages founded by the indigenous peoples of the Nayarit and Jalisco regions. In fact, Jalco was founded to protect the inhabitants from Spanish colonization. The unstated presences in the passage are the Huichole and Cora Indians who have inhabited the Sierra Madre continuously since before the arrival of the Spaniards.[17] The implication of the founding of Jalco is that it is a politically resistant space that was constructed in opposition to the colonizer. Its strategic location, along with the narrative of its founding, places Jalco within the framework of revolutionary time and space; Jalco is literally built on oppositional ground. Thus the symbolic manifestations of attack and survival are visible in the hurricanes that sweep through Nayarit regularly and the implied threat of Spanish and Mexican colonial authorities. This valorization of indigenous roots anticipates much of the rhetoric of many Chicana/o nationalist groups, who often characterized revolutionary subjectivity in indigenous terms.

The passage also offers an alternative political and community history. Rather than documenting the history of national identity through traditional historiographic methods, Galarza relies on the oral traditions of "old men" who had "heard it from the old men before them." Here, the burden of historical validity is placed on ontological experience, rather than documentary sources. By shifting the narrative focus of history from the individual "I" to a collective, oral tradition, Galarza valorizes the indigenous roots of the community while also signifying the legitimacy of communal identities. These stories are true because they've been passed down among the people. In this self-referential way, history validates the presence of a community founded in revolutionary time and space, which in turn validates the history they embody.

Jalco's revolutionary character is also signified in its landscape. The survivor of numerous storms and battles, the old walnut tree that flourishes in the arroyo backing Jalco serves as a microcosm of the revolutionary character of the village: "On the edge of the pond, at the far side, there was an enormous walnut tree, standing like an open umbrella whose ribs extended halfway across the still water of the pool. The scars on the trunk of the mighty bole showed where the arroyo had bashed it during storms of former years. But the nogal had always won these battles. The arroyo, when the storms had passed, gave up and backed away, leaving around the trunk a small beach where the pond lapped gently on the gravel" (10).

Galarza's description of the old nogal offers a model for oppositional consciousness. Though it bears the scars of its encounters with logs and other debris, the nogal has prospered in the sediment that builds around its base. Similar to the self-referential view of history espoused by the old men of the community, the fact that this tree has survived battles with the elements provides the (literal) foundation that enables it to live into the future. By logical implication, *jalcocotecanos* are able to survive the tempests of the past by preserving their indigenous character. If they don't flourish, at least *jalcocotecanos* come to understand "the difference between making a living on the mountain and working for the *patrones*" because on El Monte "you took home corn, bananas, peppers, coffee, and anything else you raised" (58). By contrast, the hated *patrones* (land owners) wield whips and use clerks "who kept numbers in a book that proved you always owed him something" (58–59).

Yet simply because the old nogal has withstood storms of the past and preserved a small beach, it is not free from the threat of further incursions. In fact, the pond that laps at the foot of the old tree retains the potential to transform into a raging tempest. Taken from this perspective it is crucial that the sediment that protects its roots remain in place. To thrive in this context is to embody the potential to oppose storms that will inevitably undermine the metaphorical roots of the community.

Since *Barrio Boy* centers on transformation, it is important to recognize that Galarza offers a complex portrayal of political agency that can be cognitively mapped onto his community. These descriptions function as implicit portrayals of how Mexicana/os—and by implication Chicana/os—are constituted by a tradition of oppositional action that dates to the pre-Columbian period. Since their spaces of origin are founded on revolutionary ground, Mexicana/os and Chicana/os are poised as nascent political beings. Therefore, part of the transformation that takes place is the revelation that Chicana/os are always already revolutionary subjects— regardless of whether their social location is Mexico or the United States. This revelation is crucial for identifying the historical roots of Chicana/o struggle.

In fact, revolutionary consciousness is replete in the narrative. Throughout his travels, Young Ernie disarmingly recounts events that portray the revolutionary character of his life and people.[18] For example, his witnessing of the rooster Coronel's mock-epic battle with a vulture underscores a variety of social imperatives that indicate his growing awareness of revolutionary consciousness: "Coronel sailed in. His wings spread, his beak half open and his legs churning over the hard earth, he struck the *zopilote* full front, doubled forward so that his beak and his spurs were at the *zopilote's* breast feathers. The buzzard flapped one great wing over Coronel and bowled him over. The rooster twisted to his feet and began making short passes in cock-fighting style, leaping into the air and snapping his outstretched legs, trying to reach his antagonists with his spurs" (31).

Coronel's fight against the *zopilote* suggests both a politics and a tactics of contestation for Chicana/os and Mexicana/os. Like those working to overthrow the forces of racism and capital, Coronel's battle seems hopeless in the face of the larger *zopilote*—a monstrous refiguring of the U.S. bald eagle. Similarly, the vulture's greed recalls the parasitic nature of the rich that Young Ernie sees in Tepic, Mazatlán, and Sacramento. Faced with the overwhelming tasks of opposing hegemonic capitalism and racism in both Mexico and the United States, Chicana/os and Mexicana/os were forced to adopt mobile oppositional strategies. Coronel's agility thus serves as a model for contemporary struggles: by utilizing the perseverance and agility that is the *jalcocotecano*'s (and by extension Chicana/o's) birthright, the disenfranchised can defeat their parasitic enemy.

The passage also (and perhaps unconsciously) reveals complex gender dynamics. Since one of Coronel's hens instigates the fight by pecking at the vulture's breakfast, there is an element of machismo in the rooster's struggle. As Carl Gutiérrez-Jones (1995) notes, to be macho in Chicana/o communities is to be *muy gallo* (literally, very rooster). Paralleling the problematic gender politics within many Chicano movement groups, Galarza's construction relies on the dual notion of women as traitors *and* repositories of family virtue. Norma Alarcón (1983) reminds us that simultaneously traitorous and maternal figure of La Malinche serves as the organizing trope for gender relations between Chicanos and Chicanas. Gloria Anzaldúa (2007) also suggests that the Aztec eagle and serpent function as metaphors for the masculine triumph over the feminine.[19] Because she symbolically functions as the mother of the race and the source of conflict with Anglo culture, the dichotomy of the mother-whore infuses this scene with its gendered charge.

Yet in a formulation that seems to underscore the problems of effecting opposition, Galarza reminds us that Coronel's victory is incomplete. Although he drives the vulture away from his hens, the *zopilote* escapes with the "chicken guts that had tempted the hen" to a "nearby tree, where he perched and finished his spoils" (31). Galarza thus suggests that any struggle that doesn't reclaim the metaphorical body of the contestants is only partial. He problematizes Coronel's *muy gallo* crowing as a premature celebration, emphasizing that projects of political empowerment that don't reconstitute the body politic are doomed to only symbolic victories.[20]

Overturning the social order becomes the focus of Young Ernie's education once the scene shifts from the revolutionary ground of Jalco, to the larger, metropolitan spaces of Tepic, Mazatlán, and Sacramento. In these spaces, Ernie experiences educational imperatives that prepare him for a life of struggle. One imperative centers on the idea of education itself. While, as Saldívar notes, Galarza's autobiography is "one of a boy's education, the manner and substance of his education are wholly different" (1990, 163). Consequently, education forms another point in the evolution of Young Ernie's radical political identity—as well as the cognitive mappings that transform his community and national consciousness.

The formal educational settings that punctuate the text emphasize the revolutionary character of Mexicana/os. For example, after his family's move to Mazatlán, Young Ernie attends classes at the local primary school. But his education focuses on more than reading, writing, and arithmetic. Instead we see the pupils prepare for revolutionary consciousness: "Don Salvador took over the class to give us lectures in history. They were more like dramatic recitals than lectures: about Hidalgo, the tragic fighting priest; Galeana, the general who chased Spaniards with his guerrillas; Guerrero, whose very name meant war. We learned about Pipila, the Indian boy who strapped a slab of rock to his back and thus armored crawled on all fours through a rain of Spanish bullets and set fire to their fortress that had withstood the whole patriot army" (Galarza 1971, 151).

While Don Salvador's rhetoric is dramatic and overblown, his message is direct: Mexican—and by extension Chicana/o—history is constituted by a revolutionary tradition. Don Salvador's stories recount famous revolutionary heroes like El Pipila, valorizing Mexico's indigenous roots in a manner that is reminiscent of the Chicano movement.[21] These heroes stand in stark contrast to their counterparts in Sacramento. Hidalgo, Galeana, and El Pipila were direct participants in the struggle for independence from Spanish colonialism. Lincoln, for whom Young Ernie's school in Sacramento is named, seems a pale technocrat by comparison. Since Lincoln was a symbolic hero of the Popular Front, the implicit critique in this comparison signals Galarza's navigation toward the militancy of insurgent nationalism.

Similarly, Mexico's revolutionary past politicizes the classroom in the narrative present (i.e., during the Mexican Civil War). Considering that Young Ernie's education begins during the Madero Revolt, it seems likely that Galarza's choice to highlight the revolutionary character of his education reinforces Don Salvador's nationalist message that "Mexicans will never bend the neck to a foreign yoke. *(Death to the foreigners.)* Not in the East, not in the West, not in the South, nay, not even in the North, is there a power capable of subjugating our national destiny or staining our national honor. *(Death to the gringos.)*" (155). Especially in relation to Don Salvador's condemnation of U.S. hemispheric hegemony, it seems that Young Ernie heeds the messages that he learns in Leandro Valle: one must be willing to take direct revolutionary action to triumph over injustice.

Young Ernie's awareness of the revolution increases as he travels toward the United States. On one level this awareness of revolution can be accounted for by the fact that the front lines of the Madero Revolt took place primarily in northern Mexican provinces. It is logical that as his family travels through Nayarit, Sinaloa, and Sonora they would have witnessed events that took place on the front lines of the revolution. But because this first-person personal narrative centers on transformation, Young Ernie's awareness of revolution locates the protagonist's *evolution* to a militant political position. It is therefore significant that as Young Ernie moves toward his ultimate destination in the United States, he witnesses direct forms of revolutionary action. Part of the transformation that takes place in Young Ernie's journey toward the United States is from the oppositional potential that constitutes his historical legacy to concrete, revolutionary action.

The transformation from oppositional potential to radical action appears in the intertwining of public revolution with private struggle. For example, Young Ernie's brother José characterizes the experience of *la lucha* in militant national terms: "Every morning was a new round in the match between us and the city. If he [José] came back with a tostón or a peso we won the round. If not, we lost. If we won, we could tell as he walked up the hill, whistling his favorite tune, 'Adios Mamá Carlota.'"[22] As Young Ernie explains, "Adios Mamá Carlota" recounts the liberation of the Mexican people from Emperor Maximilian.[23] In fact, José "whistle[s] the just deserts of Maximilian as a sign to the family that we, too, had overcome, at least for that day" (134).

José's formulation takes on a different perspective when examined from the standpoint of triangulation. By intertwining the personal and public, José suggests that the daily struggle for survival is akin to the expulsion of a colonial power. His understanding of domestic life is mediated by the project of national formation. Here, Galarza emphasizes that national consciousness is an integral aspect of the Chicana/o cause. The implication for Galarza's contemporary readers is that José's type of opposition has a place at the forefront of revolutionary struggle.

Because the Galarzas must fight to survive in both Mexico and the United States, it is important to consider how Chicana/o struggles encompass *both* sides of the border. Consequently, José's formulation problematizes simplistic readings of life *en el otro lado* (the other side). Since his struggle takes place in Mazatlán, it emphasizes that life in Mexico is never idyllic. Overcoming the labors of daily living in the city prepares Young Ernie for opposition to hegemony regardless of its physical or social location. Here, Galarza figures Chicana/o militancy as a complex struggle against injustice—regardless of its manifestation in racism, class, or political oppression.

Galarza's critique of oppressive politics reaches a climax when Young Ernie and his family move to Sacramento. In Sacramento he encounters discrimination that radically circumscribes his family's life chances. It is only when he discovers the emerging Chicana/o community in Sacramento that it is possible to grasp Young Ernie's transformation from political potential to oppositional action (symbolized in his first labor organizing mission at the end of the text). Once again, the scenes detailing Young Ernie's acculturation in the school system provide important clues to this process.

Contrasting with the revolutionary education he receives in Mazatlán, Young Ernie encounters subtle and overt forms of racism in the Sacramento school. One example comes when he works through his English pronunciation with his first-grade teacher Miss Ryan:

> She made me watch her lips and then close my eyes as she repeated words I found hard to read. When we came to know each other better, I tried interrupting to tell Miss Ryan how we said it in Spanish. It didn't work. She only said "oh" and went on with *pasture, bow-wow-wow,* and *pretty*. It was as if in that closet we were both discovering together the secrets of the English language and grieving together over the tragedies of Bo-Peep. The main reason I was

graduated with honors from the first grade was that I had fallen in love with Miss Ryan. Her radiant, no-nonsense character made us either afraid not to love her or love her so we would not be afraid, I am not sure which. (210)

While he initially submits to her suggestions about pronunciation, Miss Ryan's enforcement of English normativity constitutes an act of cultural annihilation. Her denial of Ernie's right to make sense of English through Spanish undermines his naïve desire for equal cultural exchange. In her unintelligible response to Ernie's suggestions about "how we said it in Spanish," the U.S. educational mission is clear: it enforces a specific conception of citizenship instead of encountering others according to a multicultural or pluralist perspective.[24]

It is also important that this encounter takes place in the confined space of the closet. Rather than engaging Ernie in the open classroom, Miss Ryan's indoctrination takes on the character of an interrogation. The closed space of the closet mimics not only an interrogation room but also the political position from which Miss Ryan emerges. Rather than being open to a wider cultural exchange, the closet emphasizes that Miss Ryan's world is a closed space with only one entrance and exit. There is no way through this space except through the unequal power of hegemony.

The emphasis on cultural assimilation evidenced by Miss Ryan is further underscored by Miss Hopley, the patriotic Lincoln School principal. Miss Hopley, like Miss Ryan, insists on a particular notion of citizenship. As Young Ernie notes in relation to Miss Hopley's politics:

> Miss Hopley and her teachers never let us forget why we were at Lincoln: *for those who were alien, to become good Americans; for those who were so born, to accept the rest of us*. Off the school grounds we traded the same insults we heard from our elders. On the playground we were sure to be marched up to the principal's office for calling someone a wop, a chink, a dago, or a greaser. The school was not so much a melting pot as a griddle where Miss Hopley and her helpers warmed knowledge into us and roasted racial hatreds out of us. (211; emphasis mine)

Despite Ernie's admiration of Miss Hopley's apparent antiracism, the narrative once again undermines the progressive nature of a U.S.

education. Like Miss Ryan, who rejects the chance to engage in cultural exchange, Miss Hopley characterizes immigrants as aliens. By characterizing them as aliens, Miss Hopley casts students like Young Ernie as problems that must be resolved through enforced notions of citizenship. Moreover, it is significant that her patriotism is the most rigid of any represented in the text. As the person charged with transforming young minds from aliens to U.S. citizens, Miss Hopley understands her mission well. She must "roast" out elements that do not conform to citizenship in the United States in order to "melt" these children into assimilation.

There is also an implicit comparison between Miss Hopley and Don Salvador, the principal of Young Ernie's school in Mazatlán. Where Don Salvador and Miss Hopley proclaim patriotic narratives, their messages are different. Don Salvador's dramatic recitals undermine the state by celebrating a shared history of revolutionary activity and advocating the remaking of Mexican society vis-à-vis the Madero Revolt. Miss Hopley, on the other hand, supports the state by reinforcing the status quo in the United States. Regardless of their social locations, it is significant that the two representatives of state education in the text have such different objectives for their pupils. Where Don Salvador emphasizes oppositional consciousness, Miss Hopley suggests assimilation.

Additionally, Miss Hopley's school is characterized not as a space of potential encounter (albeit of the problematic melting pot variety) but rather as a "griddle" where she "roasted racial hatreds out of us." The image of "roasting" hardly conjures a positive view of interethnic encounters at the Lincoln School. Instead, these encounters deny students of color the rights of linguistic, cultural, and social enfranchisement.

Galarza continues his critique of the U.S. educational system through his representation of the mock election. Mimicking the political process he will see later, the mock election reveals the antidemocratic nature of electoral politics in the United States. Losing the election for class president by two votes to Homer, his Irish American rival, Ernie realizes that his opponent disingenuously voted for himself in what is ironically a "demonstration of how the American people vote for president" (212). While it is to be expected that Homer would vote for himself, Young Ernie's introduction to the electoral process by Miss Hopley suggests that voting for oneself constitutes an act of bad faith. It is significant, then, that Young Ernie loses the election based on the rhetorical hypocrisy of his rival. Here, Galarza suggests that political and social enfranchisement cannot be left to the well wishes of Anglo-Americans or to the ostensibly fair electoral process. Instead this portrayal demonstrates how racial animosity is roasted in to the schoolchildren at Lincoln. For those not "lucky" enough to be "natural born citizens," the message is clear: one cannot trust the rhetoric of equality and liberal democracy espoused by the U.S. system of education.

These aspects of life in Sacramento are not limited to one national group in *Barrio Boy*. Instead, Galarza represents interethnic coalitions as basic aspects of Young Ernie's experience. For example, when describing the "lower quarter" of Sacramento, Ernie notes that "the lower quarter was not exclusively a Mexican *barrio* but a mix of many nationalities" (198). These nationalities include poor whites, Japanese, Chinese, Filipino, Hindu, Slavic, German, Portuguese, and Italian families in addition to the Mexicans and Chicana/os with whom the Galarzas affiliate. As Young Ernie explains, the barrio functions as an extended family network that provides for the newly arrived, regardless of their ethnic or national affiliation. Indeed, there is a striking level of cooperation and association between the various ethnic groups that compose the lower Sacramento barrio.

For example, Young Ernie notes how his family cooperates with fellow tenants at the family's home at 418 L Street. The "Old Gentleman"—an elderly disabled white man—"knocked on our wall when he was ready to put on his necktie and coat, a signal for me to go and help him" (218). Similarly, Ernie's mother frequently "helped the Indian lady with her wash," a favor the woman returns by taking Young Ernie to the state fair one summer (218–19). Moreover, the Galarza's "circle of acquaintances and friends" constitutes a plethora of ethnic groups, including Big Singh "the brawny Hindu" (219), the proprietor of a Chinese laundry, the owner of a Japanese fish store (220), Lettie, a black dancer (221), and Mr. Hans a German musician (217). These portrayals suggest a shared, interethnic history of struggle in the United States. While these struggles are shared unevenly by those of German, Italian, or Portuguese ancestry who would become "white," Galarza is careful to show how interethnic solidarity is an important part of Young Ernie's political formation.

These representations lay the groundwork for oppositional politics by mobilizing the inherent revolutionary character of Chicana/os in the United States. As Young Ernie notes, the most frequent topic of conversation among newly arrived Chicana/os in the barrio is the latest news of the Mexican Revolution. Galarza therefore uses his first-person personal narrative to represent oppositional consciousness as a basic aspect of the Chicana/o character, and by extension, minority and immigrant communities generally. Rather than attempting to mobilize oppositional consciousness through education and politicization, the author represents his life as a growing awareness of his organic revolutionary potential. Likewise, by documenting a tradition of direct revolutionary action, Galarza historicizes a potential foundation for oppositional projects on both sides of the border. By showing how Mexicans have fought oppression regardless of whether they were in Mexico or the United States, he offers another tool in the struggle to mobilize political consciousness.

Jesús Colón: Transforming National Consciousness through Culture

Less well known than Galarza, Jesús Colón was born in 1901 in Cayey, Puerto Rico. Colón came to the United States as a stowaway aboard the *SS Carolina* in 1918, initially settling with his older brother Joaquín in Brooklyn, New York.[25] Because he had little education beyond what he was able to glean from his experience as a *tabaquero* (cigar maker) and his homespun training, Colón was often forced to take any available job, including some that were difficult and dangerous.[26] Among these were jobs cleaning oil tankers, trucking heavy cargo on the icy docks of Hoboken, New Jersey, and manually removing labels from bottles.[27] Despite his understandable preoccupation with securing a living, he became a committed political and cultural activist.

As with contemporaries Arturo Schomburg and Bernardo Vega and predecessors like José Martí, *tabaquero* culture left an indelible mark on Colón and his writing. Winston James (1998) has noted how the *tabaquero* tradition was important to Colón's intellectual and political formation. First, the tradition of *el lector*, or the reader, exposed *tabaqueros* to political and cultural texts turning "cigarmakers (even 'illiterate' ones) into one of the best-informed and best-instructed groups in Puerto Rican society" (Quintero Rivera 1983, 27).[28] Second, because they were among the trades most adversely affected by the changes in the global economy in the wake of 1898, *tabaqueros* often assumed leadership roles in political struggles on the island, predisposing them to similar positions on the mainland.[29] Furthermore, *tabaqueros* were taught the value of cultural and aesthetic forms to political struggles. Because the tradition of *el lector* linked political issues with cultural texts, it provided cigar workers with opportunities to decode working-class cultural production in complex terms. Consequently, *tabaqueros* were among the most progressive of the working classes because they came to understand how cultural forms are reflective of collective political will.

Although he did not work in cigar production after coming to New York in 1918, Colón was permanently influenced by the radical Left associated with *tabaquero* culture. This exposure to *tabaquero* culture inclined him toward socialism and writing, first in his native Spanish and later in English. In 1923, just five years after his arrival in New York, he became one of the correspondents to *Justicia*, a publication of the Federación Libre de Trabajadores in Puerto Rico. As his command of English grew, he contributed to the Communist Party USA (CPUSA) newspapers *The Daily Worker* and *The Daily World*, as well as magazines like *Mainstream*, and the Spanish-language, anti-Franco organ *Liberación*, first edited by Colón's contemporary and fellow autobiographer Bernardo Vega. Colón also published in outlets more loosely affiliated with the party, like *Los Pueblos Hispanos* and *La Voz*. By 1955, Colón had a regular column called "As I See It From Here," first in *The Daily Worker* and later in *The Worker* (no longer daily).[30] Many of the stories included in *A Puerto Rican in New York* were originally published in his columns in *Mainstream*, *The Daily Worker*, and *The Worker*. Colón also taught at the Jefferson School of Social Science and was a frequent lecturer at universities and fraternal organizations in the New York area.[31]

Embodying Antonio Gramsci's ideal of the organic intellectual, Colón's political work wasn't limited to writing and lecturing. As Edna Acosta-Belén and Virginia Sánchez Korrol (1993) observe, Colón was involved with over twenty-five organizations dedicated to leftist politics, Puerto Rican civil rights on the mainland, and the decolonization of the island. Among these were the Alianza Obrera Puertorriqueña, the Ateneo Obrero Hispano, and the CPUSA. But his political involvement constituted more than rank-and-file membership. Colón often held influential positions, many in national organizations. He was a founding member of La Liga Puertorriqueña e Hispana, was the president of the Sociedad Fraternal Cervantes (the umbrella for Spanish-speaking lodges of the International Workers Order), held a seat on the board of directors of Casa de Puerto Rico, and served as the chair of the CPUSA's Puerto Rican Commission. Colón was also an important member of the American Labor Party, mounting two unsuccessful bids for political office under their banner.[32]

Similar to Galarza's influence on Chicana/o studies, Colón is often acknowledged as a *pionero* (pioneer) of the Nuyorican movement. This acknowledgement notwithstanding, there has been a startling lack of critical attention dedicated to Colón's work.[33] Outside of Juan Flores's foreword to *A Puerto Rican in New York*, Edna Acosta-Belén and Virginia Sánchez Korrol's "The World of Jesús Colón," Winston James's chapter on Colón and Arturo Schomburg, Silvio Torres-Saillant's (2003) article on Colón's 1969 political campaign for city comptroller of New York, Linda Delgado's chapter (2005), and Maritza Stanchich's (2010) recent chapter, little has been written about the author or his work.[34] I argue that part of this critical inattention emerges from the contradictory nature of Colón's life. Unlike many leftist intellectuals of color of his generation, Colón never broke with the CPUSA. Despite the party's purges and the sometimes problematic position it held in relation to race and ethnicity, Colón remained a member until he died in 1974. James (1998, 337–38, n99), Acosta-Belén and Sánchez Korrol, and Flores all take note of Colón's unusually consistent political position over the course of his life. In particular James points to his commitment to Stalin and Khrushchev through the 1950s and 1960s. Colón's positions were increasingly unpopular and intellectually unsafe in the climate of McCarthyism and the actions of the HUAC, before which he was summoned on two occasions.[35]

Colón was a prolific writer, authoring no less than four hundred sketches, articles, poems, short stories, and pamphlets over nearly fifty years (Acosta-Belén and Sánchez Korrol, 20–21). Despite the volume of writing he produced, I focus on *A Puerto Rican in New York* for several reasons. First, while the breadth of Colón's work is diverse, *A Puerto Rican in New York* offers a microcosm of the author's primary interests. Among the sketches included in the book, there are consistent refrains that encounter racism in the United States and Latin America, the decolonization of Puerto Rico, and the historical and cultural importance of Boricuas on the mainland. While two posthumous collections, *The Way It Was and Other Writings* (1993) and *Lo que el pueblo me dice . . . : Crónicas de la colonia puertorriqueña en Nueva York* (2001), have been issued since Colón's death, *A Puerto Rican in New York* remains the only longer work he completed during his lifetime. As such, it reveals something of Colón's thoughts about what he deemed worthy of inclusion in a longer narrative.

When we examine his triangulations, *A Puerto Rican in New York* evidences the author's transition from modes of opposition rooted in the age of the CIO to political positions that anticipate insurgent nationalism.

One place to locate such evidence is in Colón's transformation of the "I." Like Galarza, Colón transforms the "I" by matrixing subjectivity in relation to community belonging and national citizenship. For example, in the opening pages, the author notes that "We Puerto Ricans have even been subjected to treatment in the Broadway drama and a fabulously successful musical show. But invariably this treatment harps on what is superficial and sentimental, transient and ephemeral, or bizarre and grotesque in Puerto Rican life—and always out of context with the real history, culture, and traditions of my people" (Colón 1982, 9).

The play in question is the Broadway musical *West Side Story*. As an important intellectual of his generation, Colón took exception with the stereotypical portrayal of Puerto Ricans in the play. As Frances Negrón-Muntaner points out, "*West Side Story* remains the most cohesive cultural text to 'hail'—and perhaps even more important for a discussion of ethnonational shame, to *see*—Puerto Ricans as a distinctly American ethnic group" (2004, 60–61). As she goes on to argue, this ethnonational cohesion came at the expense of a negative Puerto Rican national imaginary. In his attempt to contest such racist stereotypes, Colón refuses a singular narrative identity, countering the "I" by emphasizing the collective aspects of cultural experience. This matrixed representation figures Colón's personal experiences as evocative of collective memory. His stories are reflective of the views of others, offering a composite portrait of the self that blends the "I" with Puerto Rican communities in New York City.

As a part of this blending of the "I," Colón uses multiple literary genres, including essays, vignettes, short stories, and autobiographical sketches to disrupt the linear text. Where Galarza's work overturns the liberal political self by focusing on transformation in narratives of travel and education, Colón's *A Puerto Rican in New York* remakes first-person personal narrative genres in terms of their multifaceted representations of individual subjectivity, community affirmation, and national belonging. These collective representations range from the banal (the pleasures of reading in the bathtub) to the explicitly political (a condemnation of U.S. policies in countries like Trujillo's Dominican Republic or Ibañez's Chile). Colón links these portrayals through his own position as interlocutor, revealing a collective sketch of how ordinary citizens engage with and contest their marginalization.

An example of such a multifaceted subjectivity comes when Colón describes the life of his friend José. José, a self-taught musician, historian, and music theorist, is one of the voices that constitute Puerto Rican communities in the city: "While he plays I keep wondering how many Joses [sic] are lost in the basements and top floors of New York City, with nobody telling them that they have talent, that they are perhaps geniuses. That they are a product of that ever self-renewing admirable mass of beauty and ugliness, enthusiasm and frustration we call the people" (Colón 1982, 88).

Reading this scene in terms of its triangulations reveals the myriad ways that Colón matrixes the "I" with projects of communal and national affirmation. In particular, the connection between working-class consciousness and individual intellectual production is apparent in Colón's celebration of "the people." Moreover, since the conditions of José's intellectual production mimic the author's, the musician is representative of a class of intellectuals whose labor goes unrecognized in the racialized space of New York. As Colón notes, José is the composer of one of the "hit[s] of the hour" (93). But because he does not understand the laws of capitalist production in the United States, José loses his copyright protection, and thus the royalties to which he is entitled.

In this collective sketch, Colón's reading of cultural production provides a sophisticated analysis of how people create agency for themselves. Although characters like José experience racial, labor, and housing exploitation, Colón is careful to point out that the musician continues his creative project, even in the face of his robbery at the hands of music publishers. This continuation emphasizes opposition as an organic component of cultural production in New York City barrios. Anticipating the tactics of cultural nationalist groups like the Young Lords and the Puerto Rican Student Union (PRSU), Colón validates the daily cultural expression of his community in the context of hegemonic oppression.[36]

Along these lines, it is crucial to note how *A Puerto Rican in New York* constitutes one of the intellectual forbears of insurgent nationalism. George Lipsitz (2001) explains that cultural texts often represent "movement spaces" (171) that offer locations where individuals can envision political change. The relationship between imaginative cultural texts and physical spaces helps individuals to rethink their relationships with dominant ideologies. As we see in the sketch of José's cultural work, Colón depicts actors and events that form movement spaces.

The chapter titled "Wanted—A Statue" provides another example of these dynamics in Colón's work. Here, the author argues that most ethnic and national groups in New York City are recognized through public art projects. Opening with a list of prominent figures from Italian, German, Irish, and Norwegian communities, the author notes that "there is not one statue of a Puerto Rican in all the marble and bronze figures in the city" (1982, 135). Colón's assertion that Puerto Ricans in New York need a statue offers a subtle understanding of the political implications of artistic representation: "But someone may ask: why do the Puerto Ricans or, for that matter, any nationality need a statue? Well, we might answer that statues serve as inspiration; as historical reminders of a healthful pride in one's people's contributions to the collective cultural heritage of humanity" (135). By referring to them in *national* terms, the author demands that the United States recognize Puerto Ricans as an independent historical and sociocultural unit.[37] According to this logic a statue serves as a "historical reminder" for Puerto Ricans who understand colonial domination and U.S. intervention. The statue also serves as a potential galvanizing point for (literally) concrete political action. Colón thus makes a case for recognizing Puerto Rican lives and history in the city. Likewise, because many of the inhabitants of the original Puerto Rican colonia in New York were political radicals who participated in social movements opposing Spanish and U.S. imperialisms, Colón's demand for a statue also pays homage to the historically occluded activists who lived and worked in New York City.[38]

Yet his demand for a statue transcends simple recognition in the United States, as the legacy of colonial history that underpins relations with the island requires us to consider the larger political dimensions of Colón's claim. Because statues are typically placed in parks, museums, and other public locations, they provide gathering places for political action. As well, the symbolic choices made in the urge to immortalize individual actors helps to inspire the populace. Consequently, in the disarmingly simple request for a statue, Colón makes a case for the United States to reconcile its colonial relationship with the island.

Another example of these ideas comes when the author advocates for a section devoted to Puerto Ricans in the New York Public Library. Echoing calls for Puerto Rican and Latina/o studies programs that would emerge as a central claim for groups like the PRSU, Colón demands that the New York Public Library provide an institutional space for intellectual inquiry: "If you drop into any of the branch public libraries in Manhattan you can get, for free, a list of books dealing with Puerto Rico and the Puerto Ricans living in New York" (138). But Colón understands that the symbolic incorporation of such a list is insufficient because "the library is telling the people of New York that we are a nation with our own territory, our own economy, language and culture" (13). By emphasizing intellectual production over stereotypes, Colón underscores the ways the library system already recognizes Puerto Ricans as an independent nation. Puerto Ricans are thus transformed from their popular image as marginal gang members (e.g., via the popular representation in the play *West Side Story*) to rational subjects engaged with cultural and intellectual production.

Colón's understanding of the symbolic implications of cultural representation also recognizes the hegemonic imperatives implicit in many dominant texts. Reading Kipling's famous poem of self-reliance, "If," he contests liberal political ideology that places self-sufficiency at the forefront of thinking in the United States: "'If,' by Kipling, was the poem. At seventeen, my evening prayer and my first morning thought. I repeated it every day with the resolution to live up to the very last line of that poem. I would visit the government employment office on Jay Street. The conversations among the Puerto Ricans on the large wooden benches in the employment office were always on the same subject. How to find a decent place to live. How they would not rent to Negroes or Puerto Ricans. How Negroes and Puerto Ricans were given the pink slips first at work" (40–41).

Recalling Galarza's understated irony, Colón's reading of "If" contrasts the ethos of liberal individualism with the lived experiences of working-class Puerto Ricans and African Americans in New York City. As the passage illustrates, the narrator first attempts to "live up to the very last line" of the poem, attempting to make it the mantra of his working life. Like the Irish, Italian, and German immigrants who came before him, Colón is at first hopeful that through hard work and sacrifice, Puerto Ricans can also share the bounty of the United States. But as César Andreu Iglesias observes, "some people are inclined to view the Puerto Rican experience as a historical repetition of earlier migrations to the United States, such as those of the Irish or the Italians. There are similarities [. . .] But the Puerto Rican case is more complex" (1984, xiii). Colón concluded that Puerto Rico's colonial status and the persistent racialization of immigrants from the island obviate the liberal individualism inherent in Kipling's poem.

Accordingly, Colón's ultimate rejection of the message of self-reliance in "If" emerges out of his ontological experience: "The weeks of unemployment and hard knocks turned into months. I continued to find two or three days of work here and there. And I continued to be thrown out when I rebelled at the ill treatment, overwork and insults. I kept pounding the streets looking for a place where they would treat me half decently, *where my devotion to work and faith in Kipling's poem would be appreciated*" (41–42; emphasis mine).

This ironic recognition of life in New York has its final expression when the narrator uses the physical copy of the poem and its frame to start a fire in his coal stove. Here, Colón disrupts the ideology of self-reliance that blames victims of racialization for their own lack of success through an explicit material critique. By attending to his physical survival, Colón rejects the liberal individualist ideology of the self-embodied in Kipling's poem and suggests a model of contestation for his contemporary readers by literally burning the physical manifestation of such ideologies. The myths of self-reliance and narratives of racial progress that condition relations with ethnic subjects in the United States must be consumed in the fire of direct, material contestation.

But Colón's readings of culture and artistic production are not limited to one national space. Concomitantly, nearly half of the fifty-five essays and sketches included in *A Puerto Rican in New York* deal with a variety of individuals from Latina/o communities in New York City, the island of Puerto Rico, and a variety of other Latin American locations. In fact, Colón was an early proponent of interethnic consciousness. His valorization of figures like José Martí, Simón Bolivar, and Antonio Maceo Grajales situate projects of nationalism within a hemispheric framework that emphasizes similarities between Latin Americans in the United States. Anticipating the arguments of authors like Juan González (2000) who suggest that Latin American nations share a common history of exploitation with the U.S. empire, these sketches read common cultural engagements in terms of organic interethnic alliances.

Like his contemporary Arturo Schomburg, Colón also came to identify with African Americans—in part due to his Afro-Puerto Rican heritage and the antiblack racism he experienced in the United States. As Edna Acosta-Belén and Virginia Sánchez Korrol point out, "being a Black Puerto Rican, Colón experienced racial prejudice, both on the Island and in the metropolis [. . .] and was well aware that racism and segregation had a tormented and violent history and were deeply ingrained in the fabric of U.S. and Puerto Rican society" (1993, 25). One conclusion we might draw is that Colón's matrixing of himself entailed an organic connection with other aggrieved racial and ethnic groups. Consequently, the multifaceted subjectivity he depicts is engaged with a larger project of social justice that includes Puerto Ricans and other Latina/os but is not limited to a single ethnic or national group.

For example, in the vignette "A Hero in the Junk Truck," Colón recounts an experience he and his wife Concha have after finding a portrait of Latin American nationalist Simón Bolivar (1783–1830) that is about to be loaded into a garbage truck. The story opens with the question, "How many times have we read boastful statements from high educational leaders in our big newspapers that while other countries ignore the history and culture of the United States, our educational system does instruct our children in the history and traditions of other countries" (1982, 57). Colón goes on to contest this formulation by recounting his and his wife's futile attempt to convey to the crowd the importance of Bolivar to Latin American history. In answer to questions asked by a crowd that gathers to see the portrait, he writes, "Nobody knew [. . .] Nobody seemed to care really. The questions [sic] was asked more out of curiosity than real interest [. . .] 'He is not an American, is he?' someone inquired from the crowd [. . .] My wife finally answered them with a tinge of pride in her voice. 'He is Simon Bolivar, the liberator of Latin America'" (58–59).

Colón underscores the cultural myopia of U.S. hegemony by making visible the historical and intellectual ignorance of North American readers. The crowd's ironic question, "He is not an American, is he?" contradicts Bolivar's historical desire to establish a single, hemispheric "América," reducing Puerto Ricans and other Latin Americans to stereotypes. Rather than making this irony explicit, Colón demands that U.S. readers remedy their shortcomings by acknowledging the contributions of Bolivar—as well as José Martí, Antonio Maceo Grajales, Eugenio María de Hostos, Diego Rivera, Pablo Neruda, and a host of other Latin American artists, intellectuals, and political leaders. For the reader engaged with Latin American history and culture—like the Colóns' friend John, who immediately recognizes the liberator's portrait—the crowd's ignorance sparks outrage.

It is crucial that the nexus of this critique takes place through a form of artistic representation. Recalling the fact that for Colón cultural creation bridges the gap between cognition and political action, Bolívar's portrait serves as a reminder of how revolutionary actors are marginalized in hegemonic culture. If the liberator can be tossed into a "dust bin," the symbolic implications for insurgent nationalists are clear: they must adopt new, confrontational strategies designed to effect substantive change. The passage is therefore a reminder of how culture can historicize and politicize the community. After all, even though these North Americans' opinions of Bolívar and all that he represents remain unchallenged, they are forced to confront their historical ethnocentrism by virtue of the fact that they gather in a crowd.

There are two crucial connections in each of these portrayals: first, Colón's matrixing of the self with the expression of group politics marks growing strains of militancy emerging from Puerto Rican communities and second, Colón's readings of culture emphasize connections between aesthetic production and social movements. It is at least arguable that the representation of culture in *A Puerto Rican in New York* is designed to politicize the author's community. By reading Colón's triangulations, I demonstrate how *A Puerto Rican in New York* offers a window into Puerto Rican and other Latina/o struggles against cultural and political hegemony.

Equally important is how these complex first-person personal narrative portrayals prefigure the growing militancy within Puerto Rican communities in the United States. Because of the insufficiencies of inclusive ethnic Americanism, racialized figures like Colón were forced to adopt increasingly militant strategies. With this in mind, Colón represents not only an important point in the development of insurgent nationalism but also a crucial transitional figure between older activist models and the militant politics of the 1960s.

Conclusion

Ernesto Galarza's and Jesús Colón's autobiographical texts use complex representational strategies to disrupt liberal political conceptions of subjectivity, while also representing the history and culture of their communities. Both authors embody transitional stages in the intellectual development of their communities, in part because their lives span the period between the Popular Front and cultural nationalism. By understanding how their works represent early stages in the development of insurgent consciousness, it is possible to grasp historical trajectories that inform cultural nationalism.

Galarza critiques liberal political subjectivity through the ideas of transformation and subversive education. *Barrio Boy* uses the travel narrative to portray how individual change often reflects the transformation of political consciousness within Chicana/o communities. The book also disrupts portrayals of Mexicana/os and Chicana/os as docile campesinos by leveraging indigenous resistance both within and outside of Mexico. He therefore represents Chicana/o history and culture as part of a longer trajectory of militancy that has its roots in indigenous struggles that have contested capitalism and colonialism since the conquest of the Americas.

In representing this long history of opposition, Galarza marks his personal transition from inclusive ethnic Americanism to the politics of cultural nationalism. It is of primary importance that he represents this transition through his first-person personal narrative. Because he lived through the promise of inclusive ethnic Americanism, only to experience the shortcomings of the civil rights movement and the birth of the Cold War, Galarza marks a shift in his own educational process by advocating radical modes of being for himself and his contemporaries. It is crucial to recognize that part of what takes place in *Barrio Boy* are navigations not only from Mexican to Chicano, and from individual to collective consciousness, but also from a sense of dissatisfaction with older modes of oppositional consciousness to new forms of radical politics.

Similar to Galarza's critique of liberal political subjectivity in *Barrio Boy*, Colón leverages his experience with tabaquero culture in Puerto Rico to portray the growing militant strains in Puerto Rican communities on both sides of the Atlantic. Where Galarza focuses on transformation, however, Colón uses a nascent cultural studies to critique the ways hegemony conditions Puerto Rican marginalization in the United States. The author examines complex cultural texts in an attempt to understand how Boricuas create movement spaces designed to contest dominant ideological structures.

Both authors represent their communities as moving away from inclusive ethnic Americanism and toward the militant strategies of cultural nationalism. By reflecting the militant strains emerging within their communities, their works function as movement spaces that are picked up by increasingly radical social movements and authors in the 1960s and early 1970s. As we will see in chapter 2, these strains are leveraged by authors like Piri Thomas and Oscar "Zeta" Acosta.

2

Crazy for the Nation

Piri Thomas, Oscar "Zeta" Acosta, and the Urban Outlaw

> What the state fears [...] is an alternative system of legality or rationality, rather than the unbridled and formless motion of force that has yet to be subordinated. The "irrational" appears as such through the very rationality of the state from whose homogenizing drive connects the apparent particularity of national identities to the greater homogeneity of universal history.
>
> —David Lloyd, "Nationalisms against the State"

As we have seen, Latina/o authors like Jesús Colón and Ernesto Galarza link the activism of the 1930s with the radical politics of the 1960s. In the late 1960s and early 1970s a new generation of Latina/o authors drew from these oppositional strands, further transforming them in their personal narratives. Piri Thomas, a Puerto Rican, and Oscar "Zeta" Acosta, a Chicano, are representative of this group in that their texts evidence direct engagements with insurgent nationalism.[1] Thomas's *Down These Mean Streets* (1967) and Acosta's *The Revolt of the Cockroach People* (1989b) utilize narrative strategies that challenge the foundations of democracy and its political organization through the textual narration of their individual lives.[2] Their works formulate new conceptions of what it means to be a revolutionary subject, while also revising concepts of community and national belonging. At the core of their challenges are the urban gangster and *vato loco* (crazy guy), both permutations of the familiar outlaw trope. Examining how they triangulate their multifaceted outlaw subjectivities allows us to comprehend how Acosta and Thomas pose alternatives to liberal political notions of self, community, and nation.

While the term *vato loco* is used by Acosta in relation to Chicanos, my comparative framework is designed to identify connections between the *vato loco* and the urban gangster of Thomas's work. While I am careful not to conflate these identities, I argue that Thomas's Puerto Rican and black gangsters of the 1950s share commonalities with Acosta's politicized lowriders. The *vato* and gangster evidence similar desires to disrupt dominant hierarchies (often through violence). Likewise, both are alienated from mainstream identities and notions of respectability in Latina/o communities. Both figures also reject accommodation but often do so through investments in machismo. Moreover, Acosta and Thomas endow these individual figures with collective aspirations, largely by rehumanizing them through their first-person personal narratives.

Although these representations do not offer pure, transcendent subjectivities, I suggest that the *vato loco* and gangster serve important purposes in Thomas's and Acosta's works. In their affirmations of the urban gangster and *vato loco*, they refuse to disidentify with the most despised and oppressed in their groups. Yet because both authors premise the *vato*'s and gangster's critiques of mainstream subjectivity on discourses of masculinity, they reinscribe patriarchy and homophobia. I examine Acosta's and Thomas's triangulations to comprehend how their contradictory impulses attempt to counter racism and dehumanization through the complex personhood of manhood.

Gangsters, Pachucos, *Vatos*, and Urban Alienation in the Postwar United States

In contrast to rural outlaw traditions like those documented by Américo Paredes (1998), Acosta's and Thomas's politicized gangsters are critical to forms of opposition in the city. Historian David Gutiérrez (1995) observes that broad demographic shifts after World War II account for some of the changes in oppositional strategies employed by urban Chicana/os during the late twentieth century. Factors such as the higher percentage of U.S.-born populations, access to better jobs, the rise of Latina/o middle classes, and shifts in economic production from agriculture to manufacturing brought waves of Chicana/os, Puerto Ricans, and other aggrieved minority groups to cities during and after World War II (161–65).[3] While migration patterns that brought Puerto Ricans to the United States emerged out of different economic and political contexts (Operation Bootstrap, the Jones Act, and the industrialization of the island economy during the interwar years), the demographic shifts from rural settings on the island to urban locations in northeastern cities like New York, Philadelphia, and Boston produced similar cultural, political, and social changes.

Not surprisingly, Latina/os did not experience seamless integration in cities, as they were often met with new and vehement forms of racism.

School and housing segregation, police intimidation, and voting disenfranchisement contributed to the marginalization of urban Latina/os during the postwar period. While many of these racist acts were practiced in rural environments, they manifested in new and varied forms in cities—perhaps most spectacularly in "urban redevelopment" programs.[4] In addition, because economic life in cities was organized around manufacturing or service jobs (as well as the later institution of the welfare state), urban Latina/os did not have the same level of control over production as their associates in agricultural settings. Consequently, political strategies like union organizing, work slowdowns, and boycotts did not prove as effective.

The diminished effectiveness of traditional political strategies resulted in varying degrees of alienation among urban Latina/os. In response, many young Chicana/os and Puerto Ricans began to invest in oppositional cultures that sought to redefine their relationships with the state and the entrenched power structures in their communities. The advent of pachuco or zoot suit culture during the 1940s and 1950s was of fundamental importance to Latina/o youth. Zoot-suiters signaled their estrangement from mainstream Anglo society and conventional Latina/o elites through flamboyant styles of dress and hybrid slang languages like Caló (a combination of Hispanicized English with Anglicized and archaic Spanish). Importantly, zoot suit culture affirmed cultural values and collective identification among young, urban people of color at a time when celebratory nationalism and assimilation were dominant imperatives.[5]

As the intellectual and cultural inheritors of zoot-suiters, the *vatos locos* and gangsters in Acosta's and Thomas's works shed light on the historical legacy of urban alienation.[6] Their *vatos* and gangsters reflect the disaffection that emerged out of the disintegration of the inner city and economic disenfranchisement of Latina/o communities across the United States. These authors recognize that urban racialization is already violent, something the *vato loco* or gangster knows intuitively, regardless of how unproductively they deploy this knowledge. Because *vato locos* are alienated from both Anglo society and Latina/o elites, he (and it is always a gendered "he" in Thomas's and Acosta's works) operates outside of conventional conceptions of social and community belonging.

Yet this outsider status provides the *vato* with a unique vantage point. As figures who are both a part of and apart from their communities, *vato locos* and gangsters occupy privileged positions from which to critique ideological processes. Because they understand the violent nature of hegemonic culture, these vexed characters offer important perspectives on white supremacy and state power. Considered from this perspective, *vato loco* subjectivities offer sites from which it is possible to conceive of what Chela Sandoval (2000) has described as "tactical" subjectivities—subjectivities capable of effecting counterhegemonic processes through a critical relationship with ideology. Reevaluating the gangster and *vato loco* facilitates a nuanced understanding of the history and development opposition in urban Latina/o communities.

It would, however, be irresponsible to propose these ideas without noting the *vato loco*'s or gangster's shortcomings. Thomas's and Acosta's positions on gender and sexuality are contradictory and often repugnant.[7] Likewise, their characters advocate violence, nihilism, and internalized racism that is difficult to defend. I follow Latina feminists like Angie Chabram-Dernersesian (1992), Consuelo López-Springfield (1997), Sandoval, Sonia Saldívar-Hull (2000), the Latina Feminist Group (2001), and Lisa Sánchez González (2001) who suggest that *vato loco* and gangster subjectivities are premised on gender and sexual subordination.

Thomas's and Acosta's works present additional contradictions that are not easily resolved by reading their triangulations. For example, both authors evidence tension between their desires for individual empowerment and connection with their communities. As James Smethurst points out in relation to Acosta, because many Latina/o writers invest *vatos locos* and gangsters with individualist attributes, they present a problem in figuring a "racial or national unity instead of a strictly negative resistance" (1995, 120). Thomas and Acosta often characterize these tensions in terms of alienation *from* their communities of origin. The individual is thus valorized over the community as another vector of empowerment for their protagonists. While these moments disrupt my reading of their triangulations as related to projects of community efficacy, I suggest that these contradictions expose the difficulties of constituting pure and progressive subjects within ideology. Similarly, because these authors deploy self-writing modes, these moments recall the residues of individualism present in first-person personal narrative forms.

Rather than dismissing these problematics or uncritically embracing them, I consider Thomas's and Acosta's gangsters from the standpoint of their generative contradictions. By considering the tension between their desires to contest liberal individualism and their use of the individual as a strategy for empowerment, we can better understand these vexed figures. Even as they reinscribe sexism, homophobia, and individualism, the gangster and *vato* endeavor to clear spaces for alternative forms of resistance. It is my contention that these conflicting attempts constitute important—albeit problematic—moments in the development of Latina/o oppositional consciousness.

Collapsing into Black Nationalism: Piri Thomas and *Down These Mean Streets*

Piri Thomas was born Juan Pedro Thomas in New York City's Spanish Harlem in 1928.[8] The product of a mixed-race Cuban father and a light-skinned Puerto Rican mother, Thomas's early years were characterized by "the invasions of hot and cold-running cockroaches and king-size rats."[9] As chronicled in *Down These Mean Streets*, the author first engaged in oppositional activities through his involvement with 1940s gang culture. Echoing the stories of African American autobiographers like Claude Brown and Malcolm X, Thomas details his evolution from petty street hoodlum and drug addict to hardened criminal by the age of fourteen. These criminal activities led to a prison sentence for armed robbery in 1950 (Thomas 1967, 333). After he was released in 1955, Thomas turned to writing as an outlet for his political beliefs.

Down These Mean Streets conforms to the familiar redemption narrative exemplified by autobiographers like St. Augustine, Malcolm, Brown, and Eldridge Cleaver. On closer examination, however, it is possible to grasp the insurgent roots that ground Thomas's project. In virtually every aspect of the narrative—from the author's allusions to the explicit engagement with the Nation of Islam and black nationalism in the last third of the book—Thomas utilizes complex rhetorical strategies that position his gangster persona in relation to his community and national identity. Examining his triangulations reveals how the book narrates a new ethnic subject (i.e., the Puerto Rican, or more precisely, Nuyorican) through the protagonist's strategic alignment with African Americans. Concomitantly, the narrative also posits a notion of social belonging that attempts to address the insufficiencies of both mainland and island contexts for Puerto Ricans in New York City.

While the misogyny and homophobia that Thomas represents are among its most problematic aspects, another criticism of *Down These Mean Streets* holds that the book is oriented around transcendent individualism. I will deal with issues of gender and sexual subordination later in this chapter. At this point we should reflect on the tension in *Down These Mean Streets* between hyperindividualism and communal belonging. In fact, Thomas utilizes competing narrative strategies to position his outsiders. His gangsters are related to both the individualism inherent in mainstream notions of U.S. citizenship and communal affirmation as an aspect of Spanish Harlem life.

On one hand, it is important to recall that Thomas's self-representation emerges out of the overtly racist context of the post–World War II period. As Juan González explains, Puerto Ricans migrating to the mainland during the second half of the twentieth century were subjected to a range of discriminatory practices. Puerto Ricans in New York and other cities existed within a hostile institutional and cultural framework, ranging from unfair housing policies, to the discrimination evident in public schools (2000, 81–95). Similarly, Juan Flores notes that racial stereotypes like those elaborated in the play *West Side Story* left an "indelible imprint on the popular image—and self-image—of Puerto Ricans" (1982, xii). Given the ways such racist practices functioned to debase Puerto Ricans as a group, it is plausible that Thomas would discursively assert individuality and personal dignity. This impulse is even more logical given the climate of conformity and ideologies of self-reliance that were cultural dominants during the period.

On the other hand, Latina/o first-person personal narratives often operate according to a more complex logic. Because they serve as spaces to assert collective memory and communal affirmation, Latina/o first-person personal narratives often represent the "I" as matrixed with the history and culture of the author's community. Thomas's work evidences this impulse by representing the "I" as fundamentally connected with community history and diasporic identity. Part of this community history and diasporic identification appears in the need to resist both collective and individual forms of racism. The assertion of dignity serves as an essential component of both communal belonging and individuality. Thomas's depiction of the "I" thus emerges out of the tension between individual dignity and self-worth and the impulse to register collective resistance to hegemony.

Thomas's linking of his criminality with his personal story makes these tensions evident. As an online essay, "The World of Piri Thomas: Poet, Writer, a Voice for Unity," notes, he uses his personal story to reach out to his community: "Ever since the publication of *Down These Mean Streets*, Piri has been talking to people, young and old, about his struggle for survival and identity and the effects of racism upon our children and upon himself as a Latino and a person of color."[10] Thomas further suggests that his individual identity exists in relation to larger social dynamics that criminalize his community: "But, with the knowledge that he [Thomas] had not been born a criminal, he rose above his violent background of drugs and gang warfare, and he vowed to use his street and prison know-how to reach hard core youth and turn them away from a life of crime."[11]

It is significant that Thomas describes his project as emerging from the knowledge that he was not born a criminal. The criminalization of Puerto Ricans in the United States has been more or less an institution since the second wave of immigration to New York began in the 1920s and 1930s.[12] Thomas's denial of criminalization is oppositional because it asserts the right of Puerto Ricans to think and act according to communal affirmation rather than internalized negative stereotypes. He counters dominant discourses that suggest that Puerto Ricans are gang members and criminals by arguing that he—and by implication other Puerto Ricans—was not born a criminal. In so doing, Thomas uses his story to offer a progressive view of Puerto Rican subjectivity that allows for identification outside of criminality.

Thomas also sees the motivation for his project as arising from a sense of commitment to his community. Rather than accepting the racialized norm of Puerto Rican life in the United States, Thomas transforms his "I" into a collective social, political, and racial history. Thomas's transformation of his experience as a street hoodlum, gang member, and prison inmate into a site for communal affirmation offers a key to understanding *Down These Mean Streets*.

Paradoxically, the figure of the gangster is crucial to Thomas's emancipatory project. Because only the gangster can see the nature of prejudice and exclusion in the author's work, Thomas suggests that one must move through an outlaw subjectivity (if only in surrogate form in his book) in order to effect political change. Instead of moralizing against the perils of gangster identity, Thomas shows both the possibilities and consequences associated with this form of identification—most notably in his own imprisonment at the midpoint of the text. While the outlaw is necessary for breaking out of black and white binary racial identifications in the United States, the criminalization of this outlaw silences his rebellion. This silencing is figured as the logical consequence of U.S. cultural, racial, and ideological hegemony rather than outlaw activities. Here, the criminalization of Thomas's protagonist is assured by the system of domination that creates the conditions of his criminality. It is only through the prison that the author is able to preach the conversion that offers liberatory possibilities for his community.

My goal is not to suggest that Thomas rejects liberal individualism in favor of a seamless communal subjectivity. Rather, I read Thomas's narrative strategies to unpack the tension in his work between liberal individualism and self-reliance on the one hand and communal affirmation on the other. My methodology is designed to recognize how the subjectivity that emerges from *Down These Mean Streets* constitutes an ongoing navigation between these competing impulses. In other words, my critical practice attempts to mine the tensions between competing modes and to explore the openings that emerge from Thomas's representation. It should go without saying that this approach complicates my reading strategy by shifting the focus away from linear resolution, emphasizing instead how Thomas's self-representation depicts the insufficiencies of both liberal individualism and communal values. The proto-Nuyorican subject that Thomas portrays is both a combination and a rejection of individualism and communal values.

Reading Thomas's narrative strategies also facilitates an understanding of how *Down These Mean Streets* navigates the meaning of national and multiracial belonging for Puerto Ricans in New York City. The author creates an uneasy correlation between his protagonist's identity as a Puerto Rican (understood in his work as encompassing aspects of both island and mainland subjectivities) and the dominant discourses that code him as African American in the United States. Anticipating the politics of figures like Miguel Algarín and Miguel Piñero for whom positive identification with African American subjectivities was fundamental to Nuyorican identity, Thomas consistently aligns himself with blacks in the United States.

Several critics have noted the role that blackness plays in *Down These Mean Streets*. William Luis (1998), suggests that Thomas's autobiography intervenes in the literary discourse of earlier Puerto Rican authors like Jesús Colón (1982) and Bernardo Vega (1984), who describe how Puerto Rican migrants were often subjected to antiblack, as well as anti-Latina/o, racism during the first half of the twentieth century. For Luis, Thomas interprets race in a different way (i.e., in a way that does not collapse race into class) because he does not subscribe to the socialist politics to which Colón and Vega were attached. *Down These Mean Streets* thus utilizes English, Spanish, and nonstandard street slang to signal a potential alliance between African Americans and Puerto Ricans in Spanish Harlem. Luis notes that Thomas leverages this potential alliance because "African Americans and blacks in general represent a counter discourse to the discourse of power [...] African Americans and their culture are the symbolic antithesis of the North American white power structure" (33-34).

Similarly, Lisa Sánchez González (2001) notes the relationship between "Old School" Puerto Rican writers like Pura Belpre, Arturo Schomburg, and William Carlos Williams and "New School" writers like Thomas. Where the Old School was concerned with establishing projects of social justice in the United States, New School literature "revolve[s] around more conventional genres, especially the novel, and more contemporary discourses of anticolonial resistance and civil rights" (103). Sánchez González asserts that a central aspect of this resistance is that "Piri must legitimate both his Puerto Rican and African American identities" to "conceptualize himself as both simultaneously" (108). The problem *Down These Mean Streets* encounters, then, is that these identities are too rigid to accommodate the ontology of Piri's race and ethnicity. Consequently, while "Piri craves a stable identity, and Black is an option, [...] his conflict has to do with his particular experience of Blackness as a Boricua in New York" (115).

Marta Sánchez (2005) also sees racial dynamics in Thomas's work in complex terms. But where Luis and Sánchez González understand race in *Down These Mean Streets* more or less in the same binary black and white terms operative in hegemonic society, Sánchez suggests that the book disrupts dichotomized identities. She argues that Thomas deploys a number of intercultural elements in ways that anticipate postmodern concepts of hybridity and intermixing. While she stresses that *Down These Mean Streets* disrupts racial binaries, Sánchez is also careful to point out that Thomas secures this complex racial position through the subjection of women and queers: "Piri is a victim of racism, but he compensates for the racialized and feminized abjection of black men in the United States by making the abjection of women the guarantor of his ethnic and masculine privilege" (42). Thomas thus "shakes up" the meaning of racial identities, while reinscribing sexism and homophobia in his Spanish Harlem barrio.

Marta Caminero-Santangelo (2007) concurs that the book aligns its protagonist with African Americans. But where Sánchez uses the figure of

La Malinche as a metaphor for cross-cultural representation, Caminero-Santangelo argues that indigeneity is used to defer the protagonist's relationship with blackness in *Down These Mean Streets*. In relation to the fiction that Piri's father is indio, rather than black, Caminero-Santangelo explains that "[Piri] must learn the 'lessons' of racial identity suppressed by his family and its narrated myths of origin" (52). She further asserts that in place of mechanisms of racial deferral, Piri must "embrace a construction of Puerto Rican racial identity that acknowledges a common 'peoplehood' with African Americans" (52).

While Caminero-Santangelo acknowledges that Thomas's narrative points to unstable racial categories, she argues that *Down These Mean Streets* invests in a "strategic essentialism," rather than hybridity or heterogeneity, implying that racial identity is useful in constructing solidarity. While "Thomas's autobiography [. . .] offers radical images of racial instability and nonessentialism," it also "seems to imply that [hybridity] is not always the most effective strategy for challenging the American racial system, perhaps because [it] allow[s] Piri too much 'wiggle room' for the assertion of difference from, and consequent privilege over, African Americans" (61). This leads Caminero-Santangelo to assert that in *Down These Mean Streets* no system of race is inherently conservative or radical; rather, each system of racial classification is dependent on its context. Consequently, "what is textually foregrounded [. . .] is not the issue of capitulation or resistance to racial ideology but the issue of claiming or rejecting racial privilege" (66). *Down These Mean Streets* emphasizes instead how "Piri's acceptance of 'blackness' is positioned within the bildungsroman structure as a positive step toward what we might call 'panethnic solidarity'" (67).

My position on racial representation in *Down These Mean Streets* is closest to Luis's, Sánchez González's, and Caminero-Santangelo's. I concur that Piri's alignment with African Americans is often represented as a potential model for interracial, antihegemonic activities. But where Sánchez González reads the book as a novel, I argue that *Down These Mean Streets* is better understood as a first-person personal narrative. Moreover, where Caminero-Santangelo focuses on the implications of interracial solidarity for Latinidad, and Luis on a historical understanding of racial dynamics in mainland Puerto Rican communities, my reading of Thomas's first-person personal narrative is intended to understand the tension between his individual representation and a project of community efficacy. While the book cannot fully distance itself from an investment in the individual, I argue that Thomas attempts to matrix his "self" with the history and culture of his community to contest racial discrimination in the United States in all its forms.

One manifestation of this contestation of racial discrimination appears in the navigation of Piri's blackness.[13] Because he is the darkest-skinned Puerto Rican among his family and friends, Piri is constantly marked as different. These ideas are visible when he meets a gang of Italian youths in his neighborhood early in the text:

> "Hey you," he [Rocky] said. *"What nationality are ya?"*
> I looked at him and *wondered which nationality to pick.* And one of his friends said, "Ah Rocky, he's black enuff to be a nigger. Ain't that what you is, kid?"
> My voice was almost shy in its anger. "I'm Puerto Rican," I said. "I was born here." I wanted to shout it, but it came out like a whisper. (Thomas 1967, 24; emphasis mine)

Evoking popular representations like the play *West Side Story*, the scene underscores tensions between Italian and Puerto Rican communities in the city.[14] Understanding these tensions, the questions the youths pose take on a political dimension. By simultaneously pointing out how they mark their own whiteness in opposition to Piri's *perceived* blackness, Thomas highlights how his protagonist is forced into a subordinate subject position. While Piri posits Puerto Rican-ness as a possible alternative ethnic or national identification, Rocky and his gang refuse him anything other than an African American subjectivity. They inscribe their superior position as "whites" on Piri's "inferior" black body.

It is also fascinating that Rocky and his gang engage Piri at the level of national identity. Rather than asking if he is "Spanish" (the common designator for Latina/os of many origins in New York) or asking him to identify his race, the gang asks Piri to identify his *nationality*. One way to read this conflation is in terms of the boys' confusion over the differences between race, ethnicity, and national origin. Another way to understand Rocky's mistake centers on how the racially ambiguous Piri does not conform to "legitimate" forms of social belonging in the United States. As Caminero-Santangelo explains, nationality is an important aspect of Rocky and his gang's conflation since "to have a national identity will, by the logic of race, mean that he is not black" (2007, 59). African Americans are thus figured as the negation of U.S. citizenship. In particular, the gang's use of the "slur 'nigger' renders the whole question of nationality moot in the minds of the Italian boys" (58). Because his body exceeds the ontology of U.S. racial binaries, Rocky and his gang have no frame with which to decode Piri's complex ethnoracial position.

Piri's confusion is interesting in this regard—evidenced in his halting response, "I looked at him and wondered which nationality to pick." By considering an appropriate identity for his reply, Piri seems to lack a stable sense of national, racial, and ethnic belonging. Caught between his "American-ness" and his Puerto Rican ancestry, and complicated by his phenotype, he is unable answer the gang's—or his own—query.

It is also critical to understand how the context of colonialism that places subjects like Piri in the metropolitan space of the United States infuses the scene. As naturalized citizens who have adopted U.S. rules of hypodescent, Rocky and his gang enforce both white supremacy and U.S. imperialism. It would appear that Rocky and his gang mark their own incorporation into whiteness through the performance of antiblack racism. While he cannot yet articulate an alternative to binary identities, Piri's anger and frustration indicate a need to theorize an alternative sense of national belonging. Thus his anger and whispering response: "I'm Puerto Rican [. . .] I was born here."

Thomas further encounters Piri's blackness by representing the inescapability of his "color." In a discussion with his friend Brew in the chapter "Hung Up Between Two Sticks," the protagonist displays his ambivalence about his racial identity. The chapter centers on a sophisticated discussion of the political implications of identifying as a "Negro." Significantly, Piri's claim to African American status emerges more from his ontological experience (i.e., how others perceive his race) than from Brew's argument:

> I had two colored cats, Crutch and Brew, for tight *amigos*. All the time I heard them talk about Jim Crow and southern paddies' way-out, screwed up thinking. Crutch told me once that he was sitting on the curb down South where he used to live and some young white boys passed in a car and yelled out to him, "Hey, nigger, git outta that gutter and climb down the sewer where all you black niggers belong."

It really bugged me, like if they had said it to me [. . .] Crutch was smart and he talked a lot of things that made sense to any Negro. *That was what bothered me—it made a lot of sense to me.* (Thomas 1967, 120; emphasis mine)

Despite the fact that he uses the word "amigos" to distance himself from Crutch and Brew's racial identity, Thomas represents a growing affiliation with African Americans. Instead of arguing as he does earlier for a discrete Puerto Rican identity, Piri begins to acknowledge his own blackness. To whites he not only appears "black," but his thoughts, feelings, and experiences also resonate with his African American comrades. This acknowledgement of his race is negotiated through a series of vexing incidents. Ranging from job and housing discrimination to the sexual politics associated with African American (heterosexual) masculinity, Piri's experience as a racialized subject grows as we see him mature.[15]

But Piri's racialization is not limited to public life. As the darkest member of his family, racial dynamics also operate in the domestic sphere. In a telling conversation with his mother, we see how racial logic operates at home:

"Gimme a kiss, Moms; come on, *vente*—a big *jalumbo* kiss."
"Get away, you smell bad, all full of sweat. Go, get in that bathtub and let the water and soap make you soft so the dirt has a chance to come off."
"Aw, Moms, you love me any way I am, clean or dirty, white or black, pretty or ugly."
"*Sí*, you're right, and, my son, I have to love you because only your mother could love you, *un negrito* and ugly. And to make it badder, you're dirty and smelly from your sweat!" (19)

The pairing of the terms "white and black," "clean and dirty," and "pretty and ugly," bring to mind stereotypical portrayals of African Americans as subhuman—what philosopher Charles Mills (1997) calls "subpersons" (56). Further, the conditional correlation between his mother's love and Piri's acknowledgement of their difference relies on the assumption that society does *not* love those of African descent. In fact, Piri's mother's statement that his face is one that "only a mother could love" emphasizes how blacks are constructed as outside of aesthetic and social norms. Indeed, as William Luis points out, the scene underscores how race in the United States disrupts family relationships by turning family members against one another (1998, 33–34).

Racialization intrudes on family life in a more ominous way in Piri's relationship with his father. Thomas's historical father was a dark-skinned Cuban who married the author's lighter-skinned Puerto Rican mother. In *Down These Mean Streets*, Piri's father is refigured as a dark-skinned Puerto Rican in denial about his "race." On the eve of his departure to the South, Piri confronts his father about his racial attitudes. As his father says, "maybe you see something in me I haven't seen yet, or maybe won't admit yet. I don't like feeling to be a black man. Can you understand it's a pride to me being a Puerto Rican?" (150). To which Piri responds,

> Don't say you're mixed with Caribe or Borinquén Indian blood. Poppa, don't you know where you at? Or are you seeing it, Poppa, and making like it's not there? If you're really so sure you're white, come on down South with Brew and me and see where you're really at. You don't even have to go down South. You can see where you're at right here. Only thing you don't hafta worry about is sitting in the back of trolleys or buses. But then, you only go to places where you're sure you ain't gonna have no trouble. You protect your lying dream with a heavy strain for a white status that's worthless to a black man. You protect your dream, Poppa, that's all right. There's pride galore in being a Negro, Poppa. (150–51)

Piri's argument levels important critiques of both island and U.S. racial discourses. By admonishing his father for not "know[ing] where [he is] at," Piri demands that his father recognize his social location and the realities of antiblack racism on the mainland. Moreover, his refusal of the term "Indian" uncovers metaphors employed on the island to obscure African roots.[16] As Arlene Dávila observes about island-based racial politics, "the ideas of racial syncretism promoted by Puerto Rico's nationalist ideology have historically circumvented discussions about race" (1997, 83). In a similar vein, Piri's critique reveals how his father echoes discourses of racial harmony on the island by eliding questions about his African roots. More important, Piri suggests that, while forms of discrimination are different, antiblack racism is still prevalent in Puerto Rico. By refusing to acknowledge his race in either context, Piri points to his father's complicity with white supremacy. One logical conclusion is that in *Down These Mean Streets*, to deny one's race (regardless of social location) is to deny resistance to white supremacy.

The chapter "Barroom Sociology" further elaborates these ideas as Piri and Brew meet Gerald Andrew West, a racially mixed sociology student from Penn State University. Piri and Brew, who are traveling to the Jim Crow South to better comprehend racism and thereby come to a conclusion about Piri's racial identity, stop in Norfolk, Virginia, where they meet Gerald in a bar. Gerald, who is writing a book on the "Negro situation" in the South, positions himself as an outsider who is researching from an ostensibly "scientific" perspective.[17] When confronted with the absurdity of Gerald's stance, Brew and Piri are indignant. Gerald explains that his book celebrates Negroes and "*their* wonderful capacity for laughter and strength" (170; emphasis mine). Brew becomes enraged as Gerald argues that he is untouched by racism, even distancing himself from (other) blacks by saying that he is searching for the "Negro point of view" (171). The subtext of the scene implies that when one is marked phenotypically black, no matter how subtly, one cannot escape African American identity. As Brew argues, "[Gerald] oughta go to some of them small towns whar a rock better fuckin' well know his place" (171).

The denouement of the incident centers around Gerald's personal identity—or denial of it—and Piri's and Brew's insistence that he come to terms with his African American position. To Brew's pointed question "what kinda Negro is yuh?" Gerald responds, "according to a genealogical tracer [. . .] I'm really only one eighth colored," and "I feel that the racial instincts that are the strongest in a person enjoying this rich mixture are the ones that [. . .] should be followed" (173). When Brew presses him to elaborate on his racial instincts, Gerald responds, "I—rather—feel—sort of Spanish-ish, if I may use that term. I have always had a great admiration for Spanish culture and traditions. I—er—yes—feel rather impulsed toward things Spanish" (174).

This sneering exchange emphasizes that African American identity is not a matter of choice or negotiation in *Down These Mean Streets*. Instead, Thomas suggests that there is a direct correlation between phenotype and race. Regardless of whether a person is one-eighth or one-one-hundredth black, in the eyes of dominant society one cannot escape one's appearance—especially given that the scene takes place in Norfolk, Virginia, during Jim Crow.

The spatial politics of the scene also offer a glimpse of Thomas's triangulations. Throughout the chapter, Piri is physically positioned between Gerald and Brew. Paralleling the ways Puerto Ricans and other Latina/os have shared vexed relationships with African Americans and whites in the United States, Piri occupies an intermediary space between their respective positions. Because Gerald is not quite "white" himself, he embodies a problematic in the formulation of an alternative identity. Despite his ironic preference for Spanish as an identifier, Gerald's choice suggests that Latina/o subjectivities premised on subverting African roots uphold white supremacy. It is therefore logical that Thomas navigates a Puerto Rican subject aligned with African Americans in the United States. Regardless of the fact that Piri decides he can't "hate a guy that was hung up on the two sticks that were so much like mine" (178), he continues on his journey with Brew through the South.

Gerald's imagining of himself as Spanish also highlights questions of national belonging that ground the scene. His ironic choice of Spanish underscores Piri's inability to be recognized as Puerto Rican. It is also fascinating that Gerald, like Rocky in an earlier chapter, conflates national belonging with racial identity. When we examine Thomas's triangulation, it is possible to comprehend Gerald's apparent conflation as a narrative strategy that negotiates an alternative notion of community based on the collective experiences of dark-skinned Puerto Ricans.

Thomas's representation also constitutes a call for a new political identity. It seems that Thomas did his homework while in prison during the 1950s. Like many inmates of color of his generation—including Malcolm X and Eldridge Cleaver—Thomas would undoubtedly have been exposed to fiction, philosophy, and theory produced by blacks through literacy programs in the penal system. With allusions to Malcolm X, Claude Brown, Frantz Fanon, and others, Thomas seems to appeal to a particular strain of African American radicalism.[18] By citing Cleaver, Brown, Malcolm, and Fanon as his literary antecedents and by figuring the negotiation of his blackness as a radical opposition to whiteness, Thomas navigates an identity predisposed toward black nationalism.

The evolution in Piri's thinking is evident when the narrative shifts to his prison time. In the chapter "God, Ain't You for Everybody?" Piri encounters the Nation of Islam and radical black nationalism. As Muhammad, the leader of the nation in Comstock state prison, explains to Piri, "The white devil in this country had his chance to be our brother. His chance is lost. His rule is at an end. His time is running out. His rule is almost buried under six feet of dirt decorated with his famous cross. We, the Black Muslims, are coming into our own" (292). Piri notes Muhammad's increasingly radical tone: "Muhammad turned his palms still together back on their side, only this time the hand representing the black man was on top. Muhammad's voice was now almost gentle again as he went on: 'White man—for two thousand years you've been on us—and now we're going to be on you. We want a piece of this world and we're going to get it, even if we have to take it all away from you'" (294).

Muhammad's subtext suggests that dignity for African Americans depends on an alignment with the Nation of Islam and other forms of black nationalism. Because his identity resonates with African American subjectivities, Piri is powerfully attracted to Muhammad's rhetoric: "though I didn't remain a Muslim after my eventual release from the big jail, I never forgot one thing that Muhammad said, for I believed it too: 'No matter a man's color or race, he has a need of dignity and he'll go anywhere, become anything, or do anything to get it—anything'" (297). Muhammad's explanation of racial politics provides a turning point for Piri. Rather than claiming an autonomous Puerto Rican self, Piri collapses his identity into African American subjectivity. It is therefore possible to extrapolate his claim from an earlier chapter of *Down These Mean Streets*: if the interests of blacks make sense to any African American (namely Piri), then the rhetoric of black nationalism resonates with Puerto Rican communities.

Exploring Thomas's triangulations emphasizes the importance of understanding his collapse of Puerto Rican identity into African American subjectivities in complex terms. In his attempt to constitute a politically radical position, Thomas parallels his interests with those of African Americans. This alignment allows him to leverage the history of African American radicalism in the United States in order to formulate a resistant political identity for Puerto Ricans in New York. For a population coded as "black" in a U.S. context, the racism that many Puerto Ricans experienced during the period led them to more organic affiliations with African Americans struggling for identity, rights, and space. Given the explosive historical moment—expressed effectively by Brown, Malcolm, Cleaver, Elijah Muhammad, the Black Panthers, and other voices from the radical left of black culture—it is arguable that part of what is at stake in constructing Puerto Ricans as black is a desire for political and social enfranchisement.

Moreover, by situating Puerto Rican culture in the United States as part of both a black diasporic tradition *and* an urban outlaw sensibility, Thomas galvanizes a political base and leverages an existing resistant tradition. Since his radicalization is a function of his gangster activities, it is important to appreciate the relationship the outlaw shares with black subjectivity in Thomas's work. In particular, his alignment with figures like Brown, Malcolm, and Cleaver emphasize what Michael M. J. Fischer calls "families of resemblance" (1986, 230) with radical black politics. Since these figures stress the importance of their criminal personas to the formulation of their political identities, it is logical that Thomas aligns himself with urban gangster sensibilities.

Yet as a subject who shares phenotypic and ideological interests with African Americans but who cannot be reduced to such an identity—after all, he does not pursue his relationship with the Nation of Islam upon his return to Spanish Harlem—Thomas's representation underscores how black identity, Puerto Rican identity, and all points in between form a continuum of radical oppositional politics that coincide at key points through their resistance to white supremacy. It is therefore plausible that part of what is at stake in Thomas's construction of his own black identity vis-à-vis his criminalized, gangster sensibility, is a strategic affiliation with black nationalism designed to triangulate a third subject position—a new subject that might be more accurately termed Nuyorican.

While these representations suggest a sophisticated theory of political subjectivity that anticipates the Afro–Puerto Rican identity espoused by groups like the Nuyorican Poets, it is vital to consider how Thomas reproduces gender and sexual problematics that have plagued insurgent nationalist movements. As Michael Hames-García explains, "what Thomas remains insufficiently critical of [. . .] is the potentially oppressive effects of masculinity concerning gay men and women, especially when one consciously adopts masculinity in resistance to feminization and homosexualization" (2004, 147). As a radically dehumanized individual, Thomas utilizes the discourse of masculinity to assert humanity. Yet in doing so, he reinscribes hierarchies implicit in patriarchy and homophobia.

The chapter "If You Ain't Got Heart, You Ain't Got Nada" embodies many of the problems in Thomas's uncritical adoption of patriarchal masculinity as a resistance strategy. Piri experiences a series of events, beginning with his move to another area of El Barrio, his enlistment in a gang, and an ill-fated rumble with a rival gang, the Jolly Rogers. After defeating the rival gang in hand-to-hand fighting, the Jolly Rogers breach rumble etiquette by calling for reinforcements armed with stickball bats. In the face of superior (and armed) numbers, Piri's gang runs. Rather than coding their surrender in terms of survival or strategy, Thomas describes their retreat as a shameful loss of "heart": "I felt bad those *cabrones* had made us split, but I kept running" (1967, 54). As Hames-García notes, "Piri consistently decodes the structural forces aligned against him as assaults on his hard-won masculine identity, his 'heart'" (2004, 144).

The chapter takes a fascinating turn when Thomas elaborates his final example of heart. After recounting their rumble exploits, the members of Piri's gang turn to the taboo subject of homosexuality. Alfredo, one of the older members, suggests that they go to the home of some gay men: "The talk turned way out, on faggots and their asses which, swinging from side to side, could make a girl look ridiculous, like she wasn't moving. There were some improbable stories of exploits with faggots. Then one stud, Alfredo, said, 'Say, man, let's make it up to the faggots' pad and cop some bread'" (1967, 55).

By characterizing Alfredo as a "stud" and feminizing gay, male subjectivity through the problematic use of the term "faggot," Thomas betrays his uncritical acceptance of heterosexism and patriarchy. Robert Reid-Pharr explains that, unlike other African American literary forms like the slave narrative, the threat that Piri faces isn't being brutalized or having one's woman violated but rather the threat of being homosexualized (1997, 360). Reid-Pharr's perspective aids in understanding that this disturbing portrayal, coming on the heels of the author's description of running away from the Jolly Rogers, suggests that Piri and his gang assuage their guilt over "copping out" by perpetrating violence against the bodies of the gay men, Concha, Antonia, and La Vieja. As Alfredo implies, the purpose of the gang's contact with these men is oriented around their attempt to "cop some bread," suggesting (at best) an exploitative relation.

Ironically, Thomas defers the question of Piri's homosexuality by first portraying him as a victim and subsequently conflating sexual pleasure with violence. Because, as Marta Sánchez puts it, "in Piri's masculine code, betrayal of one's gender is worse than betrayal of one's race" (2005, 52), Thomas must deflect Piri's sexual pleasure in order to maintain an "active" position for his protagonist. While it is true that Piri renders the scene hazily due in part to his ingestion of a substantial amount of marijuana, his denial of consensual homosexual sex is revealing. At several points, Piri seems dissociated from his body, suggesting that he is "paralyzed" and that his attempts to push "away at the fingers," are futile because, "they just held on tighter" (61). Even in the face of Concha's seemingly superior force, he distances himself from his pleasure by arguing, "If I didn't like the scene, my pee-pee did" (61). At the moment of his climax he feels "funny, like getting dizzy and weak and lazy" and refuses to acknowledge the orgasm, except through a complex denial: "I felt myself lurching and straining [. . .] Then I heard slurping sounds and it was all over." (61)

The erotic charge of the scene is diffused through the split between Piri's mental state and bodily experience. As Reid-Pharr argues, "Thomas maintains a distinction between himself and his sexual desire, producing, for a moment, the former as the victim of the latter" (1997, 364). Thus despite the fact that he engages in a voluntary homosexual act—without financial compensation, regardless of Alfredo's suggestion that they "cop some bread"—Thomas represents Piri as a victim in a sexual encounter oriented around asserting his masculinity. The logic of Piri's description holds that to assert masculinity, one must be prepared to commit actions up to, and including, homosexuality.

Thomas enacts a secondary denial through the conflation of sexual pleasure with violence. As he receives fellatio from Concha, Piri has a fantasy that relates his virile (heterosexual) masculinity with the fight with the Jolly Rogers:

> You keep in time with your whole body and swinging soul, and all of a sudden you're in the middle, hung up with a chick; and the music is soft and she's softer, and you make the most of grinding against her warmth. Viva, viva, viva!
> Then the Jolly Rogers walk in and everybody starts dealing. Your boys are fighting and you fall in with them. Bottles are hitting everything but the walls. You feel somebody put his damn fists square in your damn mouth and split your damn lip and you taste your own sweet blood—and all of a sudden you're glad you came. You're glad you smoked pot, you're glad somebody punched you in the mouth; you're glad for another chance to prove how much heart you got. (1967, 59–60)

By conflating his sex act with Concha first with heterosexual pleasure and then with the fight with the Jolly Rogers, Piri dissociates from the dangerous possibility of his homosexuality.[19] He denies his encounter with Concha—indeed, even his presence in the scene—by imagining violence as a constitutive aspect of virile heterosexuality. Perhaps the most important and disturbing aspect of Thomas's denial is that his fantasy is actualized. As Piri leaves the apartment following his encounter, the reader is haunted by the sound of Alfredo beating La Vieja: "I floated toward the door. I had to get air inside me. I heard the last sounds of Alfredo's anger beating out against La Vieja—blap, blap, blap—and the faggot's wail, 'Ayeeeee, no heet me, no heet—'" (61).

This violent turn culminates in the final lines of the chapter. As Piri walks downtown, heading into Central Park, he experiences a larger fantasy of economic and social empowerment, "Someday I'm gonna buy this here country Central Park—and anybody can come in, but only if they promise not to chew more than one twig or a blade of country Central Park grass" (62). While Piri's fantasy of power is figured as a condemnation of his desire to prove "heart," the scene unwittingly emphasizes the extent to which his masculinity and social power are premised on subverting homosexuality. As a subject whose heart depends on constantly asserting masculinity, this act of homosexual sex is recoded in terms of Piri's desire to claim violent mastery over his world.

Thomas evidences similar dynamics in his reproduction of patriarchal and sexist ideologies. Ranging from Piri's macho attitude toward his girlfriend Trina to the disturbing sexual assault he perpetrates against a prostitute in Texas, the protagonist's relationships with women are characterized by violence and domination. A salient example in the context of this discussion is the racialized encounter that Piri has with a white woman on the subway. In the crowded subway car, Piri's body is pushed against the unnamed woman. After apologizing for pressing his body (and his erection) against her, he reads desire in her "very damn-liberal smile" and her response, "'It's all right,' she said sweetly. 'Let me see if I can get my balance'" (136). Despite the problematic position he occupies in the scene (literally forced against the woman by the crowd in the subway car), Piri seems incapable of understanding the unnamed woman's actions in terms other than her desire for him.

Assuming that their act is consensual, the ramifications of the encounter are curious. As he remembers the events later, Piri again imagines himself as a victim:

> I wondered if the broad was rememberin' how great it was, or if she was tellin' her friends how she made a horny Porty Rican climb the side of the wall on a subway train just by wiggling her white snatch against his black cock. I frowned. I'd thought "black cock," and that meant the broad was prob'ly sayin' "nigger" instead of "Porty Rican." (141)

While Thomas's distasteful gender politics are observable in his uncritical use of words like "broad" and "snatch," his transformation of the act from one of domination to one of disempowerment reveals a deeper problematic. Piri understands the encounter in terms of how it renders him powerless to control the meaning of his identity. While he initially enjoys the liaison, his memory is spoiled by his awareness of how his phenotype overdetermines his subjectivity, leaving him feeling "hot and real stink about this funny world and all the funny people in it" (144). While Piri seems unaware of how his own imbrication in patriarchy inscribes a similar form of erasure on the body of the unnamed woman, he understands how her assumed titillation results from a misreading of his phenotype.[20] This awareness leads Piri to consider how this encounter, like many of the others he has throughout the narrative, constitutes an assault on his masculinity. Reproducing the shortcomings of insurgent nationalist ideologies, the only resistant identity possible for Piri is a masculinity premised on the subversion of women and homosexuals.

From "Flower *Vato*" to *Vato* Numero Uno: Oscar "Zeta" Acosta and *The Revolt of the Cockroach People*

Oscar "Zeta" Acosta, attorney, author, and self-described "professional revolutionary" was one of the most intriguing, if not polarizing, figures of the Chicana/o movement. Born in El Paso, Texas, in 1935, but raised in the central valley of California, Acosta pursued a variety of occupations, including farmworker, musician, Baptist missionary, civil rights organizer, and clarinetist in an Air Force band, before becoming an attorney, author, and activist. After returning to the United States in 1956 from his tour of duty and subsequent missionary work in Panama, Acosta worked his way through college and law school, passing the bar in 1966. He practiced for a short time at the Oakland Legal Aid Society but became disillusioned with law. After quitting Legal Aid, Acosta dropped out, traveling through the Southwest. He eventually met Hunter S. Thompson, with whom he remained close until his disappearance and presumed death in 1974. Acosta and Thompson cofounded the gonzo journalism style, as evidenced by Acosta's two autobiographical novels, *The Autobiography of a Brown Buffalo* and *The Revolt of the Cockroach People*, published in 1972 and 1973.[21]

In 1968, Acosta landed in East Los Angeles, where he became an influential attorney and activist involved with the Chicana/o movement. Connecting with the Brown Berets and Católicos por la Raza, he was involved in several important legal cases. As Carl Gutiérrez-Jones (1995) observes, Acosta experimented "with legal strategies that would significantly influence the litigation of Chicano civil rights groups [. . .] for years to come" (125). Among his important cases were *People v. Castro* (the East LA Thirteen) and *California v. Montez* (the Biltmore Six). In both cases, he challenged the constitution of grand juries in California and attempted to define Chicanos as a legally recognizable class facing discrimination in the United States. In addition to his legal work, Acosta ran unsuccessfully for Los Angeles county sheriff in 1970.[22] In keeping with the subversive character of his legal and political work, Acosta declared that "the history of Los Angeles County is one of violence, vice and corruption" and promised to implement a seven-point plan dedicated to the "ultimate dissolution of the Sheriff's Department" (1996, 299).

While a number of critical approaches have illuminated aspects of Acosta's literary work, it is valuable to consider the implications of reading *The Revolt of the Cockroach People*, a novel, as a first-person personal narrative. Even though events in the novel are stylized and fictionalized, critics like Genaro Padilla (1984), Ramón Saldívar (1990), Raymund Paredes (1995), and Gutiérrez-Jones (1995) have often read the novel as at least partially autobiographical.[23] Similarly, biographers like Ilan Stavans (1995) and Burton Moore (2003) have often conflated Acosta's protagonists with his life. Even though correctives by scholars like Michael Hames-García suggest that reading Acosta's "works as novels, autobiographies, or some hybrid of the two [. . .] limit[s] possible interpretations" (2004, 50), many critics continue to read the author's work as narratives of the self.

I concur with Hames-García that simplistic readings of Acosta's work as autobiography miss the complexity of his narrative reimagining of the Chicana/o movement. At the same time, I value the autobiographical resonances in Acosta's work because they make visible how he reflects and advances notions of political subjectivity espoused by the Chicana/o movement. While I am careful not to conflate the protagonists of Acosta's novels with the author, I read his triangulations in order to understand the complex political subjectivity he narrates.

While both of Acosta's novels are autobiographical, I focus on *Revolt* because of its articulations of self, community, and nation that are in dialogue with the Chicana/o movement. As Genaro Padilla (1984) reminds us, *The Autobiography of a Brown Buffalo* documents Zeta's initiation into a radical Chicano identity.[24] Through his tribulations with the legal system, dominant culture, and the counterculture during the 1960s, the reader becomes acquainted with the process through which Zeta comes to understand himself as Chicano. Yet this initiation is only a part of the story that Acosta tells over the course of the two novels. Where *Autobiography* portrays the protagonist's evolution to a radical identity, *Revolt* narrates Zeta's imbrication with the Chicana/o movement.

Of fundamental importance to identifying with the Chicana/o movement is Acosta's linking of revolutionary subjectivity with the *vato loco*. Several critics have noted the importance of the *vato loco* to Acosta's work. Raymund Paredes, for example, suggests that Acosta positions *vatos* and gangsters in relation to other subjectivities in Los Angeles in order to highlight ethnic inequality in the city: "as a self-styled cultural outlaw and ally of the downtrodden, Acosta invariably focuses his attention on those areas and features of Los Angeles that represent a disturbing reality far removed from the affluence of Bel Air and Malibu" (1995, 244). Paredes is particularly interested in Acosta's use of the *vato loco* as the locus of his rebellion: "in Acosta's mind, the most notable variety of Mexican-American cockroach is the *vato loco*," a ubiquitous figure in Los Angeles who "is the descendent of the *pachuco*, the zoot-suited rebel of the 1940s and 1950s" (245). Although Acosta "admires the *vato loco's* disdain for conventional Anglo-American values," he is "ultimately a tragic and isolated figure, another victim of Los Angeles's particular pathology" (245–46). This pathology leads Paredes to claim that Los Angeles's degradation is connected with the subjugation of Chicana/os.

James Smethurst (1995) considers the figure of the *vato loco* in his analysis of Acosta's novels. For Smethurst "the *pachuco*, the *vato* and the lowrider are [. . .] useful to Chicano writers" like Acosta because they offer "visible figures of self-consciously asserted Chicano difference from both Mexican culture and 'mainstream' United States culture" (119). But as

Smethurst points out, the *vato* doesn't provide a pure, progressive political identity; rather, he occupies an unstable position that is difficult to reconcile within the essentialist impulses many Chicana/o authors display. Consequently, while other Chicano authors often treat the *vato loco* as a rugged individualist, Smethurst argues that Acosta seizes on the *vato's* instability, problematizing static notions of Chicano identity: "In this situation, where all ethnic markers are unstable and even contradictory, but where ethnicity remains a persistent demand—from inside the narrator as much or more than from the outside world—the *vatos locos* become the perfect symbol of ethnic identity and ethnic difference" (125). Even if most of the *vatos* in the novel are self-destructive, Smethurst suggests that these impulses allow Acosta to represent the *vato* as a positive figure who is not alone in his self-destruction.

Rafael Pérez-Torres (2006) is interested in how *mestizaje*, or complex intermixing, is incorporated in Acosta's work to express resistant subjectivities like those elaborated in the *vato*. Pérez-Torres explains that culturally, "mestizaje becomes a means to articulate subjectivity otherwise, to consider ways of expressing a reworking of the self in a minor key that negotiates dominant majoritarian paradigms of subjectivity" (52). While Pérez-Torres does not explicitly engage the *vato*, he articulates the problematics associated with Acosta's alignment of masculinity with revolutionary consciousness. To this end, Pérez-Torres claims that understanding which identities are permissible and why is key to Acosta's conception of critical opposition. Identities that express an empty pluralism do little to advance struggles for social justice, while those that imply realignment or disruption offer liberatory possibilities for Chicana/o communities. For Pérez-Torres, then, Acosta's oppositional identities highlight "a sense of collectivity and political project" (53). What limits Acosta's approach is that his affirmation of *mestizaje* too readily subsumes a revolutionary consciousness that reinscribes "long-rehearsed and repressive social scripts" (66), especially those oriented around the subjugation of women and queers.

I argue that Acosta's revolutionary subject is a product of the tensions produced by various identity categories. I concur with Paredes and Smethurst that the *vato* represents a degree of instability in the author's work. By navigating between rural and urban, crazy and sane, individualist and collective, and accommodationist and oppositional positions, Acosta challenges traditional models of revolutionary consciousness. I also concur with Pérez-Torres that while Acosta's project embodies revolutionary potential, its possibilities are foreclosed by the devolution into masculinist scripts.

Where my work departs from these scholars is in my suggestion that the author utilizes a form of self-representation to politicize himself and his community through the *vato loco*. Consequently, *Revolt* provides a blueprint for exceptional identities by representing Zeta's evolution from bourgeois subject—or as some of the *vatos locos* refer to him early in the novel, "flower *vato*"—to *vato loco*. While his revolutionary *vatos* cannot transcend their limitations, I contend that their generative contradictions offer commentaries on the difficulties of constructing progressive oppositional identities within ideology.

Interestingly, Acosta's translations and definitions for the *vato* fluctuate in the novel. The *vato* is variously identified as a "warrior" (Acosta 1989b, 16), "new breed of savage" (42), "politicized lowrider" (67), "cockroach" (throughout), "Chicano street freak who lives on a steady diet of pills, dope, and wine" (89), "child of the slums" (204), and "crazy guy" (13, 248). His most elaborate definition for the *vato loco* contends,

> [The *vato loco*] learn[s] about life from the toughest guy in the neighborhood. You smoke your first joint in an alley at the age of ten; you take your first hit of *carga* [heroin] before you get laid; and you learn how to make your mark on the wall before you learn how to write. Your friends know you to be a *vato loco*, a crazy guy, and they call you *"ese"* or *"vato,"* or "man." And when you prove you can take it, that you don't cop to nothing even if it means getting your ass whipped by some other gang or the cops, then you are allowed to put your mark, your initial, your sign, your badge, your *placa* on your turf with the name or initial of your gang [. . .] You write it big and fancy, scroll-like, *cholo* print [. . .] It's like the pissing of a dog on a post. And underneath your *placa*, you always put C/S, *"Con Safos,"* that is: *Up yours if you don't like it, ese!* (90)

One reason for these definitions is that there is no precise translation from Spanish or Caló (pachuco slang) to English for the term *vato loco*. Another might have to do with the fact that, as Shimberlee Jirón-King (2008) explains, the exigencies of Gonzo journalism often emphasized visceral reaction over objectivity and authorial insight and interpretation over disinterested accounts (7). One other possibility is that the figure of the *vato loco* embodies a degree of mutability in the author's work. Ranging from "warrior" to "street freak," the *vato*'s identity changes according to his social situation. Given the variable nature of the *vato*, my methodology provides a helpful framework for understanding how mutability is necessary in the political climate of Los Angeles. As a figure who occupies multiple aspects of oppositional identity, the *vato loco* can mobilize and respond to numerous political purposes simultaneously.

One political purpose is the *vato loco*'s ability to see the truth in the complicated Los Angeles scene. In contrast to Piri Thomas's urban outlaws who focus on individual dignity and racial empowerment in New York City, Acosta's politicized *vatos* highlight macropolitical issues. Indeed, the ability to read the shifting political terrain of the city is of primary importance in *Revolt*. For example, early in the novel Zeta and the Chicano Militants (CMs) go to a meeting engineered by Dr. Francisco Bravo with Mayor Sam Yorty. Bravo, "the owner of the Pan American Bank," is a self-described spokesman (read sellout) for the Mexican American community in Los Angeles. Notwithstanding the CMs' condemnation of Bravo as a "tio taco," they agree to meet with Yorty to see if the mayor "can do anything to help with the situation in East L.A." (1989b, 72). Contrary to the stated purpose of the meeting, Zeta learns an uncomfortable truth when Yorty tells him that "the blacks picketed for years . . . for years. They marched and they did the very things you people are doing now . . . but you know something, and this is the honest-to-God truth . . . they didn't get a thing until they had Watts!" (74). By referring to the 1965 Watts Riots and subsequent reprisals by the Los Angeles Police Department (LAPD), sheriff's deputies, and the National Guard, Yorty's "advice" is actually a mean-spirited attempt to *provoke* an action. As Zeta realizes, this action will incur a repressive intervention by the LAPD.

Yet Zeta also recognizes that Yorty is "telling me the *truth*." (75). In this representation, Acosta highlights how Yorty and other icons of state power like Sheriff Peter Peaches, Chief Thomas Reddin, and District Attorney Evelle Younger tell the truth to provoke the *vato loco*. While this provocation is designed to crush opposition in Chicana/o communities, the information these representatives of state power give the *vato* enable him to better navigate the political terrain of Los Angeles. As a figure who can see the truth in a scene dominated by state intervention, the *vato loco* is well suited for oppositional consciousness in the city.

In addition, the *vato* opposes figures like Yorty, Younger, and Peaches, as well as Chicano power brokers in the novel like Bravo and Andy de Silva, "a small-time politico in East L.A. [. . .] [who] considers himself something of a spokesman for the Chicano" (94). As with Francisco Bravo, such self-described Chicano spokesmen often adopt accommodationist positions. The *vato*'s alienation from representatives of state power and accommodationist figures leaves him free from illusion about his abject place in society. He is estranged from forms of political power based on passivity or accommodation. One possible conclusion is that the *vato loco* intuitively understands how hegemonic culture co-opts Chicana/o communities. Consequently, the *vato*'s militancy is based on an organic understanding of his (and by extension other Chicana/os') relationship to structures of economic and social power.

Acosta also invests the *vato* with transformative potential because of his marginalization from both Anglo culture and traditional Chicana/o power structures. During a meeting Zeta has with the CMs at Lake Elsinore in preparation for the East LA Thirteen trial, Zeta recognizes that the *vato loco*'s ability to identify forms of oppression rests on his similarity to rural Chicana/os: "I found that some Chicanos in the city have a misconception of gringos that we farmworkers could never have. They don't quite realize they have an enemy while, in the country, the Chicano *knows* from birth he is a lowdown cockroach. *In the cities only the lowriders, the vatos locos, are in tune with this*" (67; second emphasis mine).

Like Thomas's gangsters, who explode the myths of racial syncretism in Puerto Rico and New York, Zeta and the other *vatos* underscore their racialization in the city. They recognize that the *experience* of racism in rural settings differs from the *perception* of it among Chicana/os in the city. The physical difficulty of agricultural work and overt segregation between white landowners and Mexican and Chicana/o laborers—in both their work lives and domestic situations—serve as daily reminders of the racist nature of farm life. By contrast, in cities Chicana/os and other people of color experienced a modicum of economic and social empowerment during World War II and its aftermath. Along with these economic factors is the fact that the geography of Los Angeles results in communities of color that are often in close proximity to white enclaves. Even though there are material differences between the *vato* and the farmworker, Zeta's point suggests that they share a familiarity with anti-Chicana/o and anti-Mexican racism.

Despite the fact that Acosta posits a similarity between *vatos* and rural Chicana/os at certain points in the novel, he also marks important distinctions between their political positions. One way he marks these distinctions is in the *vato*'s rejection of oppositional practices based on civil rights paradigms like nonviolent resistance. In contrast to the tactics of groups like the United Farm Workers (UFW) who practiced nonviolent resistance strategies like hunger strikes and work slowdowns, the *vatos* in Acosta's work employ confrontational, often violent, forms of opposition. As Acosta suggests, "the *vato loco* has been fighting with the pig since the Anglos stole his land in the last century. He will continue to fight until he is exterminated" (91). By linking the *vato loco* with the pachuco and other outlaw traditions, as well as with the original Californio inhabitants of Los Angeles, Acosta situates the urban gangster within a genealogy of opposition in the United States.[25] Yet this tradition of opposition is also linked with escalating violence; hence his observation that the *vato* "will continue to fight until he is exterminated." By implicit comparison, the *vato*'s revolutionary potential supersedes the actions of rural Chicana/os—at least in the more complicated Los Angeles scene. Likewise, his willingness to engage in violence eclipses the tactics of groups like the UFW, League of United Latin American Citizens (LULAC), and the Mexican American Legal Defense and Educational Fund (MALDEF).

Even though the *vato* rejects the tactics of the UFW and civil rights in the novel, it is fascinating that Zeta receives tacit approval from none other than César Chávez. As Zeta explains in advance of their meeting, "He [Chávez] believes that physical resistance to oppression only produces lesser men [...] A revolution accomplished by brute force generates but another brutal society" (44). Contrary to Zeta's expectations, Chávez suggests that there are multiple avenues for the expression of Chicana/o insurgent consciousness:

> [CHÁVEZ:] "Look," he says, a little stronger. "I *know* LA is a graveyard for organizers. You, personally, Brown Buffalo, a Chicano Lawyer, have got to help those kids. *The Militants are doing a terrific job*." (emphasis mine)
> [ZETA:] I think about his philosophy of non-violence. "I didn't know if you would approve."
> [CHÁVEZ:] "Listen *Viejo* ... It doesn't matter if I approve or if anyone approves. You are doing what has to be done."

[ZETA:] "It's not exactly what you do..."
[CHÁVEZ:] "So what? I'm a man, just like you, no? *Each of us has a different role, but we both want the same, don't we?*" (46; emphasis mine)

The context of Zeta's meeting with Chávez implicitly critiques nonviolent protest.[26] At the time of their meeting, Chávez is on his famous hunger strike of 1968.[27] As a cornerstone of Gandhian nonviolent resistance, hunger strikes are designed to evoke the revelation of truth in an oppressor. Even though he is not an "oppressor," Zeta does experience an unexpected truth: the repudiation of nonviolent strategies. Zeta's conversation with Chávez suggests that no form of resistance is applicable to every social circumstance ("Each of us has a different role, but we both want the same, don't we?"). Because they have direct access to the means of production, Chicana/os in the central valley can effect change through hunger strikes and work slowdowns. For Chicana/os in the city, however, more interventionist action is required. Consequently, Chávez argues that political actors should adapt their tactics to their social location. The conclusion that Zeta and Chávez reach is that the movement can only achieve its goals in Los Angeles by moving beyond nonviolent resistance into a policy of direct action.

Acosta extends his critique of nonviolence to students and intellectuals in the novel. In a number of scenes, *vatos locos* advocate direct action over passive forms of protest employed by intellectuals. As James Smethurst observes, "the figure of the *vato* [...] resembles that of the type of 'American' literary hero who acts rather than thinks and who embodies a pure energy" (1995, 127). Flowing from Smethurst's observation, it is important to recognize that Zeta's indictment of liberalism and passive resistance underscores his progressive move toward action—especially through clandestine activities like Molotov cocktails and bombings.[28]

It is nearly certain that Acosta's indictments of nonviolence were noted by his contemporaries. In his biography of Acosta, Burton Moore (2003) says that "Oscar was intrepid, and in his boldness sometimes angered or frightened other people. He particularly angered, or rather threatened, a lot of anointed and self-proclaimed Movement leaders. His idea of a movement was 'full speed ahead,' and "take no prisoners," to push for change rather than accommodate the *status* quo" (14).

Since many Chicana/o movement leaders in Southern California were politicized through institutions of higher learning, their politics often figured the movement in terms of reform in education.[29] Acosta rejected these ideas, insisting instead on confronting economic, social, and racial injustice. By representing the *vato* as enacting forms of social justice directly, Acosta's work intervenes in the Chicana/o movement by offering a militant subjectivity capable of demanding equality—and taking it by force if necessary.

These dynamics manifest in the tension between Gilbert (one of the *vatos*) and student activists in several scenes, including the opening chapter.[30] Beginning in medias res, the opening chapter chronicles the St. Basil's protest of December 1969.[31] After the protesters are barred from entering the Cathedral by LAPD officers disguised as ushers, Gilbert takes action that is in conflict with student activists:

> "Fuck it, *ese*. Let's get in there!" Gilbert *shouts at the student intellectuals who want to organize outside.* (emphasis mine)
> "Yeah, fuck these *putos*," Pelon puts in. Both are regular *vatos locos*, crazymen.
> "But what will happen?" [Zeta]
> "Oh, fuck that, *ese*. Let's go in." (13)

By noting the passivity of student activists who want to further organize, Acosta positions Gilbert and Pelon as men of pure action. Their forced entry into the church brings the incident to its culmination as they confront police officers. Gilbert's and Pelon's actions further politicize Zeta by rejecting his reservations ("But what will happen?"). The *vatos* subsequently enter the church through the basement, suggesting nontraditional (and mobile) modes of resistance. When barred from the metaphorical gates, the *vato* (literally) locates an underground form of movement.

These sentiments extend to similar forms of passivity as Zeta moves through various elements of the Chicana/o and activist communities in Los Angeles. His repudiation of white liberals, students, accommodationist actors like Anthony Quinn and Vicky Carr, and even the Black Panthers, locates the *vato loco* at the center of revolutionary consciousness. At about the midpoint of the text, Zeta is asked to speak as part of a rally protesting the Kent State Massacre of 1970. Ostensibly a political appearance supporting his campaign for sheriff, Zeta instead confronts the audience: "Do you realize that you'll have to shoot your mother? Do you realize that you might have to crack your uncle's head apart? Will you be willing to do that? Do you think you can slaughter your own kind? I doubt it. I seriously doubt it" (180). Here Zeta exposes the passivity that underpins many 1960s forms of activism. By pointing out the students' investments in privilege, Zeta makes a case for the *vato loco* as a more suitable figure for oppositional struggle. Since he is outside of traditional oppositional consciousness, the *vato* is better able to enact resistance uncontaminated by an investment in privilege. While this portrayal is ironic given the author's investment in the privilege of patriarchy, it is important to recognize how Acosta grounds his critique of white liberals and accommodationists. One logical consequence of Zeta's interaction with the students is that militant action is a virtual *requirement* for forms of political and social change situated in urban settings. Because these forms of political and social change exceed the bounds of law and acceptable social conduct, the *vato loco* is the logical person to engage in militant activities.

Furthermore, Zeta's indictment of student activism is figured as a violent race war. Yet because the race war that Zeta envisions can't remedy the legal system, it points to establishing a new Chicana/o nation. As Acosta notes in his "Autobiographical Essay," "You can't be a class or a nation without land. Without it, it doesn't have any meaning. It's that simple. So we are beginning to see that what we're talking about is getting land and having our own government. Period" (1996, 12). Even though his call for a Chicana/o nation might be considered naïve, disingenuous, or impractical given the heavy-handed reprisals of the state in the novel, it does provide an interesting counterpoint to discourses of passive resistance or reform in education. Where some movement groups placed heavy emphasis on educational reform, Acosta argues in favor of a new national consciousness. Genuine or not, Acosta's claim contests hegemonic notions of opposition through incremental change or accommodation. Instead, he advocates a reconfiguration of the political system designed to accommodate radical Chicanismo.

One interesting aspect of Acosta's call for an independent nation, however, is that it is not restricted to Chicana/os. Like Piri Thomas, who negotiates Nuyorican identity in relation to African Americans, Acosta depicts other Latina/os, African Americans, and even antiracist whites as important Chicana/o movement players. For example, among the organizers Zeta encounters during his first meeting with the CMs are Risco, "a curly-haired *cubano* with a slick tongue and very white teeth" and Ruth, Risco's white partner (32). In addition, in the opening pages of the novel, a central instigator of the St. Basil's protest is Duana Doherty, formerly a "street nun who once worshipped wearing black robes" but who has subsequently "joined up with the Chicanos and [become] a Cockroach herself" (17). Similarly, Jean Fisher, an African American juror (and Zeta's posttrial lover) provides information to Zeta about jury tampering during the St. Basil's Twenty-One trial. While these characters occupy secondary roles to *vatos locos* like Gilbert, Pelon, Black Eagle, Mangas, and Zeta, they suggest common political purpose between the "cockroaches" that populate the novel.[32] Even though Acosta's representation doesn't go as far as Thomas's triangulation of Puerto Rican and African American subjectivities, the novel provides a corrective by highlighting the occluded interethnic solidarities that often fueled Chicana/o movement groups.

Moreover, Acosta's positioning of the *vato loco* suggests a tension between individualism and collective consciousness. In this regard, it is critical to recall that the *vato* speaks through Zeta as much as he speaks for their social and political positions. This idea is helpful in understanding how the relationship between Zeta and other *vatos locos* is negotiated. During his defense of Corky Gonzalez, police chief Judd Davis accuses Zeta of "directing the activities of the Chicano Liberation Front" (248). Zeta responds,

> I laugh. Deep down in my gut I laugh. I can hear Gilbert laughing with me. I can hear the dudes who presently live in my own pad on Sixth Street [. . .] Right now the bastards are probably brewing up some molotov for tonight's action and here I'm being called the *mastermind*. [. . .] Those guys wouldn't do what I told them to do if their lives depended on it. They are *vatos locos! Nobody* tells crazy guys what to do [. . .] It is *they* who have converted me and driven me to this brink of madness. It is they who are watching and wondering and complaining about me. *I* am the sheep. *I* am the one being used. (248)

On one hand, Zeta recuses himself from his collective identification with other *vatos* in the novel. By suggesting that he is the victim of their excesses, he emphasizes his position as an outsider—one who is estranged even from the *vato loco*. This estrangement points to the limitations of *vato loco* subjectivity, as their nihilism and self-destructive impulses limit their potential as vectors for transcendent opposition. But Zeta's rejection of the *vato* might also be read as a desire for individual empowerment. His figuring of himself as the true outsider marks him as a distinct individual free from obligation to the *vatos* with whom he is linked.

On the other hand, as a first-person personal narrative, the self that Acosta presents offers a stylized and culturally matrixed subjectivity that implicitly critiques individualist notions of identity. Since, as Zeta argues, the *vato loco* speaks *through* him as much as he speaks *for* them, it is logical that Zeta positions himself within a collective "I." One implication of Zeta's rumination is that the *vato loco* serves as a repository for both collective opposition and a limited individualism.

In pointing out the tension between individualism and collective affirmation the *vato* embodies, I do not wish to resolve the novel's contradictions. Rather, I suggest that these contradictions are important markers of Acosta's ambivalence about individual empowerment versus projects of community efficacy. Because discourses of racialization blame individuals for their own lack of success, while simultaneously stereotyping entire classes of people, it is logical that Acosta asserts individual dignity while also valorizing community values. Likewise, another aspect of this tension is attributable to the use of the first-person personal narrative—an individualist form. I advocate reading these generative contradictions to comprehend the difficulty of constituting opposition within hegemonic culture. From this point of view, it is less important to resolve Acosta's contradictions than to examine the multiple implications they embody for individuals and social groups.

Along these lines, Acosta utilizes the *vato* to problematize simplistic notions of oppositional consciousness. As the novel progresses, paranoia pervades the characters. As historian Ernesto Chávez points out, this paranoia was well founded, given the infiltration of Chicana/o movement groups by agencies like the FBI's infamous Counter Intelligence Program (COINTELPRO) and the LAPD's Criminal Conspiracy Section (2002, 59–60). Accordingly, one aspect of the novel meditates on constituting opposition within a climate of state intervention.

These ideas crystallize in the Robert Fernández case. Fernández, a *vato loco*, is murdered by the LAPD while in custody for a routine drunk and disorderly arrest. The Fernández family asks Zeta to represent them during a coroner's inquest. Zeta's cross-examination during the inquest reveals that the police placed a sheet around Fernández's neck to make the crime look like a suicide.[33] Despite his vociferous objections to the biased actions of the inquest officers, the jury returns with a finding of suicide. After the inquest, Zeta, Gilbert, and Pelon decide to vent their frustration by "throwing a bomb." As they ride around East Los Angeles looking for a target, their conversation illuminates the difficulties of striking back:

> [ZETA:] We've got to find something, or someone . . . I'm trying to think.
> [GILBERT:] Hey man, why don't we just find a pig and shoot the sonofabitch?
> [. . .]
> [ZETA:] Hey, you guys. I'm trying to . . . And we can't just shoot anybody. You think we're a bunch of hoods?
> [GILBERT:] I'm a stone anarchist myself.
> [PELON:] I don't give a shit about politics myself.
> [ZETA:] I know. You're just a *vato loco*.
> [. . .]
> [ZETA:] We've got to find a target that's *symbolic*.
> [GILBERT:] You mean like Bank of America?
> [ZETA:] Fuck no, *ese*. That's a hippie trip. The SDS is doing that.
> [PELON:] So what? They weren't the first ones. (122)

While this exchange is rendered comically, it suggests a serious topic: the difficulty of identifying a source of power. Indeed, striking back in the social and political scene of Los Angeles is virtually impossible. Although as Zeta notes, César Chávez and the UFW are not "into bombs," Gilbert recognizes that *his* political identity demands action ("No, man. *He* isn't. But we are" [126]). In the end, the *vatos* throw a Molotov cocktail at a Safeway in their neighborhood partly because "the Farmworkers are picketing Safeway" and partly because the store's employees give Pelon's *jefita* (girlfriend) a "bad time" (126).

This scene demonstrates how the violence that Zeta and his friends enact reproduces the violence visited on their community by the state. To comprehend this point, it is important to understand that the *vatos* bomb a store in East Los Angeles. Given the economic and social conditions that pervade this space it is unlikely that the corporation would rebuild the store, leading to further devaluation of quality of life in the neighborhood. Similarly, when in the closing pages Zeta and the *vatos* detonate a bomb in the hall of justice in an attempt to assassinate Judge Alacran, the only casualty is another Latino—presumably one of the janitorial staff. These scenes underscore two important aspects of Acosta's portrayal: the only people capable of fulfilling revolutionary action are *vatos locos*, and in the hazy political and social climate of the city, these actions tend to reinscribe state violence.

The tension between fighting back and reinscribing violence points to a series of aporias in the novel. Because of their dissatisfaction with the civil rights movement, Chicanos were propelled into increasingly confrontational forms of protest. Yet when they engaged in these protests, state reprisals were virtually assured. Even in the absence of overt state violence, Acosta suggests that hegemonic culture overdetermines the outcomes of revolutionary action. Given these facts, Acosta's portrayal of the *vato loco* can be read as a meditation on political actors who embody the potential to move between and among the ideological structures composing hegemonic culture. Despite the fact that Zeta, Gilbert, and the other *vatos* fail to overturn the social order, they are able to create a critical distance from the state that enables a fresh perspective on opposition. Consequently, the novel provides a space for critical assessment of both revolutionary subjectivity and the constitution of social movements. This critical assessment makes navigation possible in the contested realm of hegemonic culture. In this way, Zeta's project of writing "THE STORY" and "THE BOOK" (22), indeed the novel itself, can be read as a reflection on the difficulties of constituting social movements in the context of state intervention.

It is therefore possible to read the protagonist's politicization vis-à-vis the *vato loco* as a triangulation from bourgeois lawyer to "*vato loco numero uno*" (16)—the position that brackets the novel. This negotiation functions partially as a blueprint for collective social action in the city. By extension, Acosta's text also serves as a political roadmap designed to instruct would-be revolutionaries on their paths from "flower *vatos*" to CMs.

Like his contemporary Piri Thomas, Acosta also detracts from his project by reinscribing gender and sexual hierarchies. Michael Hames-García explains these problematics in terms of parody: "given that the texts are satirical and the protagonists are figures for critical analysis instead of models for emulation, one might suggest that these passages offer a critical representation of sexist nationalism rather than an instance of it" (2004, 66).

While Hames-García explains that his goal is "not to 'apologize' for Acosta's portrayals of women and gay men," his reading runs counter to many feminist and queer studies critiques of Chicano nationalism that condemn positions like Acosta's for their uncritical gender and sexual problematics.

My position on these issues is that they further attest—if only unwittingly—to the difficulty of constituting opposition within hegemony. As a group marginalized by hegemonic culture, male Chicanos have an understandable stake in making a claim to personhood. Like Thomas, however, the nexus of this stake has been historically deployed via the discourse of masculinity. Consequently, Acosta often figures his and his fellows' humanity in terms of their collective manhood. In so doing, Acosta, like Thomas, falls prey to the discourse itself by reinscribing homophobia and sexism. Given Acosta's investment in the *vato loco*, it is difficult for me to read a figure known for regressive positions on sex and gender solely in terms of parody. While he does satirically point out the importance of issues like the constitution of opposition within hegemonic society and the effectiveness of striking back at power, Acosta also willingly subscribes to machismo as an organizing principle of society.

Indeed, Acosta provides evidence of this stake in machismo in his other autobiographical writings. For example, he argues in his "Autobiographical Essay" that "we have a way of life that we've learned from childhood. The concept of *la familia*, the respect of elders is not Sunday-school bullshit with us. It's part of our culture. A Chicano can no more disrespect his mother than he can himself. Which means he can, but at great cost to himself" (1996, 11–12). Predicated as it is on female passivity and problematic characterizations of women as either mothers or whores, this notion of masculinity is challenged by a subsequent generation of Latina and Chicana feminists in the postsixties period.

If a culturally matrixed subjectivity informs first-person personal narrative traditions in Chicana/o communities, then what Acosta triangulates in *The Revolt of the Cockroach People* is a politicized outlaw identity. This outlaw identity resonates with the community in Los Angeles because lowriders, gang members, and *vatos locos* offer intriguing possibilities for coalescing militant social movements. Recalling Acosta's assertion that the *vato loco* has been fighting the "pig" since his lands were stolen, we see that the insurgent consciousness that reaches into the past for Acosta is actually a triangulation of radical forms of resistance that have been ongoing in Chicana/o communities for over a century. From this perspective the *vato loco* is not *entirely* crazy. Rather, he forms the basis for a movement of freedom fighters who are the direct antecedents of the Californios—the very "*vatos locos*" who first resisted the oppression of Mexican Americans during the nineteenth century.

Conclusion

Thomas and Acosta utilize the complex personhood of manhood to claim individual rights, while also contesting the racism and ethnic exclusion that limit life chances for their communities. The nexus of each author's challenge is the outlaw—in Thomas's case the black gangster, in Acosta's the *vato loco*. While each author's deployment of the outlaw contains important differences that emerge out of the specific historical and cultural circumstances of Chicana/o and Puerto Rican communities, there are important similarities.

Thomas's self-representation constitutes a triangulation of his Puerto Rican identity with black nationalist traditions. He constructs this affiliation to leverage an already politicized militant identity for himself and his community. Acosta's militancy, on the other hand, focuses on locating appropriate forms of opposition for Chicana/os in urban social locations. Both authors therefore offer a strategic essentialism that triangulates the outsider as a potential foundation for a new social and political order.

Likewise, both authors represent outlaw subjectivities in relation to other aggrieved ethnic and racial groups. While Thomas's triangulations of African American and Puerto Rican subjectivities substantially interrogate ethnic and racial ideologies in the United States and Puerto Rico, Acosta's representations of interethnic solidarities provide a minor corrective to mainstream histories of the Chicana/o movement. In both cases, however, these authors represent organic relationships between aggrieved groups in the United States—including antiracist whites. Contrasting the essentialist rhetoric that often accompanied insurgent nationalist movements, these authors demonstrate that interethnic solidarities were important to the activism of 1960s groups.

Moreover, while both construct the outsider as the nexus of their challenges to liberal political subjectivity and forms of self-writing, they each suffer from masculinist and heterosexist impulses that limit the revolutionary potential of their protagonists. In constituting these problematics, these authors embody attempts to codify male power at the expense of women and gays and lesbians. As we will see in chapter 3, during the postsixties period, gay Chicano authors like John Rechy and feminist Latinas like Judith Ortiz Cofer offer complicated redeployments of cultural nationalist tropes that reconfigure the outsider for their own revolutionary purposes.

3

Remaking the Insurgent Vision

John Rechy, Judith Ortiz Cofer, and the Limits of Nationalist Morality

> *When the framework does not rest on a hierarchy of oppression, then every form of systemic violence and human agency must be taken into consideration.*
>
> —The Latina Feminist Group, *Telling to Live*

In previous chapters I examined Latina/o first-person personal narratives that triangulate alternative formulations of identity as the basis for projects of community efficacy. By matrixing the narration of the self with the history and culture of their communities, authors like John Rechy and Judith Ortiz Cofer respond to similar literary and political impulses. Rechy's documentary novel *The Sexual Outlaw* (1977) and Ortiz Cofer's novel *The Line of the Sun* (1989) redeploy insurgent tropes used by authors like Ernesto Galarza and Piri Thomas. Rechy and Ortiz Cofer recode these narrative strategies in postsixties contexts to contest patriarchal and heterosexist masculinity as the singular site of subject formation. Analyzing their triangulations reveals how Rechy and Ortiz Cofer leverage insurgent identities as sites of resistance to both internal *and* external oppressions, revitalizing the imagined community of the nation by clearing a space for women and queers.

In their attempts to reimagine queer and feminist subjectivities, Rechy and Ortiz Cofer also challenge discursive opposition. Their works triangulate the insufficiencies of patriarchal nationalism and the problematics internal to second-wave feminist and post-Stonewall gay liberation groups that emphasized a single identity category (gender or sexuality) over others (race, ethnicity, class). Rather than envisioning identity categories as mutually exclusive or as a hierarchy of oppressions, these authors conceptualize race, gender, sexuality, class, and national origin as mutually constitutive.

Because their texts represent queer and feminist perspectives that challenge masculinist discourses, they also embody what Gloria Anzaldúa calls *la facultad*. Anzaldúa defines *la facultad* as "the capacity to see in surface phenomena the meaning of deeper realities, to see the deep structure below the surface" (2007, 60). *La facultad* constitutes a response to the pain of oppressive experience (i.e., of being a racialized, gendered, sexualized subject).[1] Yet *la facultad* also emphasizes the alienated position of women and queers as a potential foundation for critiques of patriarchy and homophobia. While it is important not to conflate the experiences of male Latinos (both gay and straight) with Latinas, I point to the fact that Rechy and Ortiz Cofer deploy similar outsider tropes to challenge, complicate, and at times posit alternatives to patriarchal narratives accompanying insurgent nationalism.

Rhetorics of Morality: Contesting Family, Gender, and Compulsory Heterosexuality in the Imagined National Community

Chicana and Latina feminists have long pointed out that insurgent nationalisms often enforced patriarchy and compulsory heterosexuality as the foundation for revolutionary subjectivity. As the collective authors of the Latina Feminist Group note, "Latina feminists [. . .] have contested the exclusion of questions of gender and sexuality in ethnic studies curricula or political agendas. Cultural nationalism has defined some of these programs or projects, insisting on idealized notions of ethnicity, *familia*, and community. Cultural nationalists often repress women's voices by reaffirming heterosexist utopic visions of colonized peoples. At their most extreme, they discredit Latina feminists as separatist and divisive, and even bait them as 'traitors to the race'" (2001, 3).

As I show in previous chapters, texts by authors like Galarza, Colón, Thomas, and Acosta are evocative of these problematics. In their attempts to empower themselves as racialized subjects, male Latino authors uncritically incorporated patriarchy. But their incorporation of patriarchy was not value neutral. Indeed, male Latinos have a history of occluding or silencing the contributions of women and queers to the imagined national community.

Given the varieties of racism experienced by male Latinos, ranging from work and housing discrimination to hate crimes and lynching, it is logical that they would seek power within their circumscribed realms. As Anzaldúa notes, "the loss of a sense of dignity and respect in the macho breeds a false *machismo* which leads him to put down women and even to brutalize them" (2007, 105).² But as Carl Gutiérrez-Jones explains, despite the gains of Chicana and Latina feminisms in the 1970s and 1980s, new strategies of suppression were needed to "maintain patriarchal privilege as new rhetorics of empowerment threatened to dismantle the accepted coercion which kept Chicanas subordinate" (1995, 134). Gutiérrez-Jones's point suggests that patriarchy in male Latino culture, and particularly in insurgent nationalist movements, is neither an oversight nor an unwitting reinscription of hegemonic values. Instead, these perspectives represent a coordinated effort to maintain male supremacy as the organizing principle of Latina/o societies.

Even in putatively progressive contexts, like the Puerto Rican Socialist Party (PSP) that espoused an official platform of Latina empowerment, women and queers were often marginalized.³ As Puerto Rican movement activist Carmen Vivian Rivera recalls, "The mystique and aura surrounding the revolutionary were built on the *male* figure. The woman as revolutionary and leader was rarely understood, accepted, validated, or promoted. Therefore her projection both at the time and in the recording of our history is woefully absent. We tried to change the definition of leader itself, but we weren't always successful" (1998, 205).

As Rivera describes, revolutionary subjectivity in groups like the PSP was founded on unstated (but assumed) masculinity. As she further notes, "the rhetoric on promoting and following the leadership of women was impressive, but in practice and on a personal level they failed miserably" (203). Rivera's experience demonstrates that although many Puerto Rican movement groups officially espoused women's empowerment, they often reinscribed gender hierarchies that precluded women from leadership roles.

Such dynamics were also operative in other Latina/o contexts. Despite the presence of well-known female activists like Dolores Huerta, Paula Crisostomo, Esperanza Martell, and Elizabeth Figueroa, women were often consigned to subordinate positions in social movements.⁴ Sonia Saldívar-Hull points out that Chicanas were subject to masculinist control, being accused of perversion—literally, of being lesbians, dykes, and perverts—if they contested masculinist Chicano movement scripts. In fact, accusations of homosexuality were used as a tool to keep Chicanas within subordinate positions (2000, 29–32).

But homophobia was not only used as a tool to subordinate Latinas. Queer identities were figured as the antithesis of revolutionary subjectivity. As Luis Aponte-Parés and Jorge B. Merced observe, many queer Latina/os faced a choice between the political goals of insurgent groups and the need for sexual liberation. In relation to the "deconstructing and reassembling" of revolutionary identities within the Puerto Rican movement, Aponte-Parés and Merced note that "Latino gayness was not central to the formulation of [these] identit[ies]," identities that are "still in construction today" (1998, 297). Similarly, Aponte-Parés and Merced explain that to be gay, to be a "*maricón*," was "to be the total denial of masculinity [. . .] being called one is perhaps the worst insult to a [Latino] male" (302).

Heteronormative morality served as a predominant mode of enforcing these ideologies. As George Mosse (1985) argues in relation to European nationalisms, "the dynamic of modern nationalism was built upon the ideal of manliness. Nationalism also put forward a feminine ideal, but it was largely passive, symbolizing the immutable forces which the nation reflected" (64). Of particular importance to my analysis is Mosse's assertion that politically active masculinities are premised on passive femininity and the denial of homosexuality. Accordingly, "the family gave support from below to that respectability which the nation attempted to enforce from above" (19).

Mosse further argues that the apparatus of the nationalist state moves from idealizing friendship and male love to criminalizing homosexuality. This demonization of same-sex relations emerges in nationalist contexts because homosexuality is characterized as a deviation from devotion to family. By suggesting that the family serves as a model for national belonging, Mosse argues that the patriarchal structure of the nuclear family predisposes individuals to accept top-down, hierarchical authority that figures the supreme leader as the (gendered male) "father" of the people. Furthermore, because homosexuality deviates from gender roles associated with heteronormative family life, to be queer constitutes a threat to love of the nation. Queers are thus written out of the contract of national belonging, codifying patriarchal control within a fraternity of heterosexual men.

My point is not to argue that Latina/o nationalisms are reducible to the same ideological imperatives implicit in European nationalisms. Rather, I argue that many forms of nationalist thinking enforce gender roles hostile to women and queers. Given the historical context of insurgent nationalism alongside contemporary struggles for gay liberation like the 1969 Stonewall Uprising and the rise of second-wave feminism, it is interesting that masculinist formulations constituted the cultural dominant of many

Latina/o social movements. As Tim Libretti (2004) observes in relation to the New Left movement of the same period, the failure to embrace gay liberation was partially due to the elevation of false universals associated with revolutionary subjectivity. Libretti asserts that mainstream gay liberation movements were also culpable in their deferral of race and ethnicity as intersecting identity categories.

Libretti's observations about the New Left resonate with Latina/o insurgent nationalist politics. I argue that Rechy and Ortiz Cofer disturb nationalist ideologies by disrupting hierarchies of patriarchy and heterosexuality. Their works problematize essentialist notions of opposition by representing identity categories as mutually constitutive, rather than mutually exclusive. While they do not entirely divorce themselves from insurgent consciousness, Rechy and Ortiz Cover reconfigure outlaw tropes to enable their critiques of patriarchy and heterosexism. By triangulating the insufficiencies of patriarchal and heteronormative constructions of the nation, they challenge machismo, proposing instead intersecting subjectivities that include aspects of race, class, gender, and sexuality.

John Rechy and the Sexual Revolutionary

Similar to the works of Cherríe Moraga and Arturo Islas, John Rechy's novels document complex queer Chicana/o subjects that challenge essentialist conceptions of identity. Often, these subjectivities embody paradoxes that emerge from the contradictions in queer and Chicana/o cultures. It is in the spirit of examining Rechy's generative contradictions that I approach *The Sexual Outlaw*. Like his novels *City of Night* (1963), *Numbers* (1967), and *This Day's Death* (1970), *The Sexual Outlaw* blurs distinctions between Rechy's protagonist, Jim, and his ethnic and sexual identities. This blurring of distinctions complicates how Rechy conceives of opposition in *The Sexual Outlaw*, as Jim's outlaw activities critique both Chicana/o nationalism and post-Stonewall gay liberation.

Thematically, *The Sexual Outlaw* engages insurgency and ethnic identity from a queer perspective. The novel experiments with form and content to construct a composite portrait of Jim's experiences "sexhunting" (illicit sexual liaisons with multiple partners in public settings) in Los Angeles over the course of one weekend during the mid-1970s. Narrated in real time with flashbacks and imaginary sequences, the novel is divided between Jim's sexual exploits and essays (or "Voice Over" sections) that comment on events, ideas, and theories related to the protagonist's experiences. These implicit dialogues frame Jim's liaisons as textual examples, complications, and elaborations of ideas expressed in the essays. Rafael Perez-Torres (1994) notes that while the multiple genres are distinct, the two sections (erotic sections and essays) are mutually reliant. Consequently, the rebellion of the sexual outlaw's language and performance only appear in relation to the enclosing social commentary (208). While it is not clear whether the narrator in the Voice Over essays represents Jim, Rechy, or a combination of both, the continuity between sections suggests an affiliation between Jim, the narrator, and the author. For this reason, I refer to the Voice Over narrator as the narrator/Jim and the protagonist of the erotic sections as simply Jim.

In its exhaustive and (porno)graphic cataloging of Jim's experiences, *The Sexual Outlaw* confronts the reader, forcing us to encounter the protagonist's sexual odyssey on his terms. Throughout the novel, Jim constructs himself and his fellow sexhunters as consummate outsiders who refuse societal norms ranging from heterosexuality to prohibitions against "deviancy." He describes "public sex [as] revolution, courageous, righteous, defiant revolution" (47). To accommodate this vision, Jim and his fellow outlaws embrace promiscuity and exhibitionism, disrupting traditional romantic love and the consummation of sex within monogamous relationships. Through the representation of Jim's outlaw activities, we come to understand the protagonist's identity, while becoming acquainted with aspects of gay culture, including Southern California's underground public sex scene.

Rechy's personal estrangement from mainstream Chicano culture is helpful in understanding how he represents the tension between Jim's ethnic and sexual identities.[5] Citing the homophobia rampant in Chicana/o and other Latina/o contexts, Rechy states that "Hispanic heterosexuals, still so determinedly 'macho,' often seem to think that in order to be 'men' they must denounce homosexuals, and do so fiercely at times" (1995, 117). Rechy highlights the cognitive dissonance between queer identities and discourses of machismo that code homosexuality as the antithesis of masculinity. By rejecting heteronormative assumptions characteristic of many Chicana/o movement groups, while also complicating the stability of deracinated queer subjectivities, Rechy's work attempts to triangulate a subject that is queer, Chicano, and politically progressive.

One way *The Sexual Outlaw* grapples with these questions is by illuminating similarities between sexism, racism, and homophobia. In a 1995 interview with Debra Castillo, Rechy argues that "I view *all* discrimination as a hungry evil. It appalls me that so very often minorities discriminate against others. When I hear Chicanos screech 'faggot' and read of their initiating gay-bashings—when I learn that some Jews oppose including the names of homosexuals in a memorial to those who died in concentration camps, when I see some women cops determined to rival male cops as bullies, when I read the rantings and pantings of black conservative-darling Stanley Crouch against homosexuals and black women, when I hear about homosexual nightclubs that exclude women and minorities, I wonder . . . what's the use?" (121–22).

Rechy points out that many subordinated populations exercise forms of discrimination incompatible with struggles for social justice. Because he understands categories of oppression as intersecting, his conception of opposition is broader than groups oriented around a singular identity (the Chicana/o movement, gay liberation, etc.). His comments underscore factors that disrupt potential alliances (homophobia among communities of color and racism within queer groups). He further emphasizes links between gender and sexual oppressions by asserting that "the basis of anti-homosexuality lies in antiwoman attitudes. The majority of heterosexual males see women as inferior. Since women are supposed to desire men, a man who desires another man must have abdicated at least some of his superior 'maleness.' The homosexual male, therefore, is looked down on as a betrayer of machismo—'heterosexualismo'" (115).

Several critics have pointed to the relationship between homosexuality and other oppressed identities in their analysis of Rechy's novels. Frederick Aldama argues that Rechy's self-fashioning as a "literary saboteur" enables him to reimagine "an otherwise essentialized and/or neglected queer Chicano/a identity and experience" (2005, 48). Aldama asserts that Rechy's queer, biracial characters counterpoise the dualism inherent in most identity discourses through the mutually informing nature of ethnic and homosexual subjectivities. For Aldama, Rechy's work in general and *The Sexual Outlaw* in particular offer "new way[s] of understanding queer (ethnic or otherwise) sexuality not so much in the characterization of Jim, but in the presence of the fiction itself" (63–64). Consequently, Rechy discursively explodes essentialist categories associated with queer or ethnic subjectivities, advocating instead an identity that is "queer and Chicano, and much more" (72).

Similarly, José Saldívar (1997) has argued for what he calls Rechy's "U.S.-Mexico borderland past," including a formative event in the author's life: his witnessing of a dead Bracero worker who drowned while attempting to cross the Rio Grande. Saldívar claims that Rechy's Chicano identity "loom[s] behind his rage," informing his fight "against bigotry in Texas," and facilitating revolutionary activities as a sexual outlaw (110). Rechy's work is thus emblematic of "bridge consciousness, a consciousness that allows them [queer Chicana/o writers] to explore and exploit their double vision as both participant and observer and as displaced subjects across multiple discourses" (109).

Rafael Pérez-Torres (1994) reads these tensions in Rechy's work from a different perspective. Focusing on how Rechy problematizes the heterosocial order and simplistic forms of opposition within gay liberation, Pérez-Torres argues that *The Sexual Outlaw* constructs a "heroic homosexual liberation" that interrupts dualist categories (206). Accordingly, "sexual outlaws disrupt and destroy the operations of the heterosocial world by questioning the monological bases of its order: monogamy, reproduction, duality, stability, closure" (207). Although for Pérez Torres the novel can't articulate a fully revolutionary vision because it fails to move beyond dualism, it answers the problem of identity through appropriation and inversion that ironically mirror the world the novel seeks to invert (223).

My reading of *The Sexual Outlaw* builds on these perspectives by examining Rechy's triangulations of outlaw subjectivity. I argue that Rechy triangulates his protagonist's relationship with gender oppression, homophobia, and racism to posit a radical, queer, Chicano subjectivity vis-à-vis Jim's outlaw persona. Because Jim cannot be reduced to a single narrative identity, *The Sexual Outlaw* traverses the uneasy ground between Chicana/o nationalist morality and gay liberation. I partially agree with Pérez-Torres that Jim's subjectivity is not transcendent because it remains mired in dualism. I depart, however, from Pérez-Torres's claim that Jim's activities merely reflect and invert the world he seeks to disrupt.

I argue that Rechy's inability to divorce his protagonist from dualist contexts attests to a more complex oppositional dynamic. I contend that his critiques of the insufficiencies of Jim's Chicano and gay identities constitute an attempt to triangulate liberatory subjectivities within the heterosocial order. In other words, Rechy's triangulations attempt to navigate the tensions between racist and heteronormative ideologies in both gay liberation and Chicana/o contexts. Rather than considering his work from the standpoint of its failures, I advocate reading Rechy's novel as an attempt to disrupt multiple levels of oppression within the context of hegemony.

Moreover, where Aldama, Saldívar, and Pérez-Torres examine Rechy's novels as fiction, I advocate reading *The Sexual Outlaw* as a first-person personal narrative. I justify this claim in part due to the similarities Jim shares with the author. As journalist and biographer Charles Casillo observes, Rechy, like Jim, "felt so alienated, the only way to express his sexuality was through hustling" (2003, 24), recalling the fact that many of Rechy's protagonists engage in male prostitution.[6] Similarly, many of his protagonists are born in El Paso, Texas, to Mexican or Chicana mothers and violent Scottish fathers. Also, like the author, they frequently assume thinly veiled identities that correspond to Rechy's multiple aliases.[7] In fact, Rechy inscribes his experience in the novel, at times suggesting that he is Jim.[8] This conscious blurring of fiction and autobiography suggests an engagement with first-person personal narratives designed to enact projects of community efficacy.

While similar points can be made about Rechy's other novels, I focus on *The Sexual Outlaw* because of its self-conscious deployment of the outlaw trope. Indeed, *The Sexual Outlaw* constitutes an unlikely inheritor to Chicana/o nationalist texts in its valorization of the outlaw as the primary vector of revolutionary consciousness. As the narrator/Jim asserts, "the promiscuous homosexual is a sexual revolutionary. Each moment of his outlaw existence he confronts repressive laws, repressive 'morality.'" (28). This characterization of the sexual revolutionary suggests continuity with outlaw traditions espoused by authors like Américo Paredes (1998). But unlike literary inheritors like Rudolfo Anaya or Luis Valdez, Rechy uses the outlaw trope to interrogate the patriarchal assumptions of the movement, while also valorizing intersecting ethnic, gender, and sexual identities.[9]

For example, in the opening lines of the novel, Rechy describes Jim as a consummate outsider, ritually preparing for his outlaw activities: "He prepares his body for the hunt. A dancer at the bar. A boxer in the ring. Prepares ritualistically for the next three days of outlaw sex. The arena will be streets, parks, alleys, tunnels, garages, movie arcades, bathhouses, beaches, movie backrows, tree-sheltered avenues, late-night orgy rooms, dark yards" (21).

Like other Chicana/o texts that valorize ritualized figures, Rechy characterizes Jim as a warrior. The figuring of the warrior, Aztec warriors in particular, has a long history in Chicana/o literature and culture. Acosta,

Galarza, Anzaldúa, and Rechy in his later novel *The Miraculous Day of Amalia Gómez* (1991), figure oppositional struggle in Chicana/o communities in relation to Aztec warriors.[10] By drawing on the warrior icon, Rechy's portrayal of Jim complicates the popular imagery of Chicana/o insurgent movements. He inverts the image of the masculine Aztec warrior by aligning Jim's ritual personae with homosexuality. By reconfiguring an icon of the Chicana/o movement, the novel recodes the revolutionary subject in queer terms.

Rechy complicates heteronormative morality and recodes revolutionary consciousness by representing Jim's activities as a sexhunter and the liberatory aspects of public gay sex. Pondering "gay revolution," the narrator/Jim describes the "gay apocalypse":

> I had a vision of the inevitable gay apocalypse—of thousands of homosexuals rushing against the helmets and the sticks, the guns—thousands of gay men and women riding a tide of pent-up rage released at last. Abruptly that vision of apocalyptic violence stopped. Yes, that would be righteous—but was that indeed what the gay apocalypse would be?
> Perhaps. Yes, perhaps.
> Suddenly I laughed aloud. But might it not be, instead, the ultimate, the liberating public sex orgy? (183)

Here, the narrator/Jim questions how to constitute opposition within heteronormative ideology. Identifying the masculinist imperatives implicit in Chicana/o and gay liberation contexts, Jim recognizes how his conception of apocalyptic revolution is overdetermined. He rejects violence, embracing instead a "liberating public sex orgy." Rechy thus attempts to triangulate a masculinity that moves beyond violent social contexts.

These ideas emerge in another Voice Over section where Jim imagines delivering a public lecture about homosexuality. Encountering the hazard public gay sex poses to heterosexuals, the narrator/Jim asks, "What is the real gay threat?"

> There are, in fact, two very real threats that the gay world poses to straight society. One is of course psychic—the fear of being what religion, laws, doctors have wrongfully branded, condemned, persecuted, prosecuted, punished, forbidden.

The second is that an acceptance of homosexuality—including, importantly, its tendency toward promiscuity—would result in a traumatic questioning of what, in the extreme, become oppressive within the heterosexual norm.
> Why one wife? One husband? Why not lovers?
> Why marriage?
> Why sex with only one person?
> Why *not* open sex? . . .
> Why *only* relationships?
> Why necessarily children?

The heterosexual would thus be questioning, not heterosexuality itself, no, but the stagnant conformity of much of his tribal society. (205–6)

By exceeding respectability, the sexual outlaw questions the norms of gender relations, sex, and reproduction. He critiques romantic love and familial bonding that underpin the imagined national community. In addition, his criticism of both heterosexuality and the "stagnant conformity" of "tribal society" implies that there is more than simple bigotry at stake in the suppression of queers. Indeed, the sexual outlaw questions the logic of heteronormative morality.

But the sexual outlaw also exposes the collusion between the Chicana/o movement and Anglo bourgeois morality. Here it is important to recall that the nation is partially determined by concepts of gender and family that predispose one to submit to hierarchical authority. Since the heteronormativity of the Chicana/o movement was premised on similar gender and sexual norms, it is arguable that the narrator/Jim's critique is also designed to question the basis of hierarchy and expose its uncritical adoption by Chicana/o movement groups.

But *The Sexual Outlaw* offers more than a critique of Chicana/o nationalist homophobia. In fact, the novel examines dynamics internal to gay culture. The narrator/Jim's rejection of "gay fascism" that determines "that one *must* perform this sex act, and *must* allow that one, in order to be gay" (243) suggests a reconfiguration of traditional conceptions of homosexuality. In particular, Jim and the narrator are critical of sadomasochism (S&M) practices that emphasize humiliation and degradation as aspects of sexual consummation.[11] As the narrator/Jim notes in a Voice Over, "At its best, the gay experience is liberating, adventurous, righteously daring, revolutionary, and beautiful in its sexual abundance. At its worst it is a stark vision of hell" (242). These internal critiques suggest that Jim's outlaw activities explore the tensions between identity categories and form an alternative basis for oppositional consciousness within both Chicana/o and gay liberation contexts.

The Sexual Outlaw supports this reading by emphasizing instability, particularly in the relationship between the characterization of Jim and the intrusion of the narrator/Jim's commentary in the Voice Over sections. These generic representations underscore the thematic ones: that essentialist identity positions are inherently unstable. As the narrator/Jim argues in another Voice Over: "Unlike blacks, say, who have black fathers, black mothers, black sisters, black brothers, the homosexual is gay in total isolation in his family. He is often cast out when he is 'discovered.' There is this additional factor: Since his is a minority defined by its sexual preference, the gay energy flows into two areas—the revolution of the sex hunt and the revolution against bigotry" (245).

Because dominant society and communities of color marginalize homosexuals, the narrator/Jim contends that gays and lesbians must oppose both racism *and* heterosexism. The sexual outlaw's energies are thus driven to the sex hunt and the fight against bigotry—understood as antiracist and antihomophobic activities. The subtext of the narrator/Jim's statement indicates that to be revolutionary one must engage multiple struggles for social and political justice.

Moreover, as the narrator/Jim indicates, Rechy's figuring of oppositional identity is comprehensible only within a comparative framework. His suggestion that homosexuality constitutes a comparable frame with African American subjectivities makes an implicit connection between race and sexuality. While moments of interethnic solidarity between various Latina/o groups are scarce in *The Sexual Outlaw*, the narrator/Jim's statement leaves open the possibility of connection between aggrieved groups.

Despite the narrator/Jim's claims that queers exist in isolation, the potential for projects of community efficacy are foregrounded at key points in *The Sexual Outlaw*. In addition to the aforementioned statement of solidarity between queers and African Americans, throughout his sexual odyssey Jim often expresses a desire for a connection with other homosexual men, lesbians, women, and the straight Chicano and black men in the audience. This impulse is foreclosed, however, by the multiple levels of marginalization he experiences. For example, when the narrator/Jim watches a gay pride parade in Los Angeles, he notes, "There was plenty of dignity, and, embarrassing to admit—man—I felt the itchy sentiment that signals real pride. Here you are, and there they are, and here we are. I remember Ma Joad's proud speech of the Okies eventual triumph in 'defeat.' We keep coming, she said, because we're the people. (I didn't even let interfere with my mood the bitter knowledge that many of those very same Okies had unleashed mean red-neck children and even cops to pillage our sexhunting grounds)" (179).

While the narrator/Jim experiences a degree of solidarity, he rejects the possibility for meaningful communion with other queers. In this regard his physical position on the outskirts of the crowd mimics his marginality to mainstream gay liberation. On one hand, this marginality can be attributed to the fact that the narrator/Jim is a hustler—figures who are "dual outsiders, outlaws from the main society, and outcasts within the main gay world" (157). On the other hand, Jim's marginality points to the inadequacies of gay liberation as another monolithic identity discourse. As a subject constituted by his racial and ethnic identifications *as well as* his sexuality, he cannot comfortably identify within a single context. Consequently, while he feels pride in his association with other gays and lesbians ("here you are, and there they are, and here we are"), the narrator/Jim's connection is short-circuited by his experience as a raced and a queer subject.

While Jim also considers the potential for an alliance with working-class figures—symbolized by Ma Joad's (a character in John Steinbeck's *The Grapes of Wrath*) speech—the alliance is disrupted by the fact that lower-class figures are often the agents of homophobic repression. Rechy's portrayal also recalls that the very "Okies" who unleash "mean red-neck children" who persecute homosexuals also perpetuate racial stereotypes. *The Grapes of Wrath* provides a fascinating intertext since, as legal scholar Stephen Bender (2003) points out in his study of racial stereotypes, Steinbeck's novels characterize "Latinos as lazy, shiftless, drunken, and thieving, and Latinas as sexually irresponsible and fertile" (4). One possible conclusion is that the prevailing social order precludes interethnic, interclass solidarities due to internalized homophobia and racism.

But there is another possibility that explains Jim's marginalization at the parade. Because he often characterizes Jim's journey in hyperindividualist terms, Rechy's work evidences a tension between existential and communal identities. Frederick Aldama has pointed to these tensions by noting the similarities between Rechy's 1991 novel *The Miraculous Day of*

Amalia Gómez and James Joyce's *Ulysses*. Aldama points to Rechy's use of modernist narrative strategies that "give the reader a glimpse into the unfamiliar and chaotic underside of everyday life" (2005, 71). Like modernists who engaged existential philosophy in their attempts to produce a transcendent aesthetic, Rechy's characterization of his protagonist in *The Sexual Outlaw* can also be read in terms of Jim's isolated struggle with choice and responsibility. Under this view, his portrayal of Jim's reaction to the parade also points to a desire for individual empowerment over communal affiliation.

Rechy's engagement with existentialism underscores the limits of reading *The Sexual Outlaw* purely in terms of its triangulations. Because the novel represents Jim's struggle as a product of the tension between existentialist individualism and a desire for communal affiliation, it can never fully embrace a communal identity. Even though Rechy's protagonist disrupts Anglo bourgeois morality, Jim's sexuality precludes him from experiencing the communal values envisioned by Chicana/o nationalism. Likewise, his self-conscious adoption of a queer Chicano identity estranges him from mainstream gay liberation, rendering him marginal in both contexts. My argument is not designed to undermine or reconfigure my reading of Rechy's triangulations; rather, I point to these dynamics in the author's work to highlight the fissures in my methodology. Rather than reading *The Sexual Outlaw* as articulating a transcendent communal subjectivity, the novel blurs distinctions between the individual and the communal, as well as the fault lines between Jim's various identities in the sexual arena.

Similarly, it is important to understand how Jim figures his resistance as a sexual outlaw as a struggle against internal and external oppressions. The brownness of Jim's skin is one of the key elements to understanding this dual contestation. Authors from Anzaldúa to Richard Rodriguez (2002) have figured brownness as a primary signifier of Chicana/o and Latina/o identity. Unlike Rodriguez, who distances himself from ethnic identification, Rechy's protagonist is acutely aware of his brownness.[12] When Jim gazes at his body, he notes that "because of a mixture of Anglo and Latin bloods, his skin quickly converts the sun's rays into tan; the tan turns his eyes bluer; long-lashed eyes which almost compromise the rugged good looks of his face, framed by dark hair" (23). While Jim's ancestry includes "Anglo and Latin[o] bloods," his brown skin facilitates his success in the arena of sexual promiscuity. Since he figures revolution in terms of his ability to attract sex partners, Jim's success as a sexual outlaw is partially premised on his Chicano identity.[13]

Jim's awareness of his Chicano identity is not limited to his ability to attract sex partners. During many acts of sexual consummation, Jim is acutely aware of his brown skin. For example, when he has sex with a "well-known writer [who has] written several books," Jim notes that "his naked brown body is stark on the white sheets" (43). Their sexual transaction involves the white man's inscription of his putatively superior intellect on Jim's exotic body—exotic both because he is a hustler and because of his Chicano heritage. The subtext of the scene dramatizes the split between bodily experience (symbolized by Jim's brown skin) and the intellectual achievement of the white man: "I'm told I'm a very talented writer. So you see, I have my . . . intellect, and you, well, you have your body—that's your talent. We both have something beautiful" (43). By ironically dramatizing how the white man internalizes stereotypes about Chicano bodies, Rechy problematizes the assumptions of some gay liberation groups, suggesting instead that the sexual outlaw's potential lies in his foregrounding of intersecting identities.

The relationship between the narrator/Jim's Chicano ancestry and his revolutionary activities is explicit in another Voice Over dealing with his family. In answer to a question posed by an interviewer from a "radical gay newspaper" (66), the narrator/Jim laments his mother's death: "I sigh. 'I was born in El Paso, Texas. My mother was a beautiful Mexican woman, whom I love more than anything else in the world and whose death is a constant sorrowful presence in my life now.' *My mother . . . She had the most beautiful green—really green—eyes, and a smile that haunted you instantly. I loved her—love her, because death has changed nothing, and she loved me, and I—* . . . But that's for another time. Not now" (70).

Given the fact that the interviewer is an editor for a gay newspaper, the narrator/Jim's love for his Chicana mother destabilizes his (and by implication Rechy's) characterization as a gay writer. Moreover, the sense of loss that propels *The Sexual Outlaw* is visible in Jim's palpable grief. This loss comes to symbolize his estrangement from heteronormative notions of morality in Chicana/o nationalist contexts. It is also possible to interpret this loss as the narrator/Jim's inability to reconcile his sexual and ethnic identities.

The question *The Sexual Outlaw* poses is how to constitute revolutionary subjectivity without claiming one identity over another. Because the sexual outlaw's rebellion challenges the conventional social order, he offers the potential to transcend monolithic identity categories. As the narrator/Jim notes in a Voice Over describing the sexual outlaw's hunting grounds, "revolutionary murals in East L.A. And a dazzling frieze on La Brea: Greek statues, painted like movie stars, lounge among L.A. palmtrees; The Thinker, unusually muscular, is tanned bronze" (134). Here Rechy signals the passage of exclusive models of revolutionary subjectivity in the stops along Jim's cityscape. He invokes the revolutionary spirit of the Chicana/o movement by referencing East LA murals. But where the movement limited revolutionary consciousness to heterosexuals, the narrator/Jim complicates Chicana/o nationalist projects by envisioning a critical rebellion—signified by the bronze Thinker. The Thinker's brownness thus symbolizes the intersecting nature of Jim's revolutionary ethnic and sexual identities.

By utilizing similar tropes as the Chicana/o movement, while also problematizing dynamics internal to gay liberation, Rechy reconfigures the revolutionary subject vis-à-vis his warrior persona. One way to interpret these triangulations is to understand the sexual outlaw as exceeding the insufficiencies of multiple identity categories. Rechy is thus able to reconceptualize revolutionary subjectivity in a manner that allows his protagonist to be gay *and* Chicano without sacrificing his radical political consciousness at the altar of respectability.

Judith Ortiz Cofer: Remaking the Nationalist Vision

Like John Rechy's novels, Judith Ortiz Cofer's *The Line of the Sun* challenges masculinist narratives by representing alternative sex and gender roles. Where Rechy relies on the sexual outlaw's excesses to triangulate queer revolutionary consciousness, Ortiz Cofer portrays a range of transgressive characters that include outlaws and outcasts of many types. While her outsiders are not pure analogues to Rechy's sexual outlaw, Oscar "Zeta" Acosta's *vato loco* (crazy guy), or Piri Thomas's black gangsters, Ortiz Cofer's outcasts share critical perspectives with these figures. Among these perspectives are the outcast's firsthand knowledge of multiple forms of oppression in both island and mainland contexts. Her outsiders use their knowledge to resist their marginalization as racialized subjects in the United States, while also contesting how women and queers are written out of narratives of national belonging. But Ortiz Cofer goes beyond simply opposing racial, gender, and sexual marginalization. Her work contests and reformulates relationships between gender subordination, nationalist morality, and Puerto Rican diasporic identity.

While the details of Ortiz Cofer's life are well known, a brief summary of her upbringing on the island and in Paterson, New Jersey, contextualizes her complex understanding of Puerto Rican identity. Ortiz Cofer was born in Hormigueros, Puerto Rico, in 1952. When her father enlisted in the navy and was subsequently stationed in Brooklyn Yard, he relocated the family to Paterson. The nature of his navy work required tours of duty up to six months long. During his tours, Ortiz Cofer's mother would take young Judith and her brother back to *la casa*—the family's ancestral home in Hormigueros. Like her narrator, Marisol, in *The Line of the Sun* and the protagonist of her memoir *Silent Dancing: A Partial Remembrance of a Puerto Rican Childhood* (1990), Ortiz Cofer split her childhood between the island and the United States. After her father's discharge in 1968 and following the racial unrest in Paterson during the 1960s, the family moved to Augusta, Georgia. Ortiz Cofer has remained in Georgia for most of her adult life.

The Line of the Sun is one in a series of autobiographical works that include Ortiz Cofer's memoir *Silent Dancing* and several autobiographical essays, some of which are included in *Woman in Front of the Sun: On Becoming a Writer* (2000). While a great deal of critical attention has been dedicated to *Silent Dancing*, I consider *The Line of the Sun* for several reasons. Of primary importance is the fact that the novel is Ortiz Cofer's first book-length prose project. As a longer prose piece, it constitutes a substantial meditation on issues of diasporic Puerto Rican identity in a postsixties context. While *Silent Dancing* engages the outsider trope at certain points, *The Line of the Sun* foregrounds transgressive outsiders. Even though Ortiz Cofer's outsiders aren't as confrontational as Rechy's sexual outlaw, they share important similarities—most notably in their conceptions of intersecting identity. The outsider in *The Line of the Sun* thus represents alternative gender roles that disrupt nationalist morality and essentialist conceptions of Puerto Rican identity.

To comprehend how Ortiz Cofer disrupts simplistic notions of Puerto Rican identity, it is important to consider her conception of diaspora. A number of scholars have speculated on the role diaspora plays in the formulation of national identities. Jorge Duany (2002) understands Puerto Rican nationality in diasporic terms. For him, the Puerto Rican "nation" is "a translocal community based on a collective consciousness of a shared history, language, and culture" (4). Duany argues that Puerto Rican migration is "best visualized as a transient and pendulous flow, rather than as a permanent, irrevocable one-way relocation of people" (2). This leads him to posit the idea of *"La nación en vaevén"* or the nation on the move (2). This conception of transient migration means that national consciousness is not the sole domain of island-based nationalists. Instead, Duany reads Puerto Rican identity as an amalgamation of sending and receiving cultures. Cultural identities in Puerto Rico thus involve both an "ideological rift between citizenship and nationality" and "the constant transgression of the boundaries of territory, language, and ethnicity established by standard views of the nation" (18). This leads Duany to conclude that the situation of diaspora—nearly half of the Puerto Rican population on the island, with the other half on the U.S. mainland (13)—"entails approaching the nation as a dispersed and fragmented subject that flows across various spaces, classes, and other social locations" (36).

Wendy Walters makes a similar case in *At Home in Diaspora* (2005). She argues that diasporic authors articulate spaces of home that are more than geographical or cultural locations. While her focus is on international black writers like Chester Himes, Richard Wright, and Michelle Cliff, Walters's notion of diaspora dialogues with scholars like Duany by emphasizing a decentered, fragmented national consciousness. Key to this notion of decentered nationalism is Walters's understanding of displacement: "displacement creates a distance that allows writers to encode critiques of their homelands, to construct new homelands, and to envision new communities" (2005, viii). The term diaspora names both a displaced ethnic or racial identity and a political performance. She further contends that "The circulation of texts in transnational markets—the ability of ink itself to travel—means that a diasporic community is created through these literary acts. This is a community that is often not recognized by nation-states or by traditional models of literary study, yet it exists as a resistant social practice" (x).

Accordingly, the space of origin doesn't necessarily constitute a site of homecoming, implying that diaspora offers a home where racialized writers can metaphorically return. Consequently, Walters seeks to "move beyond traditional national boundaries," emphasizing instead how "the ever-shifting interstices" of diaspora constitute a forge in which identities are shaped and articulated (xix–xx).

Juan Flores (2009) has recently argued that diaspora constitutes a complex transactional dynamic. Flores agrees that the Puerto Rican diaspora functions according to Duany's notion of *La nación en vaevén*. But Flores extends this concept, emphasizing the role cultural remittances play in negotiating national identity on the island, in the United States, and beyond. Cultural remittances constitute an "ensemble of ideas, values, and expressive forms introduced into societies of origin by remigrants and their families as they return 'home,' sometimes for the first time, for temporary visits or permanent re-settlement" (4). Cultural remittances have become increasingly important as the Internet and other telecommunications technologies make daily contact with the home space and the metropole cheaper and easier for remigrants. For Flores, the concept of diaspora reconceptualizes national identity as transnational and national, without being reducible to either category. National belonging is thus produced in the dynamic interaction between *aquí* and *allá* (here and there).

I concur with Duany, Walters, and Flores, especially in their understandings of displacement, migration, and movement as fundamental to certain forms of identity. Their suggestions are helpful for my readings, as I argue that Ortiz Cofer reformulates Puerto Rican identity in relation to alternative circuits of circular migration. I also concur with Duany, Walters, and Flores by arguing against the idea of a pure home space that exists in opposition to a hybrid diaspora. Like them, my conception of diaspora extends to the space of origin. Like Duany, I believe that shifting the political to the cultural realm holds potential for anticolonial struggle.

Where my work is different is in my consideration of how literary texts discursively articulate diasporic spaces of identity and politics. By reading Ortiz Cofer's triangulations, we can understand her attempts to navigate unstable and transient states of migration and diaspora. While I use diasporic displacement as my starting point, I consider how Ortiz Cofer juxtaposes the insufficiencies of island and Nuyorican frameworks to disrupt the discrete identities enunciated by insurgent groups.[14] In this regard my work is similar to Flores's. I consider how the notion of a pure sending versus a receiving culture is complicated by Ortiz Cofer's work. Concomitantly, I argue that *The Line of the Sun* problematizes the race, class, and gender roles that serve as the foundation for the imagined national community.

These are not abstract issues occurring solely in the realm of scholarly debates about bifurcated Puerto Rican identity. In a 1994 interview with Rafael Ocasio, Ortiz Cofer speaks directly about these ideas:

> There used to be a time when the Puerto Rican experience was the experience of the people on the island; then it became the experience of people in New York City. Now it is the experience of people like me, who started out in New Jersey, and now I am in Georgia and it is a different reality. When I write in standard English and incorporate Spanish syntax into my sentences, or a few Spanish words, it is reflecting my reality as a person who grew up mainly in the United States but deeply influenced by my family's culture and traditions on the island. My language reflects my perception of being a Puerto Rican woman. (735-36)

While her characterization of diaspora doesn't account for the complexity of Puerto Rican migration, Ortiz Cofer's work grapples with aspects of identity-in-movement that she, like José Saldívar, calls "bridge consciousness."[15] As she further explains in an essay in her 2000 collection *Woman in Front of the Sun*: "I would not be precariously straddling the cultures [island Puerto Rican and mainland United States], always fearing the fall, anxious as to which side they really belonged; I would be crossing the bridge of my design and construction, at will; not abandoning either side, but traveling back and forth without fear and confusion as to where I belonged—I belonged to both" (13).

Although her notion of bridge consciousness implies organic syncretism, it is neither the urban syncretism favored by Nuyoricans, nor the "folklorized [. . .] images of harmonious integration" (Davila 1997, 63-64) promoted by nationalist elites on the island.[16] Instead, her work triangulates nationalist projects on the island and mainland to accommodate her conception of Puerto Rican diasporic identity.

Reflecting her diasporic understanding of Puerto Rican identity, *The Line of the Sun* is divided between Salud, Puerto Rico, and Paterson, New Jersey. Thematically, the novel offers separate but related stories. The first half is set on the island during the late 1940s and early 1950s and focuses on Marisol's maternal uncle Guzmán, a likeable trickster who exists on the margins of respectable Salud society. Indeed the first part of the novel traces Guzmán's transgressive narrative from his birth until he is about sixteen. Alongside Guzmán's narrative, we also get the stories of Marisol's mother, Ramona, and father, Rafael, her dead uncle Carmelo, and several eccentric characters populating Salud.

The struggle between Guzmán's free-spirited exploits and his mother Mamá Cielo's attempts to control them is central to the first half of the novel. Even before he is born, Guzmán causes consternation to Mamá Cielo: "They say Guzmán had been a difficult pregnancy for Mamá Cielo, who had little patience for the bouncing ball in her belly. She claimed the monkey was climbing her ribs, that she felt fingers grabbing her bladder and squeezing, so that she had to stop attending mass for the shame of urine tricking down her legs" (1).

Guzmán is a problem child, a "*niño del Diablo*" (demon child, 3), and a general troublemaker, leading him to become Mama Cielo's "obsession" for whom she does "not spare the rod" (1). Among his exploits are a propensity to skip school; his friendship with Franco el Loco, a disabled man who obsessively relives his wounding via a machete blow inflicted by an amorous rival; a series of transgressive relationships with women, culminating in a romance with Pura Rosa, the town prostitute; an ill-fated attempt to engage in a sexual liaison with the town spinster, Rosario Saturnino; an alliance with the domino parlor owner, Doña Amparo; and finally, his departure from Salud to the United States via an illegal labor recruiter.[17] While these transgressions render Guzmán marginal in Salud, we find that he has many redeeming qualities, including loyalty, independence, and a relatively enlightened attitude toward women and queers.

Set in the early 1960s when she is thirteen, the second part of the novel focuses on Marisol's coming-of-age in Paterson. Similar to Ortiz Cofer, Marisol moves to the mainland at the age of two, after her father enlists in the navy. Also like the author, Marisol, her mother, Ramona, and her brother Gabriel live in a tenement known as El Building, an "ethnic beehive" that functions as a "microcosm of Island life" for newly arrived Puerto Ricans in Paterson (170). Shortly into the second part of the novel, an adult Guzmán reappears, spending several months with Marisol's family. The central crisis of the second part of the novel centers on a spiritist (*Santería*) meeting arranged by the women of El Building.[18] Significantly, the spiritist meeting offers "almost a countercampaign" to a *huelga* (strike) "the men were planning" to protest the ill treatment and poor wages they experience in Paterson factories (232). Guzmán and Marisol disrupt the ceremony, ostensibly to protect the people of El Building from an imminent police raid. In their attempt to break up the meeting, Guzmán inadvertently starts a fire that destroys El Building, killing at least one person.

Similar to *The Sexual Outlaw*, the two sections of *The Line of the Sun* are mutually informing. While the first part of the novel is apparently related by an omniscient third-person narrator, we later find that it is Marisol who narrates Guzmán's exploits. The reader becomes aware that Marisol has no firsthand knowledge of the narrative she reveals, suggesting that she imagines much of the first part of the novel.[19] This is confirmed when the action shifts to Marisol's narrative in the second half. Where the first half is narrated in almost fairy-tale terms, the second part is related in first-person, realist fashion. Significantly, Guzmán's symbolic importance to Marisol also changes as she gets to know him with his flaws, including unflattering tendencies to drink, gamble, womanize, and smoke.

The novel takes an unexpected turn when Marisol rejects the embodied Guzmán, insisting on maintaining control of his narrative. Upon his departure for the island after a series of injuries, including a stabbing and smoke inhalation after the fire at El Building, she notes that "This broken man taking one step at a time into the belly of the airplane had little to do with the wild boy I had created in my imagination, but I loved him too. He was a good man and brave, even if finally not the hero of my myth. In a way I was glad that he would no longer be around to confuse me" (282).

Marisol's rejection of Guzmán's experience implies that she reconfigures his story to suit her narrative purpose. By the final lines of the novel, she completely calls Guzmán's narrative into question: "it is at that point [the end of the novel], when he and I tell our best lie" (291), suggesting that much of what she narrates is a collaborative fabrication.[20]

Critics have speculated on transgressive characters and situations in *The Line of the Sun*. Juan Bruce-Novoa (1992) focuses on how Ortiz Cofer represents community rituals on the island and in Paterson, only to systematically undermine them. The transgression he understands emerges from the appearance of a split that "nostalgically longs for the past, but ultimately accepts its fundamental distance from her [Ortiz Cofer]" (64). Bruce-Novoa's analysis centers on the novel's negative representation of *Santería* and the more benign *Mesa Blanca* spiritism associated with nineteenth-century European spiritual practices.[21] He argues that Ortiz Cofer undermines these rituals to "invalidat[e] them for herself" (66). Further, she discursively creates a Puerto Rican culture that is "not the island culture per se, but the new form of culture that arises from the text" (66). This alternative Puerto Rican culture imagines "new rituals for a community which incarnates itself as a habit of movement" (69).

Joanna Barszewska Marshall (2008) asserts that *The Line of the Sun* translates and rewrites the space of home. Marshall invokes Duany's notion of the Puerto Rican nation on the move, suggesting that

Marisol's translation of island and U.S. traditions transgresses one-to-one comprehension. Marisol understands that "a Puerto Rican home is 'untranslatable'—unable to exist outside the borders of the Island without becoming a 'bizarre facsimile' of the source" (258). At the same time, when Marisol returns as an adult narrator in the epilogue, she "engages in more complex acts of translation" (263) that undermine Salud as "a vindictive small town that feeds on rumor and scandal" (265). Consequently, Marshall sees the novel as an unresolved act of translation that complicates an essential home for Marisol and other Puerto Ricans in the diaspora.

Lisa Sánchez González (2001) also sees the novel in transgressive terms. While she agrees that the novel "interrogates the ghosts of a Puerto Rican past in order to make sense of the emigrant female protagonist's relative comfort and security in the present" (148), she decries the book for its bourgeois tendencies, especially the novel's "solipsistic" and "problematic (internalized) racism-sexism in the exoticized and racialized depiction of cultural difference among emigrant Puerto Rican women . . . and the Boricua community at large" (153). For Sánchez González, the novel evidences Marisol's disenchantment with Puerto Rico and Puerto Ricans, foreclosing the possibility of connection between diaspora and island communities. While Sánchez González grants that the novel is transgressive in its tacit acknowledgement of the island's colonial status and processes of racialization and misogyny in both spaces, she finds the potential for transgression short-circuited by Ortiz Cofer's "re/creational" (153) impulses, rendering the novel nothing more than a revision produced "simply for pleasure" (148).

Maya Socolovsky (2009) argues that "the novel is transgressive, enacting and depicting challenges to the regulatory paradigms of identity and narrative that society upholds in order to write a new and more productive space of home" (95–96). Socolovsky claims that Marisol's engagement with Guzmán allows her to strengthen "her own storytelling identity first by exploring aspects of Salud's society and then by identifying with the deviant and transgressive sexual behavior of the town's marginal figures." This allows Marisol to expose "the violence beneath [. . .] communal and family histories" demonstrating how "they still operate, in various forms" in Paterson (104). The novel thus reveals how Salud needs "the oppositional presence of local outcast figures [. . .] to legitimate their own established boundaries" (108)—a point Marisol underscores through her integration of island stories with her narrative in an attempt to come to terms with her budding sexuality. Socolovsky further notes that "neither Guzmán nor Marisol can write one another's story directly" allowing "Marisol's awkward and adolescent immigrant voice to observe and narrate Guzmán, creating an indirect relationship between the storyteller and her subject" (97). By creating a porous relationship between the two parts of the novel and the narrator-subject relationship, the novel transgresses traditional narratives, offering "no binary or oppositional other, but only traces and layers of otherness within the present" (97).

I build on these perspectives by pointing out that Ortiz Cofer uses transgressive characters and relationships to triangulate Puerto Rican subjectivity in the diaspora. Like John Rechy who deploys transgression to stage critical performances, Ortiz Cofer's characters transgress morality on the island and mainland to highlight their exclusion from normative culture. While I concur with Socolovsky that *The Line of the Sun* meditates on transgression generally, my argument focuses on how transgressive characters and situations serve specific political purposes. In contrast to Sánchez González, I am concerned more with the novel's attempts to disrupt patriarchy on the island and in Paterson than the specific political goals it achieves. I contend that Ortiz Cofer's attempts to disrupt patriarchy attest to the difficulties of constituting opposition within the contexts of racism and sexism on the mainland and bourgeois morality on the island.

In addition, I argue that the novel's disruptions of patriarchy operate as a foundation for Ortiz Cofer's critique of nationalist ideologies. Since machismo serves as the basis for the imagined national community—in both island and mainland contexts—one way to read Ortiz Cofer's critique of patriarchy is in terms of a desire to constitute Puerto Rican nationality from an alternative standpoint. Her critique of patriarchy reconfigures Puerto Rican nationality in the diaspora by triangulating the insufficiencies of gender and sexuality in mainland and island contexts.

In fact, the novel is replete with characters that exist outside of normative mores. Guzmán is, of course, the primary transgressor of mores in the novel. Among his transgressions in Salud are his relationship with Pura Rosa, his defiance of Mamá Cielo, his education (read delinquency) with sugarcane cutters, and his sexual liaisons with outcast women. But his transgressions don't stop when he reappears in realist form in Paterson. While in Paterson Guzmán demystifies the nuns at Marisol's Catholic school by taking her to see them hanging their underwear, is stabbed by a rival over an amorous dispute, and causes the fire that destroys El Building. Guzmán bridges the island and Paterson, implying that neither social context can accommodate characters that exceed the bounds of respectability. Perhaps Guzmán's most interesting facet is his complication of patriarchal norms in Salud. In particular, he evidences traits typically associated with female characters in the novel. Of key importance to Marisol's vision of her uncle, at least in his mythical form in Salud, is his awareness of how women are subjugated by repressive morality on the island. For example, he is attentive to how women must choose between their respectability and their autonomy. When gazing at one of the town prostitutes late one night he wonders, "what made this woman [. . .] choose the night life over marriage and respectability [. . .] Could it be for the right to own her time? No one waited up for this woman. No one asked her for explanations. She did not rise as Mamá Cielo did, as all the married women in town did, at five in the morning to cook for the day, to sweep their yards, to iron in the smoldering heat, and then at night to wait for sons or husbands, and if they were still desired as women, to continue giving of themselves" (108).

Rather than decoding the woman's activities as a sex worker in terms of the virgin-whore dichotomy, Guzmán considers her life from a nuanced perspective. He recognizes the compromises she makes to secure autonomy. His recognition of a woman's need to "own her time" points to domestic work as a legitimate form of labor. Should this woman choose a life of respectability, she would become subject to the burdens of domestic work (child rearing, cooking, cleaning, etc.). Instead, Guzmán's meditation highlights the cognitive dissonance between discourses of morality that condone the exploitation of female labor and the desire for autonomy many women in the novel experience. While it is without question that this woman's autonomy is secured at a cost (namely, the degradation resulting from sex work), Guzmán recognizes that female independence is equated with moral transgression in Salud.

Another example of Guzmán's nonnormative masculinity emerges from his relationship with Pura Rosa. We first encounter Rosa when Mamá Cielo takes a twelve-year-old Guzmán to the *bruja* (witch) seeking a *despojo* (exorcism). During the ceremony, Rosa claims that Guzmán is possessed by a Taíno "warrior, slain by [Spanish] priests" (27). She tells Cielo that she will have to keep Guzmán at her home on the outskirts of Salud to enact a cure. While in her charge, Guzmán experiences the first inklings of sexual desire, as he feels "the familiar weakness in his body, the tightness in his chest that [Rosa's] nearness provoked" (30). While his sexual attraction to her is sublimated by Rosa's pseudomaternal role at this point in the novel, later a teenaged Guzmán consummates their mutual desire during an encounter at a traveling carnival. They engage in a brief, passionate relationship that results in Guzmán leaving Mamá Cielo's house to live with Rosa. Although they are fifteen years apart in age, Rafael (Marisol's father) observes that "both Rosa and Guzmán had changed. They had both traveled toward each other: she was younger, Guzmán older" (92), suggesting that the transgressive nature of their relationship is bilateral.

Guzmán's and Rosa's transgressive relationship draws the attention of Doña Tina, head of the Holy Rosary Society, a group of church women self-appointed to enforce Salud morality. The Holy Rosary Society forces a split between Guzmán and Rosa by threatening to expose Rosa's work as a prostitute to her daughter Sarita. As John V. Waldron (2008) observes, the Holy Rosary Society shows how "Salud is controlled by the landed, wealthy classes who are authorized by the Roman Catholic Church to exert their will" (40). This authority is actualized, as Rosa is driven out of Salud by Doña Tina and her allies. Rosa's apparent destination is New York, but her banishment from the narrative is so complete that we never hear from or about her again.

Significantly, Marisol often describes Rosa and Guzmán's relationship in collaborative terms. Their level of cooperation is unusual, given the social location of early 1950s rural Puerto Rico where the typical division of domestic labor was much sharper. Indeed, nowhere else in the novel do we find male characters engaging in domestic activities like gardening, cooking, or tending to the home. For example, when he first visits Rosa, Guzmán helps her "tend her herb garden" while she teaches "him the names of each plant and what it was used for" (54). They also share the labor of preparing meals, gathering the vegetables they eat from Rosa's garden. Similarly, Guzmán is "fascinated by the ritual of beauty," brushing Rosa's hair and helping her prepare for her sexual liaison with the American overseer of the sugarcane operations (36). While Rosa's work, like the unnamed prostitute Guzmán encounters near his mother's house, entails a series of difficult choices, the labor they share underscores the progressive nature of Guzmán's masculinity. When considered from this point of view, Ortiz Cofer uses the bilateral nature of their relationship to make gender inequity in Salud visible.

Moreover, in a male-dominated world, it is Rosa who conveys knowledge to Guzmán. Rosa's dominant role in the relationship can be partially accounted for because she is around thirty years old, while Guzmán is only fifteen or sixteen. But given the fact that many of Guzmán's contemporaries (like Marisol's father Rafael) already engage in adult activities like full-time work in the cane fields, marriage, and immigration to the United States, it is significant that Guzmán takes Rosa's lead. She not only initiates him into the herbs used in her spiritist practice and her knowledge of New York but also demands that Guzmán be accountable in her home. Guzmán explains that at his mother's house, "Mamá Cielo usually just set food in front of him at the right times" (29). By contrast at Rosa's, Guzmán "only gets what [he] asks for" and must "help [Rosa] with her work" (30). While these representations portray Rosa as a strong female character, Guzmán's acceptance of her actions signifies his willingness to cooperate. We are therefore not surprised when Guzmán remarks that "he wished he could remain for an eternity" in Rosa's "perfumed arms" (38).

These points do not suggest that Guzmán is without flaws. Rather, as Sánchez González notes (150), during the second part of the novel Guzmán shows that he embodies many negative male traits, not the least of which is his tendency toward womanizing. As Marisol observes, "Guzmán naturally became the focal point for female attention. Here was an unattached man, attractive and related to the Gringo [Rafael], who had money. He relished talk *and was at his best in the middle of a group of admiring women*" (207; emphasis mine).

Indeed, José (who Marisol witnesses having sex with a married woman earlier in the novel) eventually stabs Guzmán due to an amorous dispute. While it is important to bear in mind the Guzmán that Marisol represents in the first part of the novel reflects her mainland feminist perspective, we learn in the second (realist) half that although he understands Rosa was a soothsayer and a whore, "she was and still is the most interesting woman I [Guzmán] have ever known" (205). Guzmán's positive characterization of Rosa in the realist half of the novel makes the case that Marisol's representation of him is based at least partially on Guzmán's own attitudes.

The novel's uninterrogated question is Guzmán's appeal to Marisol as the protagonist of her reimagined island life—especially given her unflattering experiences of him in the second half of the novel. In this regard, Ortiz Cofer goes against the trend of many contemporary Latina authors like Sandra Cisneros, Julia Alvarez, Cristina García, and

Ana Castillo, who seek feminist affirmation in the present by tracing a female-centered narrative past.[22] One way of encountering this question is to consider Guzmán's ability to move fluidly between feminine and masculine spaces. Unlike even relatively powerful female characters like Doña Tina, Doña Amparo, or Marisol herself, Guzmán can move freely between domestic spaces and the male-dominated realms of the cane fields, domino parlors, and labor-recruiting stations. While his sister Ramona or Mamá Cielo might offer more logical choices for Marisol's narrative about island life, Guzmán provides unmediated access to multiple labor, economic, and political spaces that were relatively restricted to women during the period.

Another way to consider Marisol's choice lies in her narrative recoding of Guzmán. By colonizing Guzmán's narrative from a mainland feminist perspective, Marisol endows her uncle with female qualities that foreground the inequities of patriarchy and homophobia. Guzmán's ability to recognize women's struggles on the island may thus reflect Marisol's narrative perspective as much as his. To this end Marisol claims that she is in control of his narrative and that the novel is a collaborative fiction perpetrated by herself and Guzmán.

While the gender dynamics of Marisol's recoding of Guzmán are the most obvious implication of Ortiz Cofer's representation, their relationship also offers an alternate model for constructing narratives of belonging. Because the novel is set on the island and in the Puerto Rican enclave in Paterson, interethnic solidarity is seldom represented. What we do get, however, are frequent meditations on possible solidarities between genders. In this regard, Marisol's relationship with Guzmán and Guzmán's relationship with Rosa offer models for intergender coalitions that defy conventional patriarchal authority.

But there is another aspect of intergender coalitions that is important to the novel's political interventions. Because (at least according to Marisol) Guzmán and Marisol collaborate on the narrative, their relationship calls into question the heterosexual coupling at the center of many national romances (Sommer 1991). Like the sexual outlaw who questions the foundations of marriage, sexual consummation, and reproduction, Guzmán and Marisol's relationship reconfigures national belonging because theirs is a familial rather than a sexual bond. Their relationship thus recasts the idea that heterosexual passion functions as the controlling metaphor of national belonging. Instead, their intergender alliance suggests an altogether different space of belonging based on filial ties rather than romantic coupling.

But Guzmán isn't the only nonnormative male character in the novel. Carmelo, Guzmán's gay brother, and Marisol's long-dead uncle, also offers a transgressive masculinity. Carmelo is often the antithesis of Guzmán's frenetic character. Where Guzmán is described as a monkey (throughout), a boxer (10), a "wild Indian" (203), and a "wild man" (216), Carmelo is a "slow-moving, melancholy sixteen-year-old" who Mamá Cielo fears has "inherited her husband's irritating love of books and solitude" (4). Even though he is Mamá Cielo's "best child" (15), she admonishes him for his seeming laziness, his "light olive skin [. . .] that would keep him from doing a man's work in a cane field," and his "fine long hands" that often engage in putatively unmasculine activities like "strumming his father's guitar or going through the books Papá Pepe kept in a painter's shed behind the house" (4). While Carmelo's role in the novel is relatively small, we find out that "Carmelo and his brother Guzmán were thrust together" (49) following the exposure of Carmelo's homosexual relationship with one of the town priests, El Padrecito César.

Although Carmelo's homosexuality lacks the overt oppositional character of Rechy's sexual outlaw, he occupies a key role in the novel. In fact, the revelation of Carmelo's homosexuality propels the first in a series of disruptions to Salud morality. When El Padrecito César comes to minister in Salud, Carmelo finds a friend in the priest "who shared his love for books" (17). Carmelo becomes "César's confidant, thus gaining access to his magnificent library" (18). Their reliance on one another culminates in Carmelo and César "taking advantage of the privacy and peace of the young priest's rooms" (18) as they are discovered with their "two heads close over a book" (49). The implication, of course, is that they use their time alone to do more than read. In fact, Leonarda, the housekeeper for César, and the senior priest Don Gonzalo, claims to catch Carmelo and César having sex "in flagrante" (47). She spreads word of the couple's relationship, making it impossible for Carmelo to remain in Salud. By way of escape, Carmelo enlists in the U.S. army, eventually dying in the Korean War by "being blasted into a thousand pieces" (53). Because so little of Carmelo's body can be pieced together, his remains are never sent home.

While Carmelo's homosexuality is the primary factor that provokes the people of Salud, his interest in books, music, and poetry first draws Mamá Cielo's ire. These pastimes are figured as the antithesis of masculine work (i.e., work as a cane cutter), equating books and learning with femininity. While Carmelo's homosexuality is what ultimately drives him from the island, it is worth bearing in mind that two women betray him: Leonarda and Isabel, a potential sweetheart. Their denunciations of Carmelo's sexuality implicate both genders in homophobia. Because of the threat his sexuality poses to the moral order of Salud, both men and women denounce him.

In another echo of *The Sexual Outlaw*, the specter of violence haunts the representation of Carmelo's homosexuality. For example, the violence with which Carmelo is written out of the narrative calls to mind how queer subjectivities are anathema to projects of national belonging on the island and mainland. In effect, he is annihilated from the narrative. The actual violence that Carmelo experiences in Korea is paralleled by the epistemological violence perpetrated against him in Salud. As Marisol notes, "They say Carmelo could not walk down the street without some shiftless person calling out to him that his trousers were too tight in the crotch or that his cologne could be smelled for miles and that if he didn't take care dogs would confuse him for a bitch in heat" (52).

By comparing him to "a bitch in heat," suggesting that his cologne is too strong and making negative comments about his trousers (and by implication the insufficiencies of his genitals), the townspeople make life untenable for Carmelo. More to the point, their actions reinforce moral authority in Salud as exclusively heterosexual.

As a result of his outcast status, Carmelo must choose between remaining or finding a space hospitable to his sexual identity. Not surprisingly, given the social and economic options available to a gay man from a rural town in Puerto Rico during the 1950s, Carmelo enlists in the army. But Carmelo's enlistment might also be read as a desire to prove his masculinity on the battlefield—perhaps the ultimate male proving ground. His desire to prove himself in battle may be intended to recuperate the respectability he loses in Salud. Unfortunately, rather than proving anything he's literally blown to bits, suggesting that any desire to fulfill the imperatives of patriarchy is doomed to utter destruction.

While Guzmán and Carmelo offer alternative masculine figures for Marisol, she also invests in transgressive female characters. The most significant seems to be Pura Rosa. Rosa is perhaps the most despised figure in Salud. Nicknamed "La Cabra" (she-goat), she is a primary object of derision for the town's moral authorities, including the Catholic Church, the Holy Rosary Society, and the town's respectable women. Rosa's home on the Red River is a three-mile hike outside of Salud, signifying a physical and intellectual break with the town and its normative prescriptions for women. While she notes Rosa's work as a prostitute and a fraudulent spiritist, Marisol recuperates her, pointing out that she is intelligent and perceptive: "In other circumstances, in another era, in a different place, Rosa might have become a student of psychology, a physician, a healer." Even though she remains "no more than a cunning fortuneteller and a whore" (97), Marisol demonstrates how her outcast status facilitates her critical view of Salud society.

As I have already noted, among her important attributes is Rosa's active and collaborative femininity. She represents a potential departure from passive feminine roles—most notably symbolized by Marisol's mother, Ramona.[23] But Rosa also serves as an alternative maternal figure for Marisol. Her home is described as having "the beauty of the Island all concentrated into a few acres with river, valley, hill, and turquoise-blue sky" (91). By figuring her home as the quintessential Puerto Rican space, Rosa and her house serve as the symbolic locus of island culture. When considered from this perspective, Rosa serves as a metaphorical mother, allowing Marisol to experience a type of return—if only discursive—to the space of origin. As Marisol later notes, "I should have grown up there [Puerto Rico]. I should have been able to play in emerald-green pastures, to eat sweet bananas right off the trees, to *learn about life from the women who were strong and wise*" (222; emphasis mine). In the absence of direct contact with women of this type, Marisol imagines a potential maternal figure in Rosa.

But Marisol's investment in Rosa is curious since she is "not from Salud" (37). Although Rosa was born in Salud, she "was away for many years" in New York (37). Consequently, there is a contradiction between Marisol's representation of Rosa and her home as quintessentially Puerto Rican and Rosa's history on the mainland. This contradiction is problematized further when we learn about Rosa's difficult life on the mainland. When describing how she became a medium, we learn that Rosa was conscripted into a prostitution ring that used spiritism as a cover. Ironically, though her experience with the prostitution ring constituted "a descent into hell" (34), Rosa utilizes her skills as a spiritist to secure a life for herself on the island. As she explains to Guzmán, "it's not that I do anything bad . . . not really. I just make a living the only way I know how [. . .] I represent a new way" (37). This "new way" signifies a departure from island discourses that portray Nuyoricans as either culturally deficient or assimilationist. Instead, Ortiz Cofer's depiction of Rosa suggests a complex identity that disrupts the opposition of a discrete home space on the island with a hybrid diaspora. As Rosa's syncretic Santería practice demonstrates, her work is characterized by cultural remittances that accrue from New York.

Another important female character is Doña Amparo. As the owner of the local domino parlor, Amparo engages in many legal and illicit transactions that are usually the exclusive domain of men. In addition to allowing gambling and drinking, Amparo holds cockfights and provides a refuge for Salud's men when they fall out of favor with their wives. But Amparo does more than exercise business acumen. Instead, she chooses "power over respectability" (124), never regretting the choice. She knows "that in order to compete in a man's world of property ownership, she had to make others dependent on her in as many ways as possible" (124). To secure a space of feminine agency in a patriarchal world, Amparo must explode respectable values.

While she doesn't hold maternal appeal for Marisol in the same way as Rosa, Amparo offers a model of feminine agency on the island oriented around monetary and social power. Given the historical circumstances of early 1950s Puerto Rico (industrialization, the divestment of the rural economy, and migration to the mainland), it is significant that Amparo experiences financial success without traveling to New York. Although she preys on an already marginalized group of people (the cane workers of Salud), Amparo's skills as a businesswoman disrupt stereotypes about women on the island as passive and sexually permissive. Instead, she offers another way for women to own their time—albeit within an exploitative capitalist framework.

Again, it is important to qualify these portrayals. Because the negotiations that women like Amparo and Rosa engage in are problematic, the implications of their actions complicate pure and progressive readings of their characters. As a prostitute and an illicit businesswoman, Rosa's and Amparo's activities have as much potential to destroy them as to liberate them. They are partially complicit with patriarchal culture, even as they try to counter it. Like Rechy's sexual outlaw, however, their contradictions offer spaces that facilitate Ortiz Cofer's attempts to triangulate alternatives for women and queers. Under this view, Amparo's and Rosa's willingness to exceed respectability not only allows them some semblance of autonomy and agency but also interrupts discourses of nationalist morality.

Further, the novel's transgressive characters (both male and female) point to Marisol's navigations of her identity in the present. Because she cannot identify with either island or Nuyorican frameworks, she, like the author, attempts to navigate a new identity for herself and people like her. Marisol explains, "I would always carry my Island heritage on my back like a snail" (273), implying that her heritage is both a burden and a space of safety. But this identity is also portable: it allows her to carry her home—including aspects of island *and* mainland life—with her. By figuring Marisol's identity and home as portable, Ortiz Cofer disrupts discourses that tie the nation to a specific geographical or cultural space. Ortiz Cofer thus triangulates a space of national belonging for women like Marisol that locates identity in diaspora.

Conclusion

Rechy and Ortiz Cofer use narrative strategies that disrupt the rigid sex and gender roles inherent in nationalist projects. The primary vector of their contestations of respectability is the figure of the outlaw or outsider. By countering rigid, patriarchal subjects, both authors clear spaces for feminine and homosexual subjectivity within the imagined national community.

While Rechy's primary focus is on homosexuals, his deconstruction of revolutionary subjectivity is complex and multiply determined. Since he is marginalized by both Chicano and gay liberation contexts, the sexual outlaw is estranged from multiple identity categories. These multiple forms of oppression allow the sexual outlaw to understand his identities as mutually constitutive, rather than mutually exclusive. While he does not always use this knowledge productively, Rechy's sexual outlaw does offer a model for navigating new forms of racial and sexual identity in a postsixties context.

Likewise, Ortiz Cofer's feminist approach destabilizes gender and sexual roles that underpin the imagined community of the nation. She critiques essentialist notions of identity that locate Puerto Rican subjectivity either on the island or in New York. Instead, she posits diaspora as a more inclusive space of identity for Puerto Ricans in multiple social and political contexts. As we will see in chapter 4, this project of recasting identity in diaspora is one that is taken up by contemporary Latina authors like Julia Alvarez.

4

I Can't Be Me without My People

Triangulating Historical Trauma in the Work of Julia Alvarez

> *At first glance, [Trujillo] was just your prototypical Latin American caudillo, but his power was terminal in ways that few historians or writers have ever truly captured, or, I would argue, imagined. He was our Sauron, our Arawn, our Darkseid, our Once and Future Dictator, a personaje so outlandish, so perverse, so dreadful that not even a sci-fi writer could have made his ass up.*
>
> —Junot Díaz, *The Brief Wondrous Life of Oscar Wao*

> *Indeed, the terror [of Trujillo's regime] was so appalling that it has been described more readily in literature than in history.*
>
> —Lauren Derby, *The Dictator's Seduction*

As we have seen, Latina/o authors often use first-person personal narratives to triangulate new forms of individual identity and plural models of group formation. Julia Alvarez works in this vein by complicating the stability of history, personal memory, and fiction in her literary construction of a Dominican Republic based on a transformative history of the self. Because of the collective trauma inflicted by Rafael Leonidas Trujillo's brutal thirty-one-year dictatorship and the bifurcated nature of Dominican life due to migration and exile in the wake of the regime, a plausible univocal history of the nation can no longer be constructed.[1] To combat historical silence, Alvarez foregrounds the problematics of historical narratives through the self-conscious blending of genres.[2] By situating historical considerations in her novels as more than mere setting, Alvarez complicates what constitutes a valid historical narrative, leading her to reimagine and reclaim history. This chapter considers Alvarez's first four novels, *How the García Girls Lost Their Accents* (1991), *In the Time of the Butterflies* (1994), *¡Yo!* (1997b), and *In the Name of Salomé* (2000), to understand how she creates a composite (though fragmented) narrative of Dominican history. By renarrativizing the traumatic history of the Trujillo period and its legacies, Alvarez triangulates a national subject that attempts to resolve the contradictions of diasporic identity. Concomitantly, she counterpoises the insufficiencies of the United States and the island to triangulate a new cartography of belonging for herself and others who share this traumatic history.

There are two issues I should acknowledge before proceeding. First are the conceptual difficulties involved in correlating Dominican history with the experiences of Dominicans living in the United States—matters that are particularly salient considering the history of U.S. intervention on the island. Second, there are trade-offs involved in my reading, given that it spans ethnic and area studies. Because Alvarez's work encompasses spaces that cannot be demarcated by a single disciplinary framework, deploying multiple methodologies makes visible the complex identity position she articulates in relation to historical trauma.

By historical trauma I denote a shared emotional and psychological injury that is the result of catastrophic events. Historical trauma accrues over the span of an individual life and across generations. As Adam Lowenstein (2005) explains, "To speak of history's horrors, or historical trauma, is to recognize events as wounds. Auschwitz. Hiroshima. Vietnam. These are names associated with specific places and occurrences, but they are also wounds in the fabric of culture and history that bleed through conventional confines of time and space" (1).

Lowenstein's definition suggests a disruption in historical continuity, a rupture in the fabric of time and space that defies resolution.[3] In this chapter I refer to the historical trauma resulting from Trujillo's dictatorship. As Alvarez's work documents, life in Trujillo's Dominican Republic was characterized by torture, surveillance, and paranoia—experiences exacerbated by the activities of Trujillo's secret police force, el Servicio de Inteligencia Militar (Military Intelligence Service or SIM).

The concept of historical trauma sheds light on how silence is both incorporated into and resisted in Alvarez's work. Historical trauma allows us to understand Alvarez's contradictory impulses to, in Lowenstein's words, "navigate the tensions between those who feel a certain traumatic event *cannot* be represented and those who feel the same event *must* be represented" (1). I suggest that Alvarez provides *one* model for working through conflicting impulses in her first-person personal narratives. By returning to these events over the course of her novels, Alvarez reimagines this history to transform it into a trajectory leading to a more positive future. By telling the story of "what happened," she breaks the silence enforced by the regime, creating a historical foundation for the nation based on affective truth, rather than official doctrine.[4]

Like many of her generation and class, Alvarez was born in New York City in 1950. When she was three months old, her family returned to the Dominican Republic, where her father—a prominent physician—became involved in a resistance movement. After the discovery of the movement by forces loyal to Trujillo (a.k.a. El Jefe), the Alvarez family fled to the United States where they remained after the dictator's assassination. Alvarez now splits her time between Vermont, where she teaches creative writing at Middlebury College, and the Dominican Republic, where she and her husband own and operate a model farm dedicated to sustainable, organic, shade-grown coffee and to promoting literacy in rural island communities.

An interesting aspect of Alvarez's first four novels is that she alternates between autobiographical and historical fiction. Alvarez being typical of the authors I examine in this book, her first and third novels, *How the García Girls Lost Their Accents* and *¡Yo!*, are often considered fictionalized autobiographies.[5] While I heed critics like Raphael Dalleo and Elena Machado Sáez (2007) who suggest that Alvarez's turn to historical fiction is premised on "the apparent exhaustion" (134) of her personal story as a source for her writing—and by extension a source for her commitment to progressive politics—I argue that first-person personal narrative traces remain in her historical novels. Alvarez superimposes her story on characters in her historical novels to complicate the meaning of community and national identity for Dominicans on the island and in the United States. Her discursive identity is thus marked by mapping diasporic spaces of belonging. As Lucía M. Suárez (2004) asserts, Alvarez uses her "writing to cross-examine gaps in memory and to explore the ways in which these allow her to think about Dominican-American identity on both sides of the hyphen" (121). These diasporic identifications go beyond essentialist notions of the nation, complicating how Alvarez conceives of belonging in mainland U.S. and island contexts.

For example, in "Doña Aida, With Your Permission," Alvarez responds to a comment made to her by Doña Aida Cartagena Portalatín, "the grand woman of letters in the Dominican Republic," at a Caribbean studies conference in the Dominican Republic.[6] Cartagena Portalatín suggests that Alvarez write in Spanish, imploring her to "come back to your country, to your language. You are a Dominican" (1998, 171). Alvarez resists Cartagena Portalatín's admonition, arguing that "I am not a mainstream American writer with my roots in a small town in Illinois or Kentucky or even Nuevo México. I don't hear the same rhythms in English as a native speaker of English. Sometimes I hear Spanish in English (and of course, vice versa). That's why I describe myself as a Dominican-American writer. That's not just a term. *I'm mapping a country that's not on the map*, and that's why I'm trying to put it down on paper" (173; emphasis mine).

While she initially resists the essentialist position Cartagena Portalatín asserts through an elaboration of diasporic identity ("That's why I describe myself as a Dominican-American writer"), Alvarez falls back on rhetorical strategies rooted in nationalist ideologies. These ideologies are national because they conceive of the space of belonging as "limited and sovereign" (Anderson 2007, 6)—hence her desire to map "a country that's not on the map." This mapping departs from traditional conceptions of the nation, constituting what Kelli Lyon Johnson calls Alvarez's "emerging cartography of identity and exile" (2005, xix). Alvarez's work encounters spaces that are neither *aquí* nor *allá* (here nor there), blending geography, memory, and personal history. The geography she discursively navigates goes beyond the island's borders, grounding her conception of national belonging in diaspora.

Throughout her first-person personal narratives, Alvarez figures diasporic identity as a consequence of the traumatic history of the Trujillato and its legacies. Trujillo's rule was characterized by paranoia and silence. In addition to torturing and murdering political opponents, the regime cultivated a network of informants designed to root out insurgency. As historian Lauren Derby notes, "everyday life during the Trujillato was characterized by pervasive insecurity and atomization as an ever expanding apparatus of espionage developed, which by the 1950s rivaled the formal political apparatus itself in organizational strength" (2009, 139). Literally anyone could be an informant in Trujillo's Dominican Republic. Even informal opinions against the regime were punishable by exile, imprisonment, torture, the "nationalization" (read theft) of property, and potentially death. Not surprisingly, Dominicans learned silence as a matter of survival.

Coupled with this culture of silence was the understandable need to deny the regime's excesses. Ranging from Trujillo's well-known torture techniques to the sexual depredations that became, as Derby (109–15) argues, one of the regime's signature tactics, the Trujillato was characterized by inconceivable abuses of power.[7] The events of the post-Trujillo era did little to facilitate national reconciliation. Beginning with Ramfis Trujillo's murderous rampage after his father's assassination, dictatorial politics dominated the Dominican Republic until the late twentieth century.[8] Dominicans thus faced the choice of remaining on the island and experiencing trujilloism without Trujillo or migrating to the United States, Puerto Rico, Spain, or other countries.

Like other authors this book considers, Alvarez does not present pure or transcendent subjectivities. Alvarez and her family were part of the light-skinned elite on the island. After the family's flight to the United States, her father established a successful medical clinic that provided the family with middle-class advantages unavailable to most Dominican immigrants. While these facts do not disqualify Alvarez's work, there is a seeming inattention to race and a disturbing reinscription of island class hierarchies in her novels.

For example, nowhere in her novels or other writings are there serious discussions of how race functions on the island or in a Caribbean context—a preoccupation of Caribbean intellectuals since at least the early twentieth century.[9] Given Trujillo's racialist project of whitening the population, one would expect at least tacit acknowledgement of racial politics on the island.[10] As Stephen Knadler (2005) explains in relation to *In the Name of Salomé*, even though Alvarez's work ostensibly rejects antiblack racism, her novels display residual anxiety around African identity in both mainland and island contexts. In fact, race in her novels often elides the question of blackness altogether, figuring racism as either anti-Latina/o or anti-immigrant discrimination in the United States, or in vague references to racial politics on the island.[11]

Similarly, the author's privileged class position is often reflected in her work. Although many of her novels are set primarily in the Dominican Republic, there is little awareness of either working or campesino classes. In fact, nearly every major character in her work is from the elite—a fact that is treated as transparent in her novels.[12] In addition, novels like *In the Time of the Butterflies* treat antitrujillista organizations like the Fourteenth of June Movement as manifestations of the bourgeoisie. It is without question that Trujillo fell only with the cooperation of upper-class Dominicans and the tacit consent of the CIA. But Alvarez's work overvalues upper classes on the island, paying little attention to rank-and-file Dominicans who struggled to overthrow the dictator. Consequently, while Alvarez opposes Trujillo and all that he stood for, her work does not evidence awareness of how her privilege occludes her historical and aesthetic vision.

I advocate reading Alvarez's work in terms of these generative contradictions. Even though her representations are rooted in classed and racialized ideologies of liberal individualism, I contend that her triangulations offer a partial but important step toward reconstructing traumatic histories. While she focuses her narratives through privileged white figures, she combats the historical silence enforced by the regime. Her work attempts to offer an alternative trajectory for the future. If we note the problematics, while also comprehending how Alvarez combats historical silence, it becomes possible to understand her work within the larger context of historical trauma.

Genre Anxiety: Testifying to Collective Trauma through Alternative Historiography

One place to locate evidence of historical reconfiguration is in Alvarez's genre blending. While I do not wish to rehash well-known debates about the oppositional political capacity of postmodernism by scholars like Fredric Jameson (1991), Linda Hutcheon (1989), and Chela Sandoval (2000) or studies of hybridity by Néstor García Canclini (1995), Anibal Quijano (2000), Walter Mignolo (2000), or Rafael Pérez-Torres (2006), it is important to recognize that genre instability often signals a larger political intent.[13] George Lipsitz (2001) suggests that genre instability can indicate broad changes in society because it shows how "the old stories [are] inadequate or at least incomplete" (186). Flowing from this observation, postmodern literary genre blending can signal more than play. Indeed, genre instability can indicate that cultural stories are dysfunctional, revising how individuals relate with social structures.

While Alvarez's work does not always use the same tropes as authors like Don DeLillo, Thomas Pynchon, or Salman Rushdie, her novels do explore a number of postmodern literary techniques, including genre blending, fragmentation, metatextuality, shifts in narrative perspective, episodic pastiche, discontinuity, and reflexivity. Considering her writing within the rubric of postmodern literature makes visible how Alvarez inverts the hierarchy of fact and fiction to reveal the constructed nature of historical narratives. There is no clear boundary in her work between the personal, the political, and the fictional—a point Alvarez underscores by noting, "In my familia, fiction *is* a form of fact" (1998, 124). She purposefully combines history, fiction, and personal narrative to transform the personal into national terms.

Alvarez uses two primary narrative strategies to triangulate traumatic historical narratives. First, she self-consciously superimposes her story on Dominican historical figures—most notably in *In the Time of the Butterflies* and *In the Name of Salomé*. As I will argue, the interview woman who opens *Butterflies* and the conversations between Camila and Marion in *Salomé* function as "stand-ins" (Lifshey 2008, 439) for the author and her experiences of exile and migration. These first-person personal narrative resonances allow Alvarez to blur distinctions between personal memory, history, and fiction, reimagining the national story of the Dominican Republic. As she explains in relation to the Mirabal sisters in "Chasing the Butterflies," "And so it was that my family's emigration to the United States started at the very time their lives ended. These three brave sisters and their husbands stood in stark contrast to the self-saving actions of my own family and of other Dominican exiles. Because of this, the Mirabal sisters haunted me" (1998, 198).

While this passage could be interpreted as survivor's guilt (and there is palpable guilt in Alvarez's work), she also represents her identity as rooted in an important history that has been lost in the United States. The haunting she underscores represents both the lingering presence of the past and the production of her mainland existence—and by extension the presence of diasporic subjects who share similarities with her.

In addition, Alvarez frequently deploys the first-person narrative point of view to construct an alternative historical account. The first-person "I" in her work masquerades as autobiography, combining aspects of the novel with life-writing genres. As Ellen McCracken (1999) points out in relation to *In the Time of the Butterflies*, Alvarez's work functions as "a kind of collective autobiography or *testimonio* of the women, both fictionally and historically reconstructed by another because the subjects themselves are not able to do so" (84). By relating her story with the Mirabal sisters' narrative, Alvarez tells "her first country's political history through important female political icons" (84). She demands that North American readers come to terms with this history, insisting that her diasporic identity forms at the moment of the Mirabal sisters' historical death. By positioning herself as the inheritor of this history, Alvarez challenges essentialist notions of the nation by self-consciously pointing to her diasporic subjectivity. Her presence in the United States is figured as a consequence of the history she documents in her novels. Beyond merely reconciling North American historical ethnocentrism, Alvarez attempts to triangulate an alternative source and a competing trajectory for the official narratives of Dominican history.

I do not suggest that all novels that employ first-person narration or that document diasporic history necessarily constitute life-writing forms. Many novels use first-person narration to various effects. But as I have shown, many Latina/o authors use first-person personal narratives to express discursive resistance. When considered from this perspective, Alvarez's use of the "I" constitutes an important attempt to give voice to Dominican history (in both U.S. and island contexts) in the wake of the Trujillato. Furthermore, my argument is intended to note how genre instability points to larger political purposes in Alvarez's work. As this book suggests, many Latina/os reconfigure life-writing genres by blending them with fiction and other literary forms in an attempt to triangulate new identity positions. By considering her historical triangulations, we can comprehend how Alvarez combines history, memory, and fiction in an attempt to navigate the omissions in and fragmentation of Dominican history.

Alvarez employs these narrative strategies in an attempt to disrupt the silence of official Dominican and Dominican American histories. While McCracken has suggested that we do not learn much historical detail from Alvarez's work, it is important to consider how this seeming lack of specificity functions within the context of working through (or psychologically healing) historical trauma.[14] Psychoanalytic literary critic Shoshana Felman and psychiatrist Dori Laub (1992) argue that the truth-value in trauma victims' accounts is not the primary point of working through trauma. Because traumatic events often overwhelm an individual's psyche, trauma victims have difficulty accurately assessing limit events. Since working through trauma depends on assembling a narrative of the episode, victims are doubly marginalized by their inability to accurately reconstruct the event in a therapeutic setting. Felman and Laub advocate that analysts and historians place less weight on details in historical accounts, focusing instead on the affective articulation of rupture (i.e., trauma) itself.[15] The process of working through should instead focus on the patient's ability to represent the unrepresentable—that is, to represent the experience of trauma itself.

While Felman and Laub describe the psychological procedures individuals use to process limit events, their analysis has implications for working through collective trauma. As I have noted, during Trujillo's rule, an entire generation of Dominicans was faced with the choice of complicity or silence. Understood from this standpoint, Alvarez's novels attempt to provide spaces where Dominicans on the island and in the United States can assimilate and renarrativize these events. By understanding her novels as documenting the return of a repressed history—rather than as an explicit engagement with historical details—we can trace how Alvarez promotes working through collective historical trauma.

Among the narrative strategies Alvarez utilizes to promote working through historical trauma is genre blending—in particular the blurring of history, memory, and fiction. Writing of postmodern feminist texts, Linda Hutcheon (1989) argues that the personal is often superimposed on the public to politicize the experiences of people who have been omitted as legitimate subjects of history. Hutcheon argues for what she calls postmodern historiographic metafiction, a literary genre blending aspects of autobiography, fiction, and other narrative forms in an attempt to make the private public: "Another related form of postmodern writing informed by the feminist revaluation of life-writing and its politicization of the personal is the kind of work that sits on the borderline between fiction and personal history, either biographical or autobiographical [. . .] The representation of the self (and the other) in history in this form is also done with intense self-consciousness, thus revealing the problematic relation of the private person writing to the public as well as personal events once lived (by the narrator or someone else)" (161).

Historiographic metafiction allows authors to capture the fractured, multiply-determined nature of history and identity, making it possible to represent the previously unrepresentable. Since postmodern aesthetic modes replicate the combination and textual polyphony that constitute historical narratives, Hutcheon advocates a deeper reading of the politics that motivate such narrative strategies. Making the personal public also centers the vexed relationship between writers and their public. Because historical discourse traditionally focuses on public acts of great men, great deeds, and grand events, female first-person personal narrativists foreground how their work is excluded from dominant discourses. By imagining the possibilities for historical events, historiographic metafiction allows authors like Alvarez to recuperate part of the absent record.

Historiographic metafiction constitutes both an alternative to the historical record and a competing mode of historical recording.

While critics like Isabel Zakrzewski Brown (2000) have considered Alvarez's work from the standpoint of historiographic metafiction, I use Hutcheon's framework differently. Where Brown shows how Alvarez's work attempts to resolve contradictions between feminism and postmodern aesthetics, I use the concept of historiographic metafiction to argue that Alvarez complicates the stability of history, memory, and fiction to promote a collective process of working through historical trauma. If, as Felman and Laub point out, traumatic narratives attest to more than historical detail, we should consider that Alvarez does not elide the traumatic history of the Dominican Republic. Rather, by destabilizing genres, Alvarez's work combines the historical, the personal, and the fictional to highlight her experience as a survivor and circumvent the narrative closure of Dominican history.

For example, in "Chasing the Butterflies," Alvarez writes of her desire to connect with the Mirabal sisters' personal history on a 1986 trip to the Dominican Republic: "What happened on that trip was that the past *turned into the present* in my imagination. As I entered the Mirabal house, as I was shown the little patio where Trujillo's secret police gathered at night to spy on the girls, as I held the books Minerva treasured (Plutarch, Gandhi, Rousseau), I felt my scalp tingle. It was as if the girls were watching me" (199; emphasis mine).

By focusing on polyvocal experience instead of documentary sources, Alvarez offers a collective alternative to the historical record. She connects with the past via direct contact with private items like books, diaries, and other personal effects. Touching these items facilitates a process whereby "the past turn[s] into the present." This entry point allows her to contest what constitutes history, leading her to comment: "everywhere we went, it seemed we could reach out and touch history. And always there were plenty of living voices around to tell us all their individual versions of that history" (207). Rather than relying on static methods of historical interpretation, Alvarez recognizes the value in "individual versions" of history.

Additionally, Alvarez's reworking of history provides a therapeutic tool for working through collective historical trauma. As she notes, the implications of the Mirabals' murder affect more than surviving family members. Indeed, their murder provided part of the rationale for deposing Trujillo. Beyond the political consequences for the regime, the Mirabals' murder was also the impetus for creating the International Day for the Elimination of Violence against Women celebrated on the anniversary of their death. Hence working through this history has hemispheric, even global, implications. Even within Dominican and Dominican American history, Alvarez's multivocal, multiperspective narratives facilitate communal understandings of the Trujillato. By positioning her novels as a space for collective remembrance and affirmation, others can access (and presumably work through) this traumatic history.

Paradoxically, Alvarez's superimposition of her personal story on historical figures offers one of the keys to working through this history. In a conversation with the radio program *Democracy Now!*, interviewer Amy Goodman asked Alvarez if she drew from her personal experience when writing *In the Time of the Butterflies*: "Well, of course! I mean, when I found out that there wasn't just the three sisters, but there was a fourth sister who survived, I thought, I know the politics of an all female family in a Latino culture. And I definitely know the dynamics that can happen when there's four of them. So, I thought, if anyone can write this story, I can do it" (1997a).

Because she claims to understand the politics of a four-sister family in a Latino culture, Alvarez emphasizes the role ordinary people play in historical struggles by investing private aspirations with public implications. Alvarez's use of the term "Latino" in a Latin American context is curious, given that the concept has different meanings outside the United States. Nonetheless, her assertion of common identification with the Mirabals situates her understanding of Dominican and Dominican American identity within both her individual story and the history of the nation. As a survivor of the regime, her story is integral to the narrative of Dominican history.

Alvarez elaborates in her essay "A Genetics of Justice." At the beginning of the essay, she writes, "Perhaps because I was spared, at ten, from the dictatorship my parents endured most of their lives, I often imagine what it must have been like for them growing up under the absolute rule of Generalísimo Rafael Leonidas Trujillo" (1998, 103). As someone who was both a part of and apart from the trauma of the regime, Alvarez can imagine the possibility of transcending Trujillo:

> When I *run through my mother's memory* of this parade, there is a scene I imagine that she has not told me about. My mother walks into El Jefe's line of vision, the parade stops... (emphasis mine)

For there, no more than ten steps away, he stands, a short, plump man sweating profusely in his heavy dress uniform. The medals on his chest flash brightly in the hot sun so that he looks as if he has caught on fire. She can see the rivulets of sweat under his Napoleonic hat, making his pancake makeup run down his face, revealing the dark skin beneath. *I invent this scene because I want my mother to see what she cannot yet imagine: El Jefe coming undone.* (107; emphasis mine)

The frame-breaking nature of the regime and Dominicans' denial of its excesses, means that they must imagine El Jefe coming undone, rather than experiencing it. By reimagining her mother's experience with Trujillo's patriarchal authority, Alvarez offers a therapeutic method for resolving traumatic history for her mother—and by extension an entire generation of Dominicans. While Alvarez invents this scene to understand her mother's experience, the legacy of these events continues to influence the present. Although the regime had been defunct for over thirty years when her essay was published, Alvarez continues to imagine Trujillo's undoing. Instead of representing a disjointed, disembodied history, she imaginatively recounts the limit event. Under this view, the parade offers a mediated reconfiguration of history vis-à-vis her mother's experience.

Alvarez also uses stories and storytellers to foreground the constructed nature of historical narratives. By foregrounding the constructed nature of history, she highlights fictions perpetuated by institutional power. When speaking of the value of Trujillo's "truth," Alvarez writes, "There was also the fiction presented to the world and acted out by Dominicans that we had a democratic form of government. Every four years the populace went out and voted for the one candidate allowed on the ballot, handpicked by Trujillo. Sometimes this candidate was Trujillo himself." (1998, 124)

As Alvarez notes, part of the fiction perpetrated by Trujillo was the idea of popular consent. These fictions constituted historical truth, implying that truth itself is often conflicted. Her valorization of stories and storytelling offer a way to combat historical contradictions that afflict Dominicans and Dominican Americans.

But Alvarez's deployment of history and personal memory is not unidirectional, since the historical also facilitates a new understanding of the "I." As she recalls in "Chasing the Butterflies," her interest in the Mirabals' story initially came from her father's prohibition of her reading a *Time* magazine story about the assassination. Encountering the article later in life, Alvarez recalls, "as I read the article, I recovered a memory of myself as I sat in the dark living room of our New York apartment, secretly paging through this magazine I was forbidden to look at" (1998, 197). By accessing the historical details of the article, Alvarez suggests that she recovers lost personal memories. The fact that this recovery takes place through a narrative structure is of primary importance. It follows that the process of recuperating personal memories is bound with narrating a collective history.

Consequently, one way to understand Alvarez's work is to consider how generic disruptions in her novels offer different windows into the representation of fragmented identity produced through political turmoil and exile. Because her experiences are constituted in terms of surviving the regime, her story becomes integral to the narrative of Dominican history. Moreover, the superimposition of her "self" on historical figures in her novels formulates a new understanding of what constitutes a legitimate subject of history. Since Alvarez's project attempts to reclaim a time in the Dominican Republic when an entire generation's history vanished due to exile, Trujillo's political assassinations, and collective silence, it is arguable that the superimposition of the self on the historical offers a way to triangulate a more positive future.

The Return of the Repressed: Reading Fragmented Histories in *How the García Girls Lost Their Accents* and *¡Yo!*

Alvarez's engagements with history range from unconscious historical interruptions to full historical imbrication. Her first-person personal narratives *How the García Girls Lost Their Accents* and *¡Yo!* form the basis of this historical continuum by attempting to resolve the trauma of dislocation, political repression, and exile. Even though this history is fragmented, it returns at key moments in both texts. As a diasporic subject whose presence in the United States is premised on Trujillo's excesses, Alvarez's work attests to more than the official historical record. Her work foregrounds the repressed to articulate the experience of historical trauma.

How the García Girls Lost Their Accents (1991) documents the experiences of the four García sisters, Carla, Sandi, Yolanda, and Sofía—who strongly resemble Alvarez's four-sister family.[16] Progressing in a series of interlocking vignettes, the novel is replete with the trappings of Latin American boom novels, including a family tree, temporal changes, and a shifting narrative perspective. Covering roughly thirty years, the novel narrates aspects of the García family's experiences of immigration, exile, gender identity, and ethnic and national affiliation. More important, the novel encounters the Dominican Republic's traumatic history, often interrupting the narrative with seemingly extraneous historical details.

These interruptions evidence Alvarez's desire to reconstruct the silence of historical trauma. For example, the opening chapter, "Antojos" (cravings), presents Yolanda García's (Alvarez's literary alter ego) return to the Dominican Republic after a five-year absence. While obvious to readers with some familiarity with Spanish, the shortened form of Yolanda's name, Yo, corresponds to the first-person personal pronoun in Spanish. Thus "Yo" can be interpreted as "I," playfully pointing to the author as an extratextual source for Yolanda's character.

Yo's return to the island is about more than a family visit. As the chapter title indicates, the cravings Yo experiences are representative of a loss that goes beyond the mere absence of family contact. One of the indications we get of this loss is in the family's reception of Yolanda as "one of those Peace Corps girls who have let themselves go so as to do dubious good in the world" (4). This figuring of Yo as a "missionary," a Peace Corps worker, and ultimately "Miss America" places her outside of mainstream island life.

Not surprisingly, given that Alvarez problematizes essentialist forms of identity, Yo also feels apart from North American belonging. Following Tía Flor's insistence that Yolanda speak "¡En español!" she thinks, "Yes, and when she returns to the States, she'll find herself suddenly going blank over some word in English, or, like her mother, mixing up some common phrase" (7). Yolanda exists on the margins between Dominican and U.S. identity. Her anxiety over her use of an idiom betrays a discomfort with pure identity in either context. Since language has historically been a unifying aspect of Latina/o and Latin American identities, Yo's confusion over her code switching offers a poignant commentary on her dislocation.[17]

This contestation of identity is further problematized in the chapter when Yo encounters a group of male farmworkers on a visit with yet another set of relatives in the mountains. After stopping for a solitary moment in the countryside, Yo muses that the quiet in the Dominican Republic is "what she has been missing all these years without really knowing that she has been missing it. Standing here in the quiet, she believes she has never felt at home in the States, never" (12). Even though her

Dominican family codes her as "Miss America," Yo's feelings of national belonging are more complex: her identifications range from Dominican to U.S. citizen and back to Dominican.

But Yo's musings on identity contain another layer of complication. When she encounters male farmworkers who "poke out of the windows, hooting and yelling" (13), identity in the Dominican Republic is destabilized by virtue of her gender, race, and class. Yo finds herself both attracted to and fearful of two farmworkers who stop to help her with a flat tire. She is attracted to the younger of the two, suggesting a symbolic desire for the island. But given that the incident takes place in a rural portion of the island, it is likely that the campesinos are dark-skinned. The fact that she fears them thus suggests her internalization of racial, class, and gender stereotypes.

Alvarez presents a complicated crisis of identity in this opening chapter that attempts to triangulate the insufficiencies of race, gender, and national identities in the Dominican Republic and the United States. Because of her relationship with racism in the United States, as well as her elite racial and class status on the island, Yo cannot easily identify with either social context. Further, as a woman coded as "Dominican" in the United States and "Miss America" on the island, she is unable to comfortably identify with either national space. An important implication is that Alvarez attempts to posit a new space of belonging grounded in the experience of diaspora.

We should, however, remember that these triangulations of Yo's identity are premised on the trauma of political exile. Although Yo is able to return to the island in the present of the novel, she bears the scars of exile. Unlike other Latina/o groups like Mexicans and Puerto Ricans who are able to move relatively freely between the United States and the homeland, many Dominicans of Alvarez's generation were unable to return due to the Trujillo regime's political persecution.[18] These facts cast the seeming lack of historical details in the novel in different terms. Rather than seeing the relative dearth of historical detail in the *García Girls* as a lack, we should instead understand it as a fragment of historical trauma.

Another example of how Alvarez represents ruptures in history comes when Yo supervises the division of a cake the family makes to celebrate her arrival. The cake, in the shape of the island and complete with candles representing the five largest cities, is to be divided among the squabbling younger cousins. As the text demonstrates, recent political history has left traces of national dispute in the psyches of Yo's cousins and their children:

> Yolanda gazes at the cake. Below her blazes the route she has worked out on the map for herself, north of the city through the mountains to the coast [...]
> Small arguments erupt over dividing the cake's cities: Lucinda's two boys both want Santiago since they went gliding there last weekend; Lucinda's girl and Carmencita's girl both insist on the capital because that's where they were born, but one agrees to cede the capital if she can have La Romana, where the family has a beach house. (11)

As the children's fighting indicates, the Dominican Republic has lingering political divisions. The route Yolanda maps is divided laterally and vertically by the clan's children. Since Santiago lies in the north central portion of the country, and La Romana and Santo Domingo along the south coast, the cake will be separated in a three-part division that recalls the factional violence that has plagued the island since its independence in 1843.[19] Because of the island's geography, some dividing lines are natural. Likewise, most countries are partitioned into smaller political and socioethnic units. Nonetheless, the way Alvarez represents the division of the cake mimics the internal factionalism that has characterized Dominican politics since the nineteenth century.

It is also significant that these divisions take place along gender and class lines. Since Lucinda's boys and Carmencita's girls are the primary combatants, the conflict is gendered. Lucinda's boys want Santiago, not for its strategic or symbolic importance, but because they went gliding there. Likewise, the ceding of La Romana is dependent upon the family's beach house. In a country where only 52 percent of the population completes grade eight (Organisation for Economic Co-operation and Development 2008, 152–53), and where, according to the United Nations Children's Fund (UNICEF), the average per capita income in 2009 was around $4500 per year, these children occupy a privileged position from which they can metaphorically divide the nation.[20]

Echoing the problematic valorization of light-skinned elites over darker-skinned campesino classes that was accentuated by Trujillo's racialist policies, the division of the cake also suggests a privileging of white over black, and *claro* (light) and *indio* (Indian) over *negro*. It is therefore typical that the North would be separated from the South. Yet because of the racial composition of these geographical areas, coupled with the fact that the privileged elite—including the fictional de la Torre/García clan—have historically been lighter skinned in the Dominican Republic, it is arguable that there is a racial component to the children's bickering.

Alvarez's engagement with history doesn't detail the island's incursions from Spanish, French, Haitian, and U.S. forces, focusing instead on representing rupture. Because of the legacies of dictatorship, racism, divisive politics, and colonial intervention, this gathering is always already affected by the island's history. It is, however, important to recall Felman and Laub's point about representing affect when working through historical trauma. Because the cake causes divisive conflict, the historical circumstances that nuance the scene help to locate the rupture in Dominican life. If children are ready to figuratively go to war when dividing a cake shaped like the island, we should consider the historical circumstances that lead to such divisive politics.

These ideas are underscored when the family cedes the division of the cake to Miss America herself, Yo. As Yo's cousin Lucinda reiterates, "It's your cake, Yoyo. You decide" (12). Yo is given final responsibility over dividing the cities of the Dominican Republic, serving as an uncomfortable reminder of how the United States has had a direct influence on the island's history and politics. The United States invaded the Dominican Republic twice during the twentieth century: the first time in 1916 and the second in 1965. The figuring of Yo as the arbiter of the Dominican cake has implications that reach beyond the historical trauma of the Trujillo regime. Here, the rupture Alvarez attempts to articulate also relates to the history of U.S. hemispheric interference that made Trujillo possible.

But Alvarez's representation of history has implications beyond individuals. She collectivizes traumatic history, pointing to how it affects Dominicans broadly. In the chapter "Daughter of Invention," Laura, Yo's mother, notes the traumatic response her husband Carlos has to her "yelp" in the night:

> There was terror in his voice, the same fear she'd heard in the Dominican Republic before they left. They had been watched there; he was followed. They could not talk, of course, though they had whispered to each other in fear at night in the dark bed. Now in America, he was safe, a success even; his Centro de Medicina in the Bronx was thronged with the sick and the

homesick yearning to go home again. But in dreams, he went back to those awful days and long nights, and his wife's screams confirmed his secret fear: they had not gotten away after all; the SIM had come for them at last. (139)

Instead of focusing on the tortures, disappearances, and murders perpetrated by the SIM, Alvarez represents the dreaded secret police through Carlos's *response*. Even though by this point in the novel Trujillo is long dead, Carlos and his wife are haunted by their fear: "In the old country, any whisper of a challenge to authority could bring the secret police in their black V.W.s" (145). By focusing on how this history affects Carlos and his family in the narrative present, Alvarez confronts the trauma visited on this generation of Dominicans. Carlos's experiences provide a narrative space where others might identify with (and potentially work through) this collective history.

Because Dominicans like Alvarez and her family lived through both the Trujillo dictatorship and the dislocation of exile, we should consider how this novel forms the basis for a historical continuum that promotes a collective working through. The author's conclusion to the *García Girls*, "I grew up, a curious woman, a woman of story ghosts and story devils, a woman prone to bad dreams and bad insomnia" (290), demonstrates how historical trauma is transferred to the next generation. Yet because of neocolonial interference by the United States, Trujillo's legacy of forcing people to become either liars or corpses and the unrest that characterized Dominican politics for the remainder of the twentieth century, it has been difficult to resolve this history. Indeed, as Carlos's night terrors indicate, the nightmare continues. In order to process that "violation that lies at the center of [her] art" (290), Alvarez is driven to represent this history to promote collective working through for Dominicans on the island and in the United States.

Alvarez continues the project of processing repressed historical trauma in ¡*Yo!* As the double entendre of the title (and the fact that the "I" is being declaimed in Spanish) indicates, the novel blends fiction and autobiography. While ¡*Yo!* is not a linear first-person personal narrative, it provides a composite portrait of Yolanda/Yo consisting of interlocking vignettes narrated by the title character's family, friends, and lovers. Yo never speaks for herself in the novel. Instead, each narrator details a telling incident that represents their relationship with Yo. Accordingly, we gain a better understanding of Yo as she is experienced by her family and friends.

The central conflict in *¡Yo!* revolves around Yolanda's transgressive use of family stories. As the novel opens, Yo is fresh from the celebrated reception of her first novel (a novel that appears similar to *How the García Girls Lost Their Accents*). She is admonished by nearly every character in the novel for using private history as the subject of her work. One important theme is the lingering effect of the dictatorship on the formation of Yolanda/Yo's identity. These self-conscious, metafictive elements continue the project of historical interruption Alvarez begins in *García Girls* by representing the history of the Trujillato as an integral aspect of Yolanda/Yo's character. In so doing, Alvarez suggests that breaking the silence perpetuated by the regime is fundamental to positing a new diasporic identity for Yolanda/Yo—and by extension, people like her.

The role of storytellers is of critical importance to the representation of history in the novel. Ranging from Scheherazade in *One Thousand and One Arabian Nights* to the family's preoccupation with Yo's transgressive use of their stories, storytellers occupy key positions in *¡Yo!*. Because storytellers aid in renarrativizing traumatic events, they create the possibility of moving beyond fragmented history. Indeed, Yolanda's mother, Laura, notes how stories sometimes revise traumatic events: "Isn't a story a charm? All you have to say is *And then we came to the United States*, and with that *and then*, you skip over four more years of disappearing friends, sleepless nights, house arrest, narrow escape, *and then*, you've got two adults and four wired-up kids in a small, dark apartment near Columbia University. Yo must have kept her mouth shut or no charm would have worked to get us free of the torture chambers we kept telling the immigration people about so they wouldn't send us back" (28).

While the legacy of dislocation, exile, and torture render the family fearful and silent, Laura indicates that stories create the possibility of transcending this history. By telling the story of their immigration to officials in the United States, the family escapes the near certain torture and death that would have been their lot under Trujillo. More to the point, by telling "the story" the Garcías transcend the "and then," recuperating the history that led to their place in the United States.

Alvarez figures Yo as responsible for the family's exile in both the *García Girls* and *¡Yo!*, suggesting that storytelling is also dangerous. Indeed, Alvarez implies that Yo is culpable in the discovery of her father's plot to assassinate Trujillo. In the *García Girls*, Yolanda brags that her father has a gun locked in a closet, tipping off SIM agents who subsequently search the

García home. By virtue of his connections with Tío Vic (a likely CIA operative in the Dominican Republic), Carlos and his family escape to the United States. Alvarez continues this story line in Laura's chapter in ¡Yo! Laura catches Yolanda (probably around eight or nine years old at the time of the vignette) going through her closet in the family home in the Dominican Republic, potentially finding the gun. Even though it appears that Yolanda either does not comprehend the gun's significance or just does not see it, Laura is threatened by her daughter's possession of this knowledge. Stories in this sense transgress the silence required for survival under the regime. In fact, as Laura points out, stories can get one killed.

But storytellers embody another layer of complexity in ¡Yo! Since stories potentially offer alternative versions of history, they offer a powerful tool for processing trauma. In "The Suitor," Dex, Yo's Southern American lover, fails to maintain his relationship with her in part because of his lack of facility with stories. Following her to the family compound on the island, Dex is confounded by the elaborate web of stories Yo weaves to explain his presence. Despite her liberal leanings in the States, on the island Yo feels compelled to retain the illusion of a chaste Catholic woman. This leads Dex to question the utility of stories, causing Yo to note, "It's all one big story down here, anyway. The aunts all know that their husbands have mistresses but they act like they don't know. The president is blind but he pretends he can see. Stuff like that. It's like one of those Latin American novels that everyone thinks is magical realism in the States, but it's the way things really are down here" (197).

By self-consciously deploying stories as alternatives to official versions of truth, Alvarez promotes the recovery of affective aspects of history. Yo indicates that there are *many* forms of truth on the island, including official versions that, while they might not be "true," keep people alive. From this standpoint certain fictional versions of events offer a more accurate historical account than mainstream records. Rather than understanding storytelling as occluding the veracity of historical truth, stories in Alvarez's work facilitate the reconstruction of traumatic histories.

By deploying stories as alternatives to official truth, ¡Yo! also develops different historical trajectories. Thus when Carlos and other characters in ¡Yo! are confused by the inconsistencies between Yolanda's versions of historical events and their personal memories, we see how storytelling plays a crucial role in working through historical trauma. As Carlos notes late in the book,

Sometimes I get confused as to what exactly happened. I don't think it is only because I am now an old man. *It's also because I have read the story of those years over and over as Yo has written it, and I know I've substituted her fiction for my facts here and there.* Many times I don't even realize I've done so until I get together with my old cronies from the underground. I'll say to one of them, "Maximo, hombre, do you remember that secret closet you helped me build in the new house?" And Maximo will look at me funny and say, "Carlos, you better get that cholesterol checked." (299; emphasis mine)

Rather than figuring his inability to distinguish Yo's stories from his memories as a lack of understanding, Carlos's confusion is symptomatic of a desire to make stories a valid form of historical narrative. Moreover, Carlos's recognition of a historical narrative in Yo's novel (and by implication Alvarez's), playfully suggests that the author views her work as a type of history. More to the point, because he has made sense of his traumatic history through Yo's stories, Carlos understands events in a different light. These fictions provide an alternative to the official record, offering Carlos a space where it might be possible to resolve the trauma of political repression and exile.

In the final lines of the book, Carlos empowers Yolanda/Yo, making her the keeper of the family stories. By encouraging her to tell "The Story," he urges her to facilitate a process of working through: "My daughter, the future has come and we were in such a rush to get here! We left everything behind and forgot so much. Ours is now an orphan family. My grandchildren and great grandchildren will not know the way back unless they have a story. Tell them of our journey. Tell them the secret heart of your father and undo the old wrong. My Yo, embrace your destino. You have my blessing, pass it on" (309).

One way to read Carlos's encouragement that Yo "embrace [her] destino" is as a woman writer's need for paternal approval. Another way to read Carlos's imperative is as a desire to reconstruct old connections. Because this family feels a loss of continuity with the homeland, Carlos suggests a way to integrate their experiences with their fellows. The unity Carlos desires can only occur through the processing of historical trauma and the possibility for a return—however incomplete—to the homeland. By telling the story of their dislocation and their journey through life in the United States, Yo reconstructs the narrative of her family's flight from the island, suggesting that reconciling these events *is* possible.

But processing historical trauma in this context does more than simply propel the machinery of Alvarez's narrative. Her desire to reconstruct occluded aspects of Dominican history also represents an attempt to triangulate an alternative space of diasporic identity. Likewise, in her desire to disrupt the regime and its surrogates' official versions of history, Alvarez's first-person personal narratives attempt to navigate an alternative historical trajectory that could lead to a transformative future. Alvarez furthers her resolution of collective trauma by superimposing her story on Dominican historical figures in *In the Time of the Butterflies* and *In the Name of Salomé*.

History and Transformative Identity in *In the Time of the Butterflies* and *In the Name of Salomé*

Alvarez's historical novels *In the Time of the Butterflies* and *In the Name of Salomé* move beyond unconsciously interrupting a fragmented history. They offer complex historical representations that reconstruct the history of the Dominican Republic and posit new possibilities for a transformative understanding of the self. Alvarez links the personal with history by filtering historical details through the psyches of her characters, foregrounding individual memories and subjective judgments. By "immers[ing her] readers in an epoch in the life of the Dominican Republic [. . .] that can only finally be understood by fiction, only finally be redeemed by the imagination" (1994, 324), Alvarez attempts to reclaim the historical by imagining real events from alternative viewpoints.

In the Time of the Butterflies chronicles the stories of Minerva, María Teresa (Mate), and Patria Mirabal, upper-class sisters who grew up in Ojo de Agua, Salcedo, Dominican Republic. The Mirabals, code named *las mariposas* (the butterflies) were involved with the insurgent Fourteenth of June Movement—named after a Castro-supported attempt to overthrow Trujillo in 1959. The Mirabal family first came into conflict with the regime at a party held at Trujillo's mansion in San Cristóbal on October 25, 1949. During the party, Trujillo was rebuffed in his attempt to seduce Minerva. The Mirabal family subsequently left the outdoor party during a storm, breaching an unspoken code of the regime—that no one should leave a function before Trujillo. Angered by these snubs, Trujillo ordered the imprisonment and torture of the family patriarch Enrique Mirabal. After Enrique's release, Trujillo continued to harass the family, imprisoning Enrique and Minerva on several occasions and divesting family businesses. As a result of the torture and abuse he suffered, Enrique Mirabal developed a heart condition that contributed to his premature death in 1953 (Méndez, Cueto, Rodriguez Deynes, eds. 2003, 311). El Jefe also intervened in Minerva's education, allowing her to complete undergraduate studies and a law degree at the University of Santo Domingo but barring her from obtaining a license to practice.

These insults led Minerva (generally seen as the leader of the sisters) to become an important antitrujillista. She was a vocal opponent of the regime, causing Trujillo consternation on several occasions. María Teresa and Patria followed suit, as all three sisters became members of the Fourteenth of June group. Owing to their insurgent activities, Minerva and Mate were incarcerated in Trujillo's infamous torture prison La 40 in January of 1960. All three of the sisters' husbands were also imprisoned due to their involvement with the movement. Under pressure from the Catholic Church and international human rights organizations, Trujillo released the women but kept the husbands incarcerated. On November 25, 1960, Trujillo's henchmen intercepted the Mirabals and their driver, Rufino de la Cruz, as they returned from a visit with the men in prison. They were led into a sugarcane field where they were beaten to death. After the murders, they were placed back in their jeep and pushed over a cliff in an attempt to make the assassination look like an accident.

In the Time of the Butterflies tells the Mirabals' stories in generally accurate historical detail, moving in chronological progression from 1943 until their deaths in 1960. The novel alternates between the women's narrative perspectives, detailing Minerva's oppositional politics, Patria's liberation theology, and Mate's epistolary diary entries. By presenting multiple perspectives, Alvarez utilizes a variety of narrative strategies that translate the sisters' personal experiences into public opposition to the regime.

In addition to the three sisters who died, the novel also chronicles the story of Dedé, the fourth sister, who survived and who relates the story in the narrative present, 1994. As the book opens, a character known as "the interview woman" meets Dedé at the Mirabals' home in Ojo de Agua. At the interview woman's prompting, Dedé provides access to the murdered sisters' belongings and relates the story as she understands it. The novel thus consists of four interwoven layers of narrative structure: (1) the interview woman's recording of Dedé's story, (2) Dedé's account, (3) the sisters' voices as they're channeled through Dedé's consciousness, and (4) Alvarez's fictionalized version of the events.

Although the bulk of the story is devoted to the Mirabal sisters, it is fascinating that the interview woman frames the narrative Dedé recalls. While she is never identified by name, Alvarez's physical description of the interview woman is consistent with her literary alter ego Yolanda García, as well as portraits of the author that have accompanied her work. The interview woman's consultations with Dedé in the novel are also consistent with the account Alvarez provides in "Chasing the Butterflies"—in which she details her real-life meeting with the surviving sister in 1992 (1998, 202–3). By virtue of her physical description and the intertextual references the interview woman embodies, *Butterflies*, like *¡Yo!*, blurs distinctions between author and character.

While a few critics (Brown 2000, 100–101; Dalleo and Machado Sáez 2007, 135–36, 156) have commented on this aspect of the novel, I argue that the interview woman's presence is fundamental to the history the novel reveals. My analysis of the novel therefore focuses on the relationship between the interview woman and Dedé. It is my contention that the interaction between Dedé and the interview woman places the Mirabals' narrative within the context of the author's self-representation. Their interactions creatively rearticulate aspects of the past in order to work through the history of the Trujillato and to promote alternative conceptions of island and diasporic identities.

An aspect of this creative rearticulation of the past is Alvarez's invocation of the Latin American *testimonio*. As commentators like John Beverly (1993) have described, *testimonio* constitutes a creative mixing of literature and history produced through a narrative collaboration between an interlocutor (typically an academic or other privileged individual) who records the story of a (usually) subaltern subject. While they are not always "factual," *testimonios* often provide revisionist versions of events from subaltern viewpoints. Flowing from this observation, the interview woman is the interlocutor for a history revealed as it is told to her. By invoking the *testimonio* tradition, Alvarez correlates the history Dedé reveals with private moments of lived experience. Rather than recapitulating official details of the Mirabals' lives, Alvarez instead provides a "way to travel through the human heart" (1994, 324) that attempts to reconstruct affective features of the sisters' stories.

Moreover, by overlaying her experience as a member of a four-sister family in the Dominican Republic onto the Mirabals, Alvarez foregrounds herself in the narrative production of this history. Foregrounding herself has important implications for her experience as a survivor and member of the diaspora. As she notes in the postscript to *In the Time of the Butterflies*,

> When as a young girl I heard about the "accident," I could not get the Mirabals out of my mind. On my frequent trips back to the Dominican Republic, I sought out whatever information I could about these brave and beautiful sisters who had done what few men—and only a handful of women—had been willing to do. During that terrifying thirty-one-year regime, any hint of disagreement ultimately resulted in death for the dissenter and often for the members of his or her family. Yet the Mirabals had risked their lives. I kept asking myself, What gave them that special courage? (323)

Alvarez's impetus for the novel seems to be the fact that the Mirabals had the courage to maintain subversive activities despite the certainty of violent reprisal. Alvarez's father's relationship to these events is the unstated presence; since he was also involved with the Fourteenth of June Movement, Alvarez questions his decision to flee the regime. Although this narrative impulse can be read as survivor's guilt, another way to interpret this portrayal encounters questions of collective complicity on the part of Dominicans. While many Dominicans opposed the regime and its excesses, the majority remained silent, cooperated, or left. By focusing on the Mirabals' courage, the interview woman implicates herself and others who chose self-preservation over collective resistance.

The interview woman's place in the novel is also crucial for unpacking Alvarez's narrative strategies. In fact, the interview woman prompts Dedé's account in the opening chapter, shaping how the novel unfolds. Unlike historians and mainstream media representatives Dedé has met in the past, the interview woman focuses on microdetails of the Mirabals' lives. This focus contrasts with traditional historiographic methods like documentary sources and corroborated testimony. Instead, the interview woman asks Dedé to place herself (in terms of birth order) in the row of portraits in the entryway of the family home. When confronted by Dedé's desire to repress the past by providing a prepared story or by focusing on "the happy moment[s] in [her] head," the interview woman presses Dedé to talk about her affective experience ("tell me about one of those moments"). The response Dedé gives provides the fictive framework for the rest of the narrative: "Dedé hesitates, but her mind is already racing backwards, year by year by year, to the moment she has fixed in her memory as zero" (7).

These exchanges reveal how the novel's rhetorical strategies contest what constitutes a legitimate historical narrative. By prompting Dedé to relay *her* version of events, Alvarez emphasizes memory over historiography. Because the novel is a framed narrative that purports to relay events as they are told to the interview woman, it is filtered through two separate memories: (1) Dedé's and (2) the interview woman's. These memories are then recorded by the interview woman who subsequently fictionalizes them. Here, Alvarez suggests that by imaginatively reconstructing this narrative, one can rearticulate the experience of collective historical trauma.

As a representative figure for an entire generation of Dominicans who absented themselves due to political persecution, lived in exile, or practiced complicity it is crucial that the interview woman hears Dedé's story. Here, I invoke the psychoanalytic concept of witnessing. According to psychoanalysts and psychoanalytic critics from Freud to Felman and Laub, trauma victims often need the support of a therapeutic witness to work through traumatic events. By offering a combination of emotional support and prompting, witnesses assist the victim in reconstructing a narrative of the event. In this regard, the interview woman's status as a member of the diaspora is crucial. Her witnessing of Dedé's story creates the possibility of connecting a *gringa dominicana* (U.S.-Dominican woman) with her island-based contemporaries. Since the interview woman's identity is tied to the same circumstances that resulted in the Mirabal murders, mapping her history onto the story of the sisters makes retaining a sense of Dominican identity in the absence of the homeland possible.

For example, in the opening chapter we see that the interview woman helps Dedé focus on events that occur before the "future began" (8). This future begins at the moment Dedé has fixed "in her memory as zero" (7).[21] But because this moment has implications for the interview woman, and by extension many Dominicans of this age and class, this zero moment also functions as a foundation for diasporic identity. By locating the origin of this history within the contested space of fiction, Alvarez filters historical details through Dedé's consciousness, suggesting that this moment is the basis of a historical trajectory that leads to Dedé and the interview woman in the present. Dedé's recounting of the past therefore contains the possibility for processing traumatic history emerging from the rest of the novel.

This introductory section also sets up the political stakes of the novel. While we come to know and eventually sympathize with the sisters, we are denied catharsis at the moment of their death. This narrative choice is curious, given that working through the sisters' murder is a likely purpose of the novel. Yet Alvarez refuses to recount the murder, foreclosing any possibility of understanding the singularity of the event.[22] This narrative refusal mimics the silence enforced by the regime, leaving at best only the traces of events we deduce from second- and thirdhand accounts of the murders Dedé compiles in the final chapter.

If we focus on the lack of catharsis at the time of the women's deaths, it is possible to miss the repercussions of the narrative Dedé reveals. Indeed, Dedé functions as a collective witness, compiling various accounts into a coherent narrative. The implications of Alvarez's representation are suggestive for my reading of historical trauma: since Dedé compiles the narrative of her sisters' deaths, she attempts to give voice to an event that is ultimately unknowable, the experience of death itself. Yet the symbolic load these events carry also implicates the inscrutability of the regime and its heavy-handed tactics for silencing opposition. Consequently, Dedé's act of recording—and ultimately recounting this history to the interview woman—constitutes an act of resistance to the historical silence perpetuated by the Trujillato. As Dedé muses, "When did it turn, I wonder, from my being the one who listened to the stories people brought to being the one whom people came to for the story of the Mirabal sisters? When, in other words, did I become the oracle?" (312). As Raphael Dalleo and Elena Machado Sáez note, Dedé only speaks in the first person in the epilogue, suggesting the discovery of a prophetic voice (156). By figuring herself as an oracle, Dedé breaks the silence of Dominican history, potentially leading to a transformative understanding of the present.

While oracles often predict the future in inscrutable ways, Dedé's comprehension of the past attempts to posit an alternative trajectory for the post-Trujillo era. It is only after she reimagines the trauma of the past that Dedé offers an interpretation of the future. After one of her friends suggests that "it's still 1960 for you," imploring her to recognize that "this is 1994, Dedé, *1994!*," Dedé responds, *"I'm not stuck in the past, I've just brought it with me into the present. And the problem is not enough of us have done that.* What is that thing the gringos say, if you don't study your history, you are going to repeat it?" (313; emphasis mine). Dedé insists on remembering, making it possible for her to work through history instead of repressing or circumventing traumatic events. By remembering and keeping this history an active and generative source for the present, it becomes possible to imagine working through to change the future.

In fact, Dedé realizes that memory is key to working through traumatic history. As she notes, "'after the fighting was over and we were a broken people'—she shakes her head sadly at this portrait of our recent times— 'that's when I opened my doors, and instead of listening, I started talking. We had lost hope, and *we needed a story to understand what had happened to us*'" (313; emphasis mine). Because she renarrativizes these events, Dedé uses the imaginary to transform this history into a trajectory leading to a more positive future. In addition, the interview woman notes that Dedé "shakes her head sadly at this portrait of *our* recent times," suggesting that she shares this historical legacy. The interview woman implicates herself by underscoring her relationship to these events. By logical inference, the interview woman's status as a *gringa dominicana* can be explained in part by the historical events the novel chronicles. Alvarez thus promotes a conception of Dominican history that includes the diaspora.

This questioning of the present vis-à-vis the past becomes a dominant theme in the novel's conclusion. When Dedé questions whether the sacrifice of the butterflies was worth the imposition of global capitalism, neocolonialism, and the increasing divide between rich and poor in the Dominican Republic, we see that this version of history opens spaces for alternative social organization:

> It comes to me slowly as I head north through the dark
> countryside—the only lights are up in the mountains where the
> prosperous young are building their getaway houses, and of course,
> in the sky, all the splurged wattage of the stars. Lío is right. The
> nightmare is over; we are free at last. But the thing that is making
> me tremble, that I do not want to say out loud—and I'll say it once
> only and it's done.
>
> Was it for this, the sacrifice of the butterflies? (318)

By suggesting that Dominicans have avoided accounting for the legacies of the Trujillato by substituting bourgeois prosperity for freedom and political enfranchisement, Dedé's assessment contains a melancholic charge.[23] She points to the fact that, even in the mid-1990s, the island had yet to work through the circumstances that led to Trujillo. It is also crucial to recall that the Mirabals' struggle was Marxist-Leninist in its orientation, implying a communitarian vision of society. Under this view, Dedé's seeming melancholia can be reframed in terms of a process of mourning the victory of liberal individualism and capitalism over communitarianism and socialism. Her questioning of their sacrifice requires that contemporary readers come to terms with the specificity of the Mirabals' vision, including the details of their contestation of El Jefe. Alvarez therefore represents both the affective experience of their murders and the occluded details of their historical struggle. Because the only person who understands this process is a *gringa dominicana*, national belonging is stripped of its essentialist and geographical aspects. In so doing, Alvarez articulates a diasporic conception of identity that recasts the legacies of Dominican history as a hemispheric phenomenon.

Alvarez continues to work through the historical narrative of the Dominican Republic in *In the Name of Salomé*. Like *Butterflies*, *Salomé* chronicles actual historical figures: Salomé Ureña (hereafter referred to as Salomé), the inspiring female poet and educator, and her daughter Camila Henríquez-Ureña. Born in 1850, Salomé wrote "patriotic hymns that often played a defining role in Dominican nationalism" (Knadler, paragraph 15). Besides her status as a literary figure, Salomé was a leading feminist and educator influenced by the Puerto Rican intellectual Eugenio María de Hostos. Salomé also created the first women's institution for higher education (Instituto de Señoritas) on the island in 1881. She died of tuberculosis in 1897.

The novel also chronicles Salomé's daughter, the important feminist Camila Henríquez-Ureña.[24] Henríquez-Ureña was the youngest and only daughter of Salomé's four children. Born in 1894, just three years before her mother's death, Henríquez-Ureña received her PhD in 1917. She became a prominent Latin American intellectual, spending extensive time in Cuba in the 1930s where she organized a number of feminist cultural organizations. During the 1940s, Henríquez-Ureña worked in U.S. universities, beginning with an appointment at Vassar College in 1942. In 1959, she moved back to Cuba, devoting most of the remainder of her life to supporting Castro's revolution. She died in 1973 on a return visit to the Dominican Republic.

Where *Butterflies* attempts to work through twentieth-century history on the island, *Salomé* delves into the period of Dominican independence. As part of this excavation of nineteenth-century history, Alvarez collapses the historical into the personal, foregrounding the relationship of the individual with her past. The primary mode Alvarez uses to express this link with the past is a virtual conversation between Salomé and Camila. As Raphael Dalleo and Elena Machado Sáez observe, both *Butterflies* and *Salomé* "interpolate the stories of heroic women [. . .] with the narratives of those who have inherited their stories—Dedé, the Mirabal sister who survives by declining to participate in her sisters' revolutionary activities, and Camila, Salomé's daughter, who comes to the United States and becomes a professor" (2007, 144).

By focusing on the inheritors of the political legacies of the Dominican Republic, Alvarez attempts to triangulate an alternative future. Her focus on women who must live with these legacies allows the author to counter the patriarchal nature of Dominican politics with a history grounded in feminism and social justice.

While the first-person personal narrative traces that propel *Salomé* are less obvious, the virtual conversation between Camila and her mother shares similarities with the actual conversation that takes place between the interview woman and Dedé in *Butterflies*. Like the interview woman and Dedé, Camila and Salomé witness each other's historical experience—if only in highly mediated forms. As a result, they construct a composite record of Dominican history that accounts for events that lead to Trujillo. While I do not claim that the representation of either Salomé or Camila is directly linked to Alvarez, I suggest that their textual exchange connects the history they narrate to the author's diasporic status.

For example, *Salomé* opens in 1960, a year after the Cuban Revolution and one year before Trujillo's assassination. Camila, retiring from a teaching job in New York, has decided to join Castro's revolution. On their way to Florida, Marion—Camila's occasional lover and lifelong friend—attempts to talk Camila out of leaving the States. But Camila wants to "give herself completely to something" so she can be committed to creating a new patria like her mother. To Marion's insistence that she justify her decision, Camila answers, "I have to go back a ways [. . .] I have to start with Salomé" (7). Camila's answer collapses her story into her mother's, suggesting both the symbolic importance of motherhood to national consciousness and Salomé's historical significance to Dominican independence.

As Marion presses Camila to tell her "the story," Camila responds again, saying "as I said, I'll have to start with my mother, which means at the birth of la patria, since they were both born about the same time" (8). Alvarez figures Salomé's birth as coinciding with the origin of the nation, merging the personal and the political. This merging of the personal and the political locates the struggling nation in the figurative body of Salomé. By locating the nation in the body of a woman, Alvarez writes against masculinist historiographic processes. Rather than centering on Santana, Báez, the Reds, the Blues, or the history of the caudillos, Alvarez focuses her narrative on a mother-daughter combination forgotten in the United States.[25]

In highlighting these two women, Alvarez imagines history from a different standpoint, triangulating a potential trajectory leading *away* from Trujillo. These ideas are visible when Marion presses Camila to "finally talk about [her]self," to which Camila responds, "'I *am* talking about myself,' she says—and waits until they have passed a large moving van, a sailing ship afloat on its aluminum sides—before she begins again" (8). The sailing ship evokes an image of the conquistadores who colonized the island of Hispañola. But because it appears on an aluminum moving van, we get a sense of the collapse of the present into the past. It is also important to consider that Camila and Marion pass the moving van before she recounts her story, suggesting that one must work through the legacies of colonialism before generating a transformative understanding of the present. Through Camila's desire to connect with her mother, we also see that longing is often tied to the aspiration to create a new patria. Because Camila, Salomé, and *la patria* all emerge from the same historical circumstances, Camila's story is a part of the same historical context that shaped her mother and her country. Camila and Salomé must therefore situate their personal identities within the historical context of the nation.

We get a stronger sense of Camila's historical context in Salomé's first chapter. Where Camila's story begins at the end of her life, Salomé's opens with her birth—and the birth of *la patria*. In the chapter "El ave y el nido" (The Bird and the Nest), the title character explains "the story of my life starts with the story of my country, as I was born six years after independence, a sickly child, not expected to live. But by the time I was six, I was in better health than my country, for la patria had already suffered eleven changes of government" (13). As Salomé notes, coming just six years after independence from Haiti, the country has had nearly a dozen governments. Alvarez thus compares Salomé's health with the health of the nation, metaphorically linking the destiny of the individual with the collective.

Alvarez's linking of Salomé with the growth and development of *la patria* is elaborated as Salomé recounts her importance as an inspiration for patriotic nationalism. As she grows older, Salomé realizes that her poetic voice stems from a desire to understand the question "what is la patria?" (15). This question propels her to write patriotic poetry in an attempt to understand the abstract concept of the nation. Using the pen name Herminia, Salomé "work[s] at setting la patria free" (62). Salomé's figuring of national consciousness as related to her poetry suggests a collective function to her literary work. This linking of artistic production with national consciousness recalls Benedict Anderson's (2007) assertion that the nation is in part dependent on the literary imagination. But this transaction also works in reverse, since Alvarez correlates the fight to establish a patria with Salomé's personal identity. As she works to set *la patria* free, Salomé also works to establish personal freedom vis-à-vis her alter ego Herminia. Although "sometimes [her] hand would shake as [she] wrote," Salomé becomes "the brave one" who is "not in thrall to her fears" (2000, 62).

As the novel develops, storytelling and the imaginative retelling of history become increasingly important. At roughly the midpoint of the novel, Camila poses for a statue of her late father that will be dedicated to the new Cuban regime. Domingo, the sculptor commissioned to create the statue, has struck up a relationship with Camila. During the course of their relationship, they also imagine Salomé's importance to the nation: "Mostly she talks about her mother. She has told him Salomé's story, and he joins in, as if he knew the national poet, who at thirty married a young white man from a prominent family. Back and forth they go, conversing and weaving the imagined fabric of Salomé's life from what Camila already knows and *what she is discovering by talking openly with him about her mother*" (160; emphasis mine).

By renarrativizing the events of her mother's life, Camila better understands her mother's importance to nationalist struggle, including resisting the denial of Salomé's African heritage (Knadler 2005, 17). More important, Camila and Domingo focus on the personal details of Salomé's life, recalling the interview woman's approach to history in *Butterflies*. Significantly, it is only through the collaborative imagination that Salomé's life takes shape for Camila and Domingo. By "weaving the imagined fabric of

Salomé's life," Camila comes to a new understanding of her mother and her significance to *la patria*.

The collapse of the personal into the political reaches a climax in Camila's discovery of Salomé in Castro's Cuba. Because her metaphorical search for her mother is equated with *la patria*, the personal and the political combine to produce alternatives for both individual identity and social relations. Like Alvarez's project in *In the Time of the Butterflies*, a transformative understanding of the self is premised on the resolution of collective history:

> But still, I longed for her—a longing that would well up in me in the middle of the night and send me wandering through houses, apartments, wherever it was I was living at the time. I tried all kinds of strategies. I learned her story. I put it side by side with my own. I wove our two lives together as strong as a rope and with it I pulled myself out of the pit of depression and self-doubt. But no matter what I tried, she was still gone. Until, at last I found her the only place we ever find the dead: among the living. Mamá was alive and well in Cuba, where I struggled with others to build the kind of country she had dreamed of. (2000, 335)

For Camila, resolving the personal implies a collective struggle for a better world. Camila's yearning is thus satisfied by recognizing her mother in the struggle for an emancipatory nation. The final message we get is to "keep trying to create a patria out of the land where we were born. Even when the experiment fails, especially when the experiment fails" (342).

But national consciousness isn't limited to one national space in *In the Name of Salomé*. Following Latin American thinkers like José Martí, Eugenio María de Hostos, and Simón Bolívar, the nation is often figured as a hemispheric phenomenon. For example, Salomé's relationship with Hostos is often characterized as a hemispheric alliance. Salomé is in "moral love" with Hostos, a "moral love that took over my senses and lightly touched my whole body with an exquisite excitement whenever [Hostos] was in the room!" (172–73). While Salomé's "moral love" is never consummated, it recalls Doris Sommer's (1991) assertion that romance often serves as a metaphor for national belonging. By symbolically linking characters in romantic relationships, authors like Alvarez suture the internal differences that are frequently a barrier to national unity. It is important, however, to recognize that Hostos is not Dominican. Indeed, Alvarez sutures a notion of hemispheric unity that anticipates contemporary discussions of *latinidad* in the United States.

Camila's relationship with Cuba treads similar hemispheric ground. Besides spending portions of her youth in Cuba, Camila engages in the aforementioned relationship with Domingo. While part of their erotic charge is Domingo's desire for surrogate contact with Salomé, another aspect of their relationship suggests symbolic coupling between Cuba and the Dominican Republic. As the daughter of the "first woman of the island" (176), Camila represents a connection with the political history of the Dominican Republic.

More important, Camila's relationship with Cuba symbolically unifies oppositional projects on both islands. When she applies for Cuban citizenship, Camila recognizes the (literal) connection between Cuba and the Dominican Republic: "If she is to struggle for freedom here, she might as well join her fate to this country. And as Martí once said to their uncle Federico, why speak of Cuba and Santo Domingo, when even the underwater cordillera that runs from island to island knows they belong together" (164).

By citing Martí as an intellectual forebear, Camila recognizes the hemispheric connections that bind anticolonial struggles in the Caribbean. The underwater cordillera that connects the two islands signifies links between projects of national freedom in Cuba and the Dominican Republic—and throughout the Caribbean. One logical conclusion is that Alvarez projects contemporary understanding of interethnic Latina/o consciousness onto the historical characters she documents in her novels. By linking projects of national consciousness in the Dominican Republic with Puerto Rico and Cuba, she makes a case for organic, hemispheric connections between Latina/o groups, even before their arrival to the United States.

Because Alvarez's story is matrixed with the history and politics of the Dominican Republic, the collapse of the individual with the history of the nation in her historical novels functions as a symbolic negotiation of the self. Part of the reason to continue to struggle to "set la patria free" is to understand how identity must be resolved from the fragmentation and dislocation produced through the project of defining the nation. Consequently, she characterizes national belonging as a hemispheric phenomenon, relocating national belonging to the diaspora.

Conclusion

To understand how Alvarez aligns first-person personal narrative traces with the history of the Dominican Republic, it is productive to examine her first four novels. Alvarez reimagines history to resolve the trauma of dislocation and exile, while also clearing a space for diasporic identity. By examining these novels from the perspective of historical trauma, we are able to understand that the history of the nation is based on a transformative history of the self.

Alvarez's first-person personal narratives *How the García Girls Lost Their Accents* and *¡Yo!* attempt to resolve the collective trauma visited upon Dominicans who either were complicit with Trujillo or fled the country. These novels offer a potential therapeutic process by suggesting a procedure for renarrativizing Dominican history. By locating this therapeutic historical process in a first-person personal narrative form, Alvarez provides a different perspective on the nation—one that includes Dominicans living in the diaspora.

Alvarez alternates between her autobiographical and historical novels to provide a more thorough negotiation of this therapeutic process. By contesting "official" versions of Dominican history, she suggests a process that transcends individual pathology, positing an alternative trajectory for the future. This alternate trajectory is based on a different historiographic method that contests patriarchal imperatives that deny women legitimate roles as subjects of history. It also facilitates a better understanding of the conditions that led to Trujillo, positing a hope for a better future.

Conclusion

New Millennial Triangulations

> My attention to the nation and my interest in differentiating amongst different nationalisms do not stem from a reactionary desire to reinstall the nation-state or nationalism as privileged categories of cultural analysis. Rather, I believe that transnationalist agendas, which I share, are poorly served by denying the continuing, though discernibly declining, power of the nation-state.
>
> —Shalini Puri, *The Caribbean Postcolonial*

Thus far, my analysis of Latina/o triangulations has focused on first-person personal narratives written during the last third of the twentieth century. I have attempted to highlight how the works I consider posit communal identities that contest liberal individualism, racism, and white supremacy. As I have also shown, many of these narrative strategies engage insurgent nationalist politics—although authors like John Rechy, Judith Ortiz Cofer, and Julia Alvarez transform this rhetoric during the postsixties period. While twentieth-century texts contain important elaborations of Latina/o identity, it is important to consider how Chicana/o, Puerto Rican, and Dominican writers in the United States continue to navigate self, community, and nation in the post-9/11 and (allegedly) postracial world.[1] In particular, I am interested in how new millennial Latina/o authors constitute forms of opposition that mediate the imagined community of the nation with forms of transnationalism.

Increasingly, twenty-first-century cultural texts engage aspects of opposition that are distinct from traditional epicenters of Latina/o cultural resistance. Juanita Heredia observes that "in the 21st century, Latina writers in the United States have developed a transnational perspective in their narratives by representing migrations between Latin America and the United States in a global context" (2007, 340). As a result of the younger and more frequently foreign-born population of U.S. Latina/os that have no living memory of the cultural nationalist period, the touchstone of the nation has in many ways become a historical anachronism.[2] At a time when Chicana/o studies, Latina/o studies, and especially Puerto

Rican studies have moved toward transnational perspectives, it is vital to think about how—or indeed whether—the nation as a category is functional within current theoretical and cultural paradigms.[3]

It is my contention that if we are too quick to dismiss the nation as a category of social belonging and critical analysis, we miss some of the dynamics that compose opposition in the twenty-first century.[4] In fact, the specter of the nation and traditional identity discourses that accompany it continue to haunt the imaginary of Latina/o cultural texts. Shalini Puri (2004) distinguishes between transnationalisms, which exceed the boundaries of the nation-state, and postnationalism, which treats the nation as a bankrupt category of analysis. Rather than conceiving of transnationalism and nationalism in opposition, Puri proposes that the nation and transnation make continual accommodations to one another. Following Benedict Anderson, she argues that nationalism is not an ideology but a framework for political activity. Reification of *the* nation and *the* state occlude varied practices of nations, states, and political opposition (9–10). This leads her to conclude that much celebrated conceptions of hybridity and intermixing as possible "antidotes" to the nation actually work to reinforce the imagined community. While "hybridity might reveal the nation is a lie, [. . .] it can also enable the lie to function. Not disruption, but consolidation of the nation-state, then, has been one historical function of hybridity" (49–50).

While Puri focuses on the Caribbean, I extend her analysis to U.S. Latina/o literature for several reasons. First, and perhaps most obviously, groups like Puerto Ricans and Dominicans emerge out of and are shaped by historical and cultural legacies of the Caribbean. More important, as the first point of contact in the colonization of the Americas, the Caribbean offers prototypes for ideologies of race, conquest, and genocide that shape historical and cultural trajectories throughout Latin America— and by implication Latina/os in the United States. Finally, because of the residue of the nation I trace throughout this book, I concur with Puri that nationalism and the nation remain important categories for expressing opposition to hegemonic culture. As Puri asserts, "Against deconstructions of 'the people' as a fabricated identity, I defend the idea of imagining 'the people' in democratic and egalitarian ways as a political *achievement* worth struggling for. Such negotiations might involve reconceiving the relationship of different elements within and amongst nations, and struggles by disenfranchised groups over law, policy, allocation of resources, and cultural representation, that is, intervening in the relationship between elements of the nation and the state" (12).

In keeping with a model of the nation oriented around concepts of political, social, and racial justice, I concur with Puri in arguing that the nation remains an important—although not indispensible—mode of political expression. As a form of political expression, it maintains an influence on articulations of Latina/o opposition, even in light of the diminished authority of cultural nationalism. Emerging out of contexts in the Caribbean, Central America, and South America that are influenced by U.S. hemispheric domination and the drive for transnational development in the global south, many recent Latina/o arrivals are caught between conflicting currents of nationalism and globalization. As Puri suggests, one way to resist these influences is by asserting nationalist consciousness.

In addition, Puri underscores the fact that celebrations of globalization, hybridity, and *mestizaje* (complex intermixing) often misunderstand the multifaceted relationships cultural workers have with nationalism and transnationalism. It is important in this regard to consider that models of political empowerment based on nationalism are not necessarily mutually exclusive from transnationalism. Indeed, nationalism is often a precondition for transnationalism.

Moreover, David W. Noble (2002) argues that modern nationalism has always involved transnational strategies. He explains that nationalism is a manifestation of transatlantic bourgeois attempts to divine the nation from various states of nature. Noble shows how Enlightenment figures like Jefferson and Washington saw the medieval world as a pattern of traditions created by human imagination (i.e., culture). They believed that the laws of nations should be discovered by human reason, thereby divining what occurs in nature and naturalizing a social and cultural process. But Noble marks a shift in nationalist thinking during the post–World War II period that accommodates the contradictions of nationalism and global capitalism. He links the collapse of the "aesthetic authority of the international marketplace to the collapse of the aesthetic authority of the national landscape" by showing how "bourgeois elites since the 1940s have transformed [the] hope of transcending history as an unpredictable flow of time to the global marketplace" (xxxvii). As such, there is a paradox in the national narrative: national history operates as a transnational cultural pattern because it represents the spreading of bourgeois culture, rather than the purification and isolation of a national culture. For Noble, then, contemporary globalization and transnationalism would not be able to function if it were truly transnational—in part because transnationalism depends on the existence of national borders.

My point is not to insist on nationalism as *the* dominant frame for political activity in the new millennium. Rather, I ask that we take a partial step back to consider the historical, cultural, and material circumstances that continue to structure oppositional practices. It is my contention that the nation remains an important touchstone for political resistance, even as Latina/o authors in the twenty-first century move increasingly toward forms of transnational social belonging. In fact, the nation often serves as a bastion of resistance to the homogenizing power of global capital as it manifests in discourses of globalization. So while the category of the nation is increasingly unstable, the residue of late twentieth-century insurgent nationalism persists in its influence on contemporary Latina/o texts. I concur with Puri that struggles for social justice depend on acknowledging the power the nation may still hold as a force for coalescing political movements. Likewise, I agree with Noble that nationalism has always existed as a transnational phenomenon.

But where Puri is primarily interested in how hybridity has been misapplied in the Caribbean (and Noble with explaining the paradoxes of nationalism and capitalism), my concern lies in understanding how twenty-first-century Latina/o first-person personal narratives triangulate the national and transnational to formulate alternative structures of social and political belonging. In particular, I focus on how first-person personal narratives from the twenty-first century reinvent narrative forms to accommodate their visions of political, social, and racial justice. While new millennial authors do not maintain a singular focus on the nation, their narrative strategies utilize the imagined community as one of a number of competing political modes that composes a field of opposition to persistent and intractable forms of racism and social inequality.

New Millennial Latina/o Literature and the Postracial Novel

Twenty-first-century novels such as Junot Díaz's *The Brief Wondrous Life of Oscar Wao* (2007), Salvador Plascencia's *The People of Paper* (2005), and Sandra Cisneros's *Caramelo* (2002a) share many formal qualities that characterize the texts I examine in this book. From the use of the bildungsroman to a conscious blurring of distinctions between author and narrator or protagonist, these novels extend narrative trajectories associated with twentieth-century Latina/o first-person personal narratives. In addition to their narrative strategies, the protagonists of these novels are often matrixed with the history and culture of their communities in ways that recall works by Piri Thomas, Judith Ortiz Cofer, and Julia Alvarez. As Celaya Reyes, the adolescent narrator of Cisneros's *Caramelo*, puts it in relation to the historical strands that bind her with her grandmother and father, "one can't be reached without touching the other. Him inside her, me inside him, like Chinese boxes, like Russian dolls, like an ocean full of waves, like the braided threads of a *rebozo* [. . .] And we are all, like it or not, one and the same" (2002a, 425).

Yet these texts also evidence what Ramón Saldívar (2009) describes as the postracial turn in contemporary Latina/o literature. In contrast to mainstream media assertions of a postracial United States, Saldívar does not signal the end of racialization—and therefore a presumed end to governmental and structural regimes like affirmative action that are designed to remedy historical inequality. He explains that "race and racism, ethnicity and difference are nowhere near extinct in contemporary America. In the early twenty-first century, race remains a central problem of American modernity, but one no longer defined exclusively in shades of black or white" (1). Consequently, Saldívar explores "the aesthetic principles guiding the emergence of a body of literature dealing with, to paraphrase W. E. B. DuBois, the strange meaning of race in the dawning of the twenty-first century" (1).

For Saldívar, postracial novels are characterized in part by the tension between a desire for racial and social justice and the impossibility of achieving this desire through traditional discursive or political processes. This aporia requires new millennial writers to reassess "the relationship between race and social justice, race and identity, and indeed, race and history," requiring them to "invent a new 'imaginary' for thinking about the nature of a just society and the role of race in its construction" (1). While these writers often paradoxically and ironically deploy narrative strategies that combine the fantasy of "coalescing with reality," favored by romantic authors, the "defamiliarization of reality" used by modernists, and "the ludic play of metafiction" (22) characterizing postmodernists, they do so with a twist. They require "us to read the story of the histories of conquest, colonization, diaspora, and struggle[s] for social justice in the Americas by forging links between the fantasy of the imaginary and the real of history" (22–23). These reinvented narrative strategies recenter traumatic histories of colonization, racism, and genocide in the Americas, while also emphasizing the "*constant* and *complete* rupture between the redemptive course of American history with its origins in conquest and the psychic facades that bar the way to memories of that traumatic past" (23). Saldívar further claims that "in twenty-first century postrace fiction, neither literary realism, nor modernist estrangement, nor postmodern play, nor even magical realist wonder can suffice as *formal* stand-ins for the concrete *content* of justice" (24).

Saldívar's emphasis on *content* points to the fact that authors like Díaz, Plascencia, and Cisneros refuse to disidentify with social justice. They remain committed to egalitarian politics even after the disappointments of the civil rights and ethnic power movements of the late twentieth century. Their narrative strategies also respond to postmodern aesthetic modes that dissolve the hope for political transcendence through pastiche and play. They attempt to constitute narrative modes that "perform the critical work of symbolic action, denoting the public work of the private imagination, but only after routing it through the pathway of fantasy in the service of the profoundly unsymbolic racialized imagination" (25).

I concur with Saldívar's analysis of postracial novels—in particular, his conception of twenty-first-century novels as responding to the tension between a desire for social justice and the impossibility of its fulfillment through traditional means. But where Saldívar's conception of the postracial novel concentrates on dialectical development between aesthetic form and political implications, my object of study is somewhat different. I am concerned with how the dynamics Saldívar describes in relation to form are analogous to the complex representations of the self I investigate in this book. My work elaborates on how we might read contemporary Latina/o authors' triangulations as continuing to articulate complex forms of self that are related to group identity and projects of community efficacy. Indeed, many twenty-first-century Latina/o novels demonstrate a simultaneous engagement with and disavowal of conventional modes of political opposition, including the imagined national community. Examining Latina/o triangulations allows us to decode the political implications of these narratives in terms that remain filial to, yet exceed, the nation.

Concomitantly, if we take Saldívar's assertion that twenty-first-century Latina/os—indeed aggrieved racial and ethnic authors generally—reinvent narrative forms to accommodate their commitments to projects of social and political justice, then it is important to consider how they constitute opposition.[5] In other words, by examining how Díaz, Plascencia, and Cisneros triangulate new forms of political resistance, it is possible to comprehend their mediations of nationalism and transnationalism with other forms of political and social practice. As Mikhail Bakhtin (1981) argues, nothing from the past ever disappears. Every word we utter, write, or think is inextricably bound to a historical and cultural context. I argue that political forms are similar to Bakhtin's assessment of language; even when the realities of nations change, nationalism still persists as a political project and moral geography.[6] By examining their triangulations, it is possible to begin decoding these conflicting impulses in the postracial novel.

Triangulating the (Trans)Nation in Sandra Cisneros's *Caramelo*

I turn now to a brief reading of Sandra Cisneros's *Caramelo*. Like Díaz's *The Brief Wondrous Life of Oscar Wao* and Plascencia's *The People of Paper*, *Caramelo* uses narrative strategies that combine aspects of postmodern play and modernist defamiliarization.[7] While the novel's size and complexity makes complete analysis impossible within the scope of this conclusion, I offer a partial reading that outlines how *Caramelo* triangulates an alternative sense of social belonging for Celaya Reyes and her family. By vacillating between the national and transnational, Cisneros mediates aspects of both, depending on context and social situation. For Celaya, there is no single way to be Mexican; rather, there are many histories, racial identities, and national contexts that contribute to her sense of herself and her relationship with structures of social and (trans)national belonging.

At 439 pages, *Caramelo* offers a sprawling narrative covering over 100 years and three generations of Reyes family history in three parts. Although the three parts share only a loose relationship, together they provide a composite portrait of Celaya and her family that suggests she is the amalgamation of family histories. Part 1 narrates a series of trips the family makes from their home in Chicago to Mexico City. Like Cisneros's family, the Reyeses make their annual pilgrimage to visit Celaya's paternal grandmother—known alternately as the Awful Grandmother, the Grandmother, and Soledad (her given name). Part 1 culminates in a side trip to Acapulco during the last summer visit (roughly 1962). In Acapulco, a monumental conflict arises between Celaya's father, Inocencio, and her mother, Zoila. While the cause of the fight remains a mystery in part 1, we subsequently learn (150 pages later in part 3) that the fight centers on the revelation that one of the Awful Grandmother's servants, Candelaria, is the unacknowledged daughter of Inocencio.

Part 2 moves back in time before Celaya was born, when she was "dirt." As Celaya explains, "when I was dirt . . . is how we begin a story that was before our time. Before we were born" (89). Part 2 focuses on the history of the Awful Grandmother, known in this section as Soledad. While Soledad is the narrative center of part 2, there are a series of digressions that tell the stories of the Little Grandfather (Narciso), as well as Celaya's paternal great grandmother Regina and great grandfather Eleuterio. Soledad's narrative excavates repeating patterns that plague the Reyeses, including a history of overvaluing male children while neglecting and abusing female ones. These gender dynamics partially explain how the Awful Grandmother became awful by documenting her deplorable childhood, complete with the death of her mother, her father's abandonment of her, and the sexual abuse she suffers at the hands of her Uncle Pío. Things don't get much better for Soledad when she marries Narciso, as he is a philanderer whose only concern—true to the root of his name, narcissism—is his own pleasure.

Importantly, part 2 also lays the groundwork for the Reyeses' many migrations. Beginning with the family patriarch, Eleuterio's move from Spain to the New World, and moving through Narciso's and Inocencio's early migrations to the United States, Cisneros documents the Reyeses' century of movement. This emphasis on circular migration and return, as opposed to unidirectional immigration, complicates the characters' relationships with structures of national and transnational belonging by disrupting any conception of stasis or stability.

Part 3 offers the longest and most linear of the sections. Where part 1 is rendered in interlocking vignettes through the young Celaya (she ranges in age from about five to eight or nine) and part 2 through flashbacks narrated collaboratively by Soledad and Celaya, part 3 progresses more or less teleologically. It focuses on Celaya's coming-of-age in late-1960s Chicago and San Antonio. As a part of her development (both in terms of character development and maturation) Celaya must come to terms with her family's complicated binational history. Paralleling the struggles for a space of belonging we have seen in the work of Judith Ortiz Cofer and Julia Alvarez, part of Celaya's task is to determine where she feels most at home. But because she represents the literal combination of her Chicana mother,

Zoila, and Mexican national father, Inocencio, any unilateral sense of home is insufficient. While the critical response to *Caramelo* is strikingly limited given that it has been in print for nearly nine years, a few commentators have noted how the novel represents the tension between the national and transnational. Juanita Heredia (2007) compares Cisneros with Peruvian American author Marie Arana to argue that many new millennial Latina writers deploy transnational perspectives that complicate essentialist conceptions of the nation. Heredia is particularly interested in how Cisneros uses Mexican "heritage culture as a discourse of intervention in the Mexico-United States borderlands" (343). This emphasis on heritage culture disrupts discourses of assimilation in the United States, monolithic notions of Chicana/o nationalism during the 1960s, and simplistic conceptions of the borderlands that privilege U.S. perspectives over Mexican ones. Heredia further argues that Cisneros's use of these narrative strategies "contests dominant forms of oppression in the formation of the protagonist" (343). In so doing, Heredia argues that there is a discernable move from the national to the transnational as it manifests in Celaya.

Gabriela Gutiérrez y Muhs (2006) also notes transnational dynamics in *Caramelo*. Gutiérrez y Muhs focuses on figures from Mexican popular culture like Tongolele, Toña la Negra, Augustín Lara, and a host of others appearing in the novel. She claims that Cisneros uses pop cultural references to contribute "to the project of globalizing Chicana literature, and historicizing Chicano/Mexicano culture" (24). Gutiérrez y Muhs argues that the novel likely wouldn't be as readable or as popular were it not for its intersection with the Internet—perhaps the ultimate manifestation of globalization. She further suggests that popular culture figures in the novel were carefully selected by Cisneros because of their involvement with projects of social justice. Consequently, the figures Cisneros selects serve as links to resistant subjectivities on both sides of the border. This has the effect of "globalizing Chicana/o protagonists" in order to bring "Mexican subjectivities into the pot of what is American, thereby expanding Aztlán into various directions and discourses, as well as continents" (34).

In contrast to Heredia and Gutiérrez y Muhs, Bill Johnson González (2006) focuses on language and translation in *Caramelo*. While his analysis is directed at Cisneros's defamiliarization of English through literal translations (formulations like "what a barbarity / ¡Qué barbaridad!" or "how exaggerated / ¡Qué exagerado!"), Johnson González also sees transgressive aspects in the novel's national and transnational dynamics: "what makes Cisneros's work unlike so many other Chicano texts, which tend to depict that community's struggle to preserve its cultural difference from the dominant culture of the United States, is precisely the novel's exploration of the tensions and critical differences within the Mexican/Chicano community" (3). Johnson González explores these tensions to determine how "Celaya's linguistic perplexities are [. . .] compounded by the fact that she is intellectually located in the interstices between two fiercely nationalistic (and often politically opposed) cultures" (4). While each of these national languages and cultures attempts to institute stability, Celaya's marginality provides her with a privileged perspective. Thus for Johnson González Cisneros does more than critically interrogate the nation; she refracts it into an entirely different space of belonging that is hybrid and new.

My perspective on these issues is that the novel engages in a series of triangulations of the national and transnational. But where Heredia and Gutiérrez y Muhs subsume the novel within an emerging transnational body of literature, I argue that Cisneros does not entirely divorce the novel from the national. I suggest that the novel mediates the national and transnational to triangulate a new sense of social and political belonging for the Reyeses. A primary way that *Caramelo* represents this process is through movement. Rather than engaging in static representation, the novel invests in tropes of movement, transition, and renewal. In this sense my reading is closer to Johnson González's analysis of language. I agree that Cisneros continually refracts the purely national or transnational into something altogether different.

We see these dynamics from the novel's opening pages. After a series of epigraphs, disclaimers, and introductions, the novel proper opens in medias res on one of the aforementioned trips to Mexico: "Uncle Fat-Face's brand-new used white Cadillac, Uncle Baby's green Impala, Father's red Chevrolet station wagon bought that summer on credit are racing to the Little Grandfather's and Awful Grandmother's house in Mexico City" (5). From the start, movement is emphasized, as our first glimpse of the Reyes family is inside of their automobiles en route to Mexico City. By representing her characters on a journey south to Mexico, Cisneros complicates the traditional axis of east and west movement operative in U.S. travel narratives by authors like John Steinbeck and Jack Kerouac.[8] In addition, by relocating the red, green, and white colors of the Mexican flag to an interstitial space inside the United States, she questions the stability of national symbols. This formulation is further problematized: while the cars are currently in the United States, they won't be there for long, implying that national identifications are subject to revision depending on geographical and cultural contexts.

But movement is not limited to the United States in *Caramelo*. Indeed, we see a series of road trips, side trips, boat cruises, and border-transgressing journeys in Mexico and the United States, emphasizing that movement is the only constant in the novel. One of the most important journeys is the trip to Acapulco that brings part 1 to a close. As the event that links part 1 with the rest of the novel, the trip to Acapulco provides a framework for movement in *Caramelo*. After a disastrous birthday party for Inocencio during which the ceiling in a remodeled room in the Awful Grandmother's house collapses, the family travels to Acapulco while the ceiling is repaired. As Zoila notes, the trip will provide a welcome respite from the usual boredom of their trips: "Every time we come to Mexico it's the same old crap. Nothing but living rooms, living rooms, living rooms" (68). While Zoila gets her trip, she doesn't get the break from Inocencio's family she desires. Instead, the Reyeses—all seven children, Inocencio, and Zoila—are accompanied by the Awful Grandmother, Aunty Light-Skin and her daughter, Antonieta Araceli, and Candelaria.

Although the physical movement Cisneros represents through the trip to Acapulco is important, she also emphasizes motion through the narrative itself. Particularly in part 1, Celaya's narration progresses through a hyperfragmented style reminiscent of Cisneros's other work—especially her 1984 novel, *The House on Mango Street*. But the stakes of this style are different in *Caramelo*. Where *The House on Mango Street* depicts its protagonist Esperanza in a state of stasis, *Caramelo* represents Celaya in perpetual transition. For example, when describing the family's arrival in Acapulco, Cisneros writes, "Acapulco. In a house shaped like a boat. Everything curled like the fronds of a fern. The ocean. Our hair. Our sandals drying in the sun. The paint on the boat-shaped house" (73). By narrating isolated images, rather than detailed description or character development, the text signifies movement even as the Reyes family reaches Acapulco. The short, choppy sentences and emphasis on sensory perception evoke a sense of progress. In addition, the house where the family stays (owned by Catita, the sister of Aunty Light-Skin's employer and likely lover, Señor Vidaurri) is shaped like a boat, implying movement in the home itself—traditionally a space of stability. Moreover, even though the Reyeses stay in Catita Vidaurri's home, they are on vacation—a state of transition in itself.

This section of the novel also evidences a proleptic narrative style. When preparing for the trip to Acapulco, Celaya describes Candelaria's preparations. During her description, however, we are suddenly transported to the future:

> So at the last minute, Candelaria is sent to her rooftop room to fetch a plastic shopping bag filled with a few raggedy clothes. But Candelaria's village is in Nayarit. She's never seen the ocean. Before the eight days are up, she will be sent back on the next Tres Estrellas de Oro bus to Mexico City with the Awful Grandmother's address pinned to her underslip to prevent her from becoming one of the countless unfortunates seen hiccuping [sic] terrible tears on the television's public announcements . . . *If you recognize this young lady, please call* . . . since she is new to the city and can neither read nor write, because a huge Acapulco wave will knock her over, and the ocean will come out of her mouth and eyes and nose for days when it is discovered Candelaria can't take care of the babies without someone first taking care of her. (69)

The sudden shift in time between the third and fourth sentences ("Before the eight days are up") suggests a different type of movement: one oriented around a competing notion of history. In this regard, Candelaria's near drowning and subsequent banishment from the narrative (we hear almost nothing about her after the trip to Acapulco) provide the impetus for the fight that occurs between Inocencio and Zoila at the end of part 1. Because the fight functions as a cliff-hanger that remains unresolved until part 3, parts 1 and 3 are intrinsically linked. But part 2 is also linked in this genealogy, as it provides the context for understanding the fight and its implications through an excavation of Reyes family history. The past is thus linked to the future, suggesting fluidity of time. This continuity between history and the future allows us to conceive of events that seem unrelated as integral to the structure of the novel. Consequently, while Candelaria is a marginal character in terms of the relative space she occupies in the narrative, she becomes central due to her importance to the events in Acapulco.

While these features of the novel don't depict physical movement, they do emphasize instability and mutability as essential aspects of Celaya's and her family's lives. The movement associated with the trip to Acapulco is thus physical (the family *drives* there) and epistemological. In the fluidity between the past and the future, as well as shifts in narrative structure, Cisneros implies that change and instability are integral to the narrative process—and by implication to the Reyeses' lives. When considered from this viewpoint, Celaya's identity contradicts the stability vital to nationalist discourses on both sides of the border.

This is not to say that psychological or epistemological movement is more important than physical movement in the novel. As I have already noted, physical movement is among the novel's dominant tropes. One implication is that many types of movement are linked with national belonging in both Mexico and the United States. In fact, Cisneros links movement with national identity through the Reyes family's history of migration from and to Mexico.[9] Beginning with Celaya's paternal great grandfather, Eleuterio, who immigrates to Mexico from Spain, and moving through the migrations from and to Mexico and the United States that Narciso and Inocencio undertake, the experience of transnational migration is central to Reyes family history.[10]

For example, after the death of the Little Grandfather/Narciso in part 3, Soledad decides to move to Chicago to be near her sons. As her move approaches, the Awful Grandmother, "who'd always sworn Mexico was the most *burro* of all nations, suddenly turned nationalist" (276). Soledad's nationalism is premised on her imminent migration to the United States. Despite her "nationalism," however, the Awful Grandmother experiences something else during her migration: anti-immigrant and anti-Mexican racism in the United States. As Soledad notes, "Something happened when they crossed the border. Instead of being treated like the royalty they were, they were after all Mexicans, they were treated like Mexicans, which was something that altogether startled the Grandmother. In the neighborhoods she could afford, she couldn't stand being associated with these low-class Mexicans, but in the neighborhoods she couldn't, her neighbors couldn't stand being associated with her" (289).

Here the experience of racism reverses popular discourses of immigration to the United States. According to these discourses immigrants come to the United States to experience a better life. Soledad, however, *leaves* a space of privilege in Mexico City, experiencing disempowerment in Chicago. As Cisneros reminds us, Soledad and Narciso are middle class in Mexico: they own their own home, employ servants, own and operate a *tlapalería* (hardware store), and rent out apartments on the lower level of their house.

By contrast, in the United States Soledad is marginalized by her poor command of English, her dependence on Celaya, Zoila, Inocencio, and other relatives, her alienation from working-class Mexican and Chicano communities in Chicago, and perhaps most importantly by her experiences of racialization. Cisneros emphasizes this disempowerment through the variable meaning of Mexican identity. To be Mexican in Mexico is to embody a *raza cosmica* that, according to Mexican nationalists like José Vasconcelos (1997), combines indigenous and European elements to produce a new, superior racial identity. To be Mexican in the United States is to occupy a lower stratum on the social and racial hierarchy. One logical conclusion is that life in the United States does not offer a seamless transition from one national space to another for Soledad. For her, the United States represents a profound backward step in her economic, class, and social standing.

But Cisneros does not romanticize Soledad's class position or the various conceptions of race in Mexico in the novel. The privilege Soledad experiences is linked with disempowering indigenous figures like Candelaria and her mother Amparo. Ironically, given that she has a high admixture of indigenous blood, the main advocate of anti-indigenous racial ideologies in Mexico is Soledad.[11] As the novel elaborates, racism is not an experience limited to the United States: it is as prominent—though in different form—in Mexico.

These points underscore that discourses of nationalism on both sides of the border are bound to ideologies of race and racism. While in the United States anti-immigrant and anti-Mexican racism disempower people like the Reyeses, the privilege they experience in Mexico is linked to their capacity for anti-indigenous racism. By highlighting these similarities between Mexico and the United States, Cisneros destabilizes nationalist desires for purity, insisting on more complex and hybrid political and social identifications. The question the novel then poses is how to constitute social belonging without succumbing to the racist impulses operative in many nationalist texts.

As a partial answer to this question, Cisneros triangulates a space of belonging driven by various contexts of the national and transnational.

One important symbol she uses to convey this complication of the national and transnational is the rebozo. Ubiquitous in Mexican culture, the rebozo is a rectangular cloth garment used by women. It is made of silk, cotton, or wool and usually has an elaborately braided fringe. The rebozo has many uses, but is often employed as a shawl or baby carrier. The importance of the rebozo to the novel is undeniable, as the term *caramelo* refers to, among other things, a prized brown and white candy-striped rebozo Soledad inherits from her mother (and presumably passes on to Celaya).

Given that it is a paradigmatic symbol of Mexican culture, it is ironic that Cisneros characterizes the rebozo in syncretic terms. In a footnote, she describes the rebozo's complex history:

> The *rebozo* was born in Mexico, but like all *mestizos*, it came from everywhere. It evolved from the cloths Indian women used to carry their babies, borrowed its knotted fringe from Spanish shawls, and was influenced by the silk embroideries from the imperial court of China exported to Manila, then Acapulco, via the Spanish galleons. During the colonial period, mestizo women were prohibited by statutes dictated by the Spanish Crown to dress like Indians, and since they had no means to buy clothing like the Spaniards', they began to weave cloth on the indigenous looms creating a long and narrow shawl that slowly was shaped by foreign influences. (96)

As Cisneros describes, the rebozo is the product of myriad influences, ranging from Chinese silk to Mesoamerican weaving. But how these influences come together constitutes the most interesting aspect of her description. Through contact via the Spanish empire, trade routes along the Silk Road, and expressions of indigenous resistance, the rebozo encompasses aspects of many cultural and geographical contexts. Indeed, an unstated premise of Cisneros's history is that no national form is free from outside cultural influences. One logical conclusion is that if a quintessentially Mexican national symbol is the product of multiple influences, then national consciousness is far from stable.

Another aspect of Cisneros's triangulation of the national and transnational has to do with conceptions of "home." In a move that recalls diasporic Caribbean authors like Julia Alvarez and Judith Ortiz Cofer, Celaya posits family as one potential site for home. James Phelan observes that *Caramelo* complicates notions of "home" and "country," suggesting that the space of home is politicized, while the nation is personalized (2006, 119). We see these dynamics when the Reyeses move to San Antonio. After Soledad's migration to Chicago, the family relocates to San Antonio—in part because they can afford a home there and in part because Inocencio's war buddy Marcelino Ordóñez (Mars), lives there.[12] Mars, a Chicano from West Texas, helped Inocencio get home after losing his life savings in New Orleans following his discharge from World War II. Mars convinces Inocencio and Soledad to move to San Antonio, providing a shop for Inocencio's upholstery business and helping the family locate a home. But their relationship sours when Mars raises the rent on Inocencio's shop and calls the Immigration and Naturalization Service (*la migra*) to harass Inocencio—likely to facilitate his eviction. The Reyeses become estranged from Mars, forcing their departure from San Antonio. In the chapter "Halfway Between Here and There, in the Middle of Nowhere," Inocencio describes his longing for "home":

[INOCENCIO]: Home. I want to go home already, Father says.
[CELAYA]: Home? Where's that? North? South? Mexico? San Antonio? Chicago? Where, Father?
[INOCENCIO]: All I want is my kids, Father says.—That's the only country I need. (380)

As Celaya points out, Inocencio's desire for a stable home is foreclosed by the multiple moves the family undertakes. Mexico, Chicago, and San Antonio are insufficient, as the ties that bind Inocencio and the Reyes clan to these spaces are severed. Inocencio's desire for home is transferred to his children ("All I want is my kids"), but this location also lacks stability, as the Reyes siblings are in various states of independence and movement. (Celaya's older brothers Rafa, Ito, and Tikis stay behind in Chicago, while she and her younger siblings remain with their father and mother.) The novel destabilizes any conception of home—even one independent of a specific geographical location. By implication, *any* form of national or transnational belonging is context driven. While neither context is inherently good nor bad, neither is sufficient for quantifying the Reyeses' relationship with social and political belonging. It is therefore plausible that Cisneros attempts to triangulate a new sense of the social that is free from static conceptions of the national, but that doesn't dissolve into the hybridity of the transnational.

These ideas become explicit during Celaya's teenage years in San Antonio. Although she has spent significant portions of her childhood in Mexico, she finds the authenticity of her identity challenged by several Chicana schoolmates. They call her "hippie," "*gabacha*" (white girl; 352), and "*bolilla*" (white bread; 354). As a result of these insults, Celaya finds herself having to defend her identity. She does so by elaborating her experiences of Mexicans—both within Mexico and in the United States: "There are the green-eyed Mexicans. The rich blond Mexicans. The Mexicans with the faces of Arab sheiks. The Jewish Mexicans. The big-footed-as-a German Mexicans. The leftover-French Mexicans. The *chaparrito* compact Mexicans. The Tarahumara tall-as-desert-saguaro Mexicans. The Mediterranean Mexicans. The Mexicans with Tunisian eyebrows. The *negrito* Mexicans of the double coasts. The Chinese Mexicans. The curly-haired, freckled-faced, red-headed Mexicans. The jaguar-lipped Mexicans. The wide-as-a-Tula-tree Zapotec Mexicans. The Lebanese Mexicans. Look, I don't know what you're talking about when you say I don't look Mexican. I *am* Mexican. Even though I was born on the U.S. side of the border" (353).

Like the *caramelo* rebozo that serves as a central metaphor in the novel, Mexican identity is not constituted by a single set of ethnic or racial characteristics. On the contrary, Celaya's familiarity with Mexican identity and culture is composed of diverse international influences that range from Asia and the Middle East to Native America. One conclusion that emerges from Celaya's complex understanding of Mexican identity is that discourses of *mestizaje* that celebrate the *raza cosmica* oversimplify the strands that compose Mexican nationality.

Celaya does, however, make another claim: Mexican, or perhaps more accurately Chicana/o, from the other side also constitutes a valid way to "be Mexican." But while Cisneros valorizes a concept of Chicana/o identity for Celaya, she is also critical of Chicana/o nationalist groups that emphasize an essential Chicanismo. As Celaya continues, "is hell Cookie Cantú and her yappy *perras* talking shit like,—Brown power! Making fists and chanting—*Viva la raza*. Or,—I'm Chicana and proud, wha'chu wanna do about it, *pendeja*?" (354). Here Cisneros lampoons the essentialism of Chicano cultural nationalism. To assert brown power, while misunderstanding the complexity of Mexican identity, is to fall into the same racialist traps operative in mainstream culture. In particular, Cisneros is critical of brown power that overidentifies with indigenous figures (particularly Aztecs). This is not to say that Cisneros is critical of indigenous identities; rather, through

Celaya's experience of multiple Mexican subjectivities, she complicates the *raza cosmica*. But it is equally important to comprehend that while Celaya's complex form of subjectivity critiques essentialism, it remains filial to a Mexican national consciousness. Consequently, although she cites Mexicans of many origins, they are still "Mexican."

Celaya thus occupies an intermediary space that is neither nationalist nor transnationalist. This intermediary space is symbolized when Celaya is confronted again by Cookie Cantú and her associates on their way home from school. As Celaya notes, Cookie and her gang "start throwing words and end up throwing rocks" (356). They chase her toward the freeway, beating her along the way. As she approaches an overpass where she plans her getaway, Celaya sees "some girls waiting there for me too," blocking her escape route. This forces Celaya to exit via the interstate highway: "There's no choice but to scramble over the chain-link fence and make a run for it through the interstate" (356). Literally stuck on the median, Celaya finds herself "too scared to run across the three lanes of traffic [. . .] and too scared to stay put" (357). By symbolically inhabiting a space between the Chicanas who chase her and an imagined national identity in Mexico, Celaya is indeed trapped between powerful poles of subjectivity. Neither on one side nor the other, and surrounded by the motion of cars speeding toward their destinations, Celaya realizes that "I never belonged here. I don't know where I belong anymore" (356). While she eventually gets off the highway to safety, this portrayal suggests that Celaya is (literally) hung up between nationalism (as symbolized by Cookie Cantú and her brown power disciples) and the forces of the transnation, signified by the incessant movement and transition of the speeding cars.

This leads Cisneros to triangulate an alternative position that encompasses aspects of nationalism, while attempting to move beyond it. In the final lines of the novel, she posits a new conception of home: "And I don't know how it is with anyone else, but for me these things, that song, that time, that place, are all bound together in a country I am homesick for, that doesn't exist anymore. That never existed. A country I invented. Like all emigrants caught between here and there" (434).

Recalling Benedict Anderson's (2007) famous characterization of the nation as an "imagined community," the "country" Celaya longs for exists in the imaginary. Yet this does not disqualify the power or appeal the imaginary country has for Celaya. As she tells us, she is "homesick" for the imagined community, suggesting a location for constructing connections with her origins and continuities between herself and her culture. Curiously, though, this space has no history and doesn't exist. Here Cisneros disrupts a unilateral sense of home, expanding the possibility of social connection to spaces that transcend the national. While Celaya is "caught between here and there," she is also empowered to make an intermediary space home. One logical conclusion is that Cisneros triangulates the insufficiencies of national cultures in Mexico and the United States and transnational dynamics that dissolve strong affiliations to a particular home. What emerges for Celaya is the possibility of existing within a context infused by national cultures, while also allowing the flexibility and mobility of transnationalism. Unlike Esperanza in *The House on Mango Street*, then, Celaya can explore the possibilities for identifying a home in the United States, Mexico, and beyond.

My analysis of Latina/o triangulations has attempted to interpret the multifaceted articulations of self, community, and nation that appear in late twentieth-century first-person personal narratives. I have traced these complex elaborations of the "I" as challenges to liberal individualism and accompanying racial discourses. But as I have shown in this conclusion, these dynamics are also applicable to the postracial novels of new millennial authors like Cisneros, Díaz, and Plascencia. In particular, these authors grapple with opposing the persistence of racism within the context of ideology. In my analysis of Cisneros's *Caramelo*, I demonstrate how, contrary to the popular rhetoric of transnationalism, not all twenty-first-century authors are ready to jettison the nation. While they are not mired in the outdated essentialism that plagued 1960s-style groups, they maintain a focus on the nation as one strategy for social and political empowerment.

By way of concluding, I would like to take a moment to outline several questions that underpin my analysis. In particular, I have been driven by a desire to understand two persistent tropes I found in many Latina/o texts as I conducted my research. The first is the frequent—almost obsessive—use of autobiographical forms. In the memoirs and autobiographies of Ernesto Galarza and Piri Thomas, or the autobiographical fiction of figures like John Rechy and Judith Ortiz Cofer, the trope of the self is a consistent thread linking texts from a number of Puerto Rican, Dominican, and Chicana/o communities. I found myself asking, Why the narrative of the self? What is it about the revelation of the self that is so appealing to Latina/o authors? Perhaps most importantly, I began to question what these authors gain by deploying alternative conceptions of the self. In other words, what surfaces by strategically positioning the self that doesn't emerge from other forms?

The second question I encounter has to do with how the autobiographical self is often presented. As I have attempted to show, one consistent theme of my analysis is that the self Latina/os narrate is often positioned in relation to the insufficiencies of a number of identity discourses. Ranging from an engagement with racial formations in the United States to complex intersections with hemispheric political forces, Latina/os often adopt narrative strategies that attempt to navigate ambiguous spaces of identity in the United States.

My conception of triangulation provides one way to comprehend these multifaceted navigations of identity. It represents an attempt to wrestle with the conflicting—and sometimes messy—formulations of identity in these texts. By focusing on the narrative strategies these authors deploy, I have endeavored to understand their triangulations as attempts to navigate the troubled racial waters of the United States. These triangulations thus provide evidence of how Latina/os contest their racialization, while also looking forward to alternative conceptions of identity and social belonging in the United States. While none of the texts I analyze "get there," they do offer instructive attempts that might serve as tentative steps toward social, political, and racial justice. It is my hope that this methodology can be productively employed in other social contexts to comprehend the sophisticated ways people engage power.

Acknowledgments

A colleague and friend recently shared with me that writing her acknowledgments was one of the more difficult aspects of her book. As I sit down to write my own, I realize that this is undoubtedly the case. I am overwhelmed by the gratitude I feel when I think of the intellectual and emotional debts this book owes.

First, I would like to acknowledge George Lipsitz. His formidable intellect has had a profound influence on my work. George has worn the mantle of mentor, friend, and supporter throughout the years. It is with great affection that I think of our many conversations about everything from my work to sports and popular culture. This book would not have been possible without his encouragement and insight.

This book began as a dissertation at the University of California, Santa Barbara (UCSB). While at Santa Barbara, I was the beneficiary of mentorship and friendship from Carl Gutiérrez-Jones and Shirley Lim. Their early and consistent support, guidance, and encouragement nurtured this project in innumerable ways. UCSB also provided me with rigorous training that pushed my intellectual development. I am especially indebted to Chris Newfield, Alan Liu, Alayce Lane, Kay Young, Elliott Butler-Evans, the late Richard Helgerson, and María Josefina Saldaña, all of whom shaped my thinking in significant ways. A special shout-out goes to Fred Moten, who taught me the value and pleasure of all things theoretical.

I have also been the beneficiary of support and encouragement from colleagues and friends near and far. I would like to especially thank Ramón Saldívar for his insightful comments to my introduction and chapter 4. Paula Moya helped to bring crucial aspects of my conception of triangulation into focus. Without her ability to envision the bigger picture, I might still be struggling. Michelle Elam read early drafts of my work and provided excellent feedback. Frances Aparicio also provided thoughtful comments, pushing me to think about interethnic solidarities across the body of my work. Susan Gillman was an important supporter who took time to read, offer encouragement, and exchange ideas. I am also grateful to Ramón Gutiérrez, David Lloyd, Barbara Tomlinson, and Linda Brodkey for their thoughts and encouragement over the years.

The presence of other colleagues and friends can be felt in this book. I would especially like to thank Adalaine Holton for our many conversations about and mutual admiration for Jesús Colón. Maritza Stanchich and Irmary Reyes-Santos also contributed to my understanding of Colón and his work. Tania Triana has been another wonderful friend and colleague who has been generous with her time and feedback since graduate school.

I am blessed with a wonderful community of scholars of color focusing on race and ethnicity here at the University of Oregon. They are not only my friends but also among my chief interlocutors. Shari Huhndorf and Lynn Fujiwara have been supportive friends and thoughtful critics. Shari has been particularly helpful, providing not only critical feedback to the project but also friendship, mentorship, and emotional support through the long and sometimes arduous process of writing this book. Michael Hames-García provided excellent comments to my introduction and chapter 2. His encouragement and suggestions have greatly improved this project. I would also like to thank Karen Ford, Ernesto Martínez, Cynthia Tolentino, Enrique Lima, the late Peggy Pascoe, Lynn Stephen, Analisa Taylor, and Priscilla Ovalle for their thoughts and comments. This book began to take shape after feedback I received during a presentation at the Center for Race, Ethnicity, and Sexuality Studies (CRESS) here at the University of Oregon. My thanks to the CRESS Center for inviting me to present an early version of chapter 2.

I have also been the beneficiary of excellent undergraduate and graduate students. My readings have been shaped by conversations I've had with students in my numerous English 245 and 363 classes. I am also indebted to fine graduate students, particularly those in my English 660 courses. I would like to thank Jocelyn Noonan, Nandini Dhar, Emily Taylor, Erin Rokita, Max Rayneard, Katie Riddle, Marci Carrasquillo, Sonja Burrows, Jordana Finnegan, Maria Cecilia Hwang, and Angela Morrill. Marci Carrasquillo also read and provided feedback to my introduction and chapters 3 and 4. This book also benefited from fine research support by C. Paul Bindel, Mary Ganster, and Carrie Netzer Wajda.

I would also like to thank the Department of English at the University of Oregon. I was able to complete large portions of this book during two research leaves arranged by the department. Thanks also to the College of Arts and Sciences and the Oregon Humanities Center at the University of Oregon for providing the funds for the index to this book. I am also grateful to Richard Morrison, Adam Brunner, Erin Warholm-Wohlenhaus, Alicia Sellheim, Sarah Breeding, and the anonymous reviewers at the University of Minnesota Press. Working with Minnesota has been nothing short of a delight. Portions of chapters 1 and 4 also benefited from comments by the anonymous reviewers at the journals *Centro* and *Latino Studies*.

Beyond the academic influences, this book also bears the traces of the many friends who have touched me. In particular, I would like to thank Bob Grier, Dave Melrose, Nancy May, and John Harman. Gilbert González and the late James "Blackie" Gandara had an indelible influence on me, regaling me with tales of their lives as *vatos locos* (crazy guys). Brooke Thomashefsky, Bill Palmer, Rip Sawyer, Don Ball, and the rest of the Friday night gang have been indispensible supports.

Most of all, I would like to thank my family. My parents, Wally and Ramona Vázquez, have been unshakable fans and supporters. Mi abuela, Gloria Vázquez, who passed before this book was completed, showed me the meaning of unconditional love. I cannot begin to acknowledge all the support that my wife, partner, and friend, Rhonda Zimlich, has given me. Her love, kindness, and affection have provided me with more comfort than I deserve. Her belief in me has sustained me through the best and worst of times. My life is richer for knowing you. Last, I would like to thank my daughters, Gabriella and Veronica Zimlich-Vázquez, for being a part of my life. Though you are too young to read these words, this book, and all it represents, are for you.

Notes

Introduction

1. I use Piri to refer to the protagonist of *Down These Mean Streets* in contradistinction to the author, whom I refer to as Thomas.

2. I should also note that, while this scene emphasizes linguistic "play," scholars like Henry Louis Gates (1988) have long noted that play constitutes one of the fields in which resistance can be constituted.

3. See, for example, Thomas's juxtaposition of life in the United States with the "paradise" described by his mother in the chapter entitled "Puerto Rican Paradise." See also Thomas's rejection of suburbia and Puerto Rico in the chapters "Babylon for the Babylonians" and "But Not for Me."

4. Of course it is important to note that while the meanings of racial, gender, and class categories are fluid, the binary nature of identity in the United States demands either/or identifications.

5. Operation Bootstrap comprised a series of industrialization policies initiated by Governor Luis Muñoz Marín in 1947 designed to attract U.S. capital industry through a series of tax breaks and incentives, including free land and factory buildings. As Laura Briggs (2002) notes, the program also included incentives designed to limit population on the island. Many of the policies associated with Operation Bootstrap thus characterized technological and social progress as a function of "women's willingness to use birth control" (118). Operation Bootstrap also promoted "emigration as a safety valve to alleviate the structural pressures of production" (Sánchez Korrol 1983, 217). Many Operation Bootstrap policies contributed to the unprecedented migration from the island to the United States during the post–World War II period.

6. As Ramón Saldívar (2009) suggests, the first-person personal narrative continues as a dominant literary mode in the work of twenty-first-century authors like Junot Diaz (2007) and Salvador Plascencia (2005).

7. As Dalleo and Machado Sáez argue, "We do not argue for an uncritical celebration of [postsixties] literature. None of these writers offers a fully articulated and easily implemented political project; in fact, their visions of politics are frequently idealistic. Nevertheless, their value lies in offering something crucial to

our postcolonial, post-Civil Rights era: serious engagement with the legacy of the past in the context of [the] present" (11).

8. The two exceptions are Jesús Colón and Ernesto Galarza who were prolific authors prior to the publication of their autobiographies. For more on their publishing careers, see chapter 1.

9. The term "Mexican American" is Padilla's attempt to maintain a distinction between nineteenth-century Californios and more contemporary understandings of Chicana/o identity.

10. Sommer points to Gramsci's concern with subjugated classes in southern Italy. Historians have argued that the characterization of this particular region of the Italian peninsula as "backward" functioned according to ethnically charged ideologies. As Sommer also notes, Gramsci's formulation suggests "other southern and subaltern perspectives" (105). While not directly corresponding to racism in the United States, Gramsci's work provides an interesting corollary to Latina/o struggles in North America.

11. For readers unfamiliar with Menchú and the controversy surrounding her *testimonio*, see *The Rigoberta Menchú Controversy* (2001), edited by Arturo Arias.

12. For more on Colón and his work, see Flores (1982), Acosta-Belén and Sánchez-Korrol (1993), and Stanchich (2010). See also my discussion of *A Puerto Rican in New York* in chapter 1.

13. Indeed, as Espinoza argues, "most individual outsiders [to hegemonic conceptions of subjectivity] are comfortable with the messy ambiguity of identity—when we're not thinking about it. When we try to counter the socially imposed categories and the oppression they represent, we find that we lack a language to express that which we have learned through experience" (17–18).

14. Another example is Gloria Anzaldúa's (2007) characterization of the borderlands as a "separate" country. This characterization leverages aspects of the nationalist agenda with a difference. By foregrounding the gender oppression experienced by Chicanas and gays and lesbians at the hands of Anglos and male Chicanos, Anzaldúa utilizes the rhetoric of cultural nationalism, while simultaneously contesting the masculinist discourse of these social movements.

15. Briefly, *vatos locos* are Chicano, urban, gang members and outlaws. In Acosta's work, they exist as estranged members of Chicana/o communities. As outsiders to both mainstream and Chicana/o communities, they offer alternative and revolutionary perspectives on power. Similarly, Rechy's notion of the sexual outlaw valorizes gay men who defy conventional sexual morality. The sexual outlaw is typically a street hustler (male prostitute) or promiscuous "sexhunter" who engages in public sex, often with multiple partners. For more on the *vato loco* and sexual outlaw, see my discussions of these figures in chapters 2 and 3.

16. Flowing from David Lloyd's (1997) suggestion to distinguish between nationalisms that support the state and those that work against it, I use the terms

"insurgent nationalism" and "cultural nationalism" to denote oppositional social movements based on ethnic affiliation (Chicana/o, Puerto Rican, or African American "nationalisms," for example). In general, these social movements are antiracist and antistatist. They are frequently (as in the case of the Brown Berets and Young Lords), although not universally, oriented around Marxist positions.

17. For more Latina/o critiques of cultural nationalism, see Moraga and Anzaldúa (1983), Chabram-Dernersesian (1992), Anzaldúa (2007), Saldívar-Hull (2000), and the Latina Feminist Group (2001). See also essays by Jorge Duany and Christina Duffy Burnett in Frances Negrón-Muntaner's *None of the Above: Puerto Ricans in the Global Era* (2007).

18. My thanks to the anonymous reviewer at the University of Minnesota Press for this observation.

19. Likewise, the terms "Hispanic" and "Latino" are complicated. As Shorris, Suzanne Oboler (1995), and others (Flores and Benmayor 1997, González 2000) point out, these pan-ethnic categories didn't exist prior to the 1970 census, when the U.S. government sought to quantify and catalog recent migrants from Latin America.

20. I am not implying that all Latina/os are immigrants or recent arrivals, nor that Latin America is a utopic space of unity. Rather, I point to affiliations that exist even within Latin America.

21. Galarza was a founding member of both the National Farm Workers Union and the Raza Unida Party. Colón was a lifelong member of the Communist Party USA, a member of several Puerto Rican nationalist groups, and an active trade union activist in New York. Acosta was involved with Católicos por la Raza and several other Chicano movement groups. He was also the Raza Unida Party candidate for Los Angeles County Sheriff in 1970.

22. Puerto Rican studies scholars have been attuned to the transnational dynamics of nationalism on both the island and mainland. Frances Negrón-Muntaner (2004) argues that Puerto Ricans compose what she calls an "ethno-nation," in part because of the bifurcated nature of the island and U.S.-based populations (roughly 3.4 million Puerto Ricans living on the mainland with 3.5 million on the island). Similarly, Jorge Duany characterizes Puerto Ricans as a "nation on the move" (2002, 2)—literally engaged in circular migrations between the island and the mainland that locate national identity in the experience of diaspora. These concepts aid in understanding how groups like the Young Lords embody a version of nationalism, despite the fact that Puerto Rico and Puerto Ricans conform to none of the traditional geographic, linguistic, or cultural terms that typically constitute nationhood. Juan Flores (2009) also emphasizes the importance of "cultural remittances" (4) from diasporic Puerto Rican communities in the United States to the constitution of island-based national identities.

23. For Hutcheon there are a variety of reasons why people cannot represent themselves in literary texts, ranging from lack of access to the means of literary

production, to methodological approaches of mainstream historical narratives. Women, formerly colonized subjects, and aggrieved ethnic and racial groups must therefore constitute their texts through always already partial and fragmentary literary forms.

1. Zigzagging through History

1. Denning dates the age of the Congress of Industrial Organizations (CIO) from roughly 1935 until 1953. For Denning, the residue of this period extends through the early 1960s.

2. While I use the International Publishers edition of *A Puerto Rican in New York* issued in 1982 in this chapter, the original Masses and Mainstreams edition was published in 1961. My analysis considers the book within the historical context of the 1930s through the 1950s, when most of the sketches were originally written.

3. Nicholas Kanellas (1989) has suggested that despite the fact that his reputation as a writer never reached the national recognition achieved by Galarza, Colón was well known in New York leftist circles. Given that he was one of the earliest Chicana/o recipients of a PhD from Columbia, Galarza likely would have appealed to Colón's nascent Latina/o consciousness. Since both moved in similar leftist circles, it is likely that they would have had at least a passing acquaintance with one another.

4. While Latina/o communities have existed in what is now the United States since at least the early *Californio* settlements of the sixteenth century, the early twentieth century was an era of rapid growth. During the Mexican Revolution (1910–20), nearly a million Mexican nationals crossed the border into the United States. At midcentury, the Bracero Program brought a new influx of Mexican immigrants. During roughly the same period, the policies of development on the island of Puerto Rico that came to be known as Operation Bootstrap sparked another major migration. The anti-immigrant sentiment and racialization that greeted newly arrived Latina/os artificially suppressed wages and life chances for migrants and immigrants. For more on the history of Chicana/o and Puerto Rican communities in the United States, see Gutiérrez (1995), Acuña (2007), Sánchez Korrol (1994), Matos Rodríguez and Hernández (2001), and Acosta-Belén and Santiago (2006). See also González (2000).

5. Many critics point to the sometimes problematic positions the Communist Party USA (CPUSA) held in relation to race and ethnicity. Figures like Richard Wright (who eventually reconciled with the party) and Ralph Ellison (whose relationship with the party, as Arnold Ramparsad [2007] notes, was more complicated than he reported) highlighted their estrangement from the CPUSA because of questions about persistent antiblack racism. During the past thirty years, much scholarship has shown that the CPUSA held a more complex view of race,

ethnicity, and class, including advocating for certain types of nationalism. See, for example, Paul Buhle (1987) *Marxism in the USA*, Philip Bart et al. (1979) *Highlights of a Fighting History*, and Winston James (1998) *Holding Aloft the Banner of Ethiopia*.

6. The San Francisco general strike began on May 9, 1934, as a work stoppage engineered by the International Longshoreman's Association (ILA). What began as a strike at ILA local chapters 38–79 grew into a citywide general strike that eventually involved nearly all maritime workers. By July 16, approximately 130,000 workers engaged in a sympathy strike, bringing much of San Francisco to a halt. The strike ended on July 27, but not before violence resulted in two deaths and sixty-seven injuries.

The Little Steel Strike of 1937 was organized and led by the newly formed CIO. The strike was designed to organize several smaller steel manufacturers (including Republic, Bethlehem, and Inland Steel) who were antiunion to that point. On Memorial Day of 1937, a crowd of workers marched on a Republic steel mill in Chicago, resulting in violent police repression that left ten marchers dead, with another eighty wounded. The Little Steel Strike was defeated, in part due to President Roosevelt's refusal to pressure the steel companies into a labor agreement.

7. Antonio Gramsci's concept of the organic intellectual was based on the idea that in advanced capitalist societies, all people are intellectuals. But those that are intellectuals by social function (academics, managers, and professionals) often serve as experts at legitimating the hegemonic order. In contrast to "traditional intellectuals," Gramsci championed the concept of organic intellectuals produced by working-class social movements. Organic intellectuals emerge from and have ties to the working class but are able to ascend the class structure by serving in social roles occupied by traditional intellectuals. For Gramsci, organic intellectuals are crucial to the mobilization of counterhegemony for two reasons. First, they are able to recruit traditional intellectuals to working-class struggles. Second is the organic intellectual's ability to reflect and advance the concerns of the working classes within hegemonic society. Organic intellectuals are charged with enacting a politics of transformation through their working lives. The organic intellectual engages in both traditional intellectual life (theorizing, writing, analysis) and in active working-class struggles.

8. Francisco I. Madero, the son of a wealthy landowner in Parras, Coahuila, ran for president of Mexico against Porfirio Díaz on a platform of land reform under the hacienda system. Madero was imprisoned after Díaz was declared president. He jumped bail and fled to the United States. In 1910, Madero led the successful overthrow of Díaz. In 1911, he was elected president, but his administration lasted only two years. He was overthrown and killed by forces loyal to Victoriano Huerta and Pascual Orozco in 1913.

9. For more on Galarza's biography, see the Online Archive of California biography that accompanies Galarza's papers at Stanford University at http://www.oac.cdlib.org.

10. The term "acculturation" is Galarza's. I should note that despite the term's ideological baggage, Galarza seems to have had a critical relationship with the concept of cultural assimilation. See, for example, my reading of Young Ernie's schooling later in this chapter.

11. I refer to the protagonist as Young Ernie in contradistinction to the author, Galarza.

12. The lack of borders in Jalco is underscored by Galarza's exhaustive description of the boundaries of each subsequent barrio: Tepic, Mazatlán, and Sacramento. For one salient example, see Galarza's description of the Mercado in Tepic (87–89).

13. Locke's "Second Treatise" (1988) suggests that securing "life, liberty, and property" is the solemn and moral philosophical duty of government. This phrase was famously glossed by Thomas Jefferson as "life, liberty, and the pursuit of happiness." As scholars such as Mills (1997) and Macpherson (1964) have noted, however, the United States has maintained the original meaning of Locke's phrase.

14. This point is underscored by Galarza's negative portrayal of civil authorities. From the rurales that "protect" the interests of *los ricos* (the rich) in Tepic, to the police in Sacramento, civil authority protects the interests of the ruling classes in the narrative.

15. Later in the text, Galarza notes that those who had ventured away from Jalco to work in the hacienda system quickly learned the differences between a subsistence economy and the demands of capitalist exploitation: "in the company store every centavo you earned was taken back by a clerk who kept numbers in a book that proved you always owed him something. If a peon left the hacienda before his contract was over and his debts were paid, he became a fugitive" (58–59).

16. Galarza and his family move to Jalco from the town of Miramar. While Galarza was born in Jalco, he emphasizes his *arrival to* a space that is characterized by its long—and separate—historical context.

17. Galarza notes that the "proof [of this history] were the Coras and Huicholes themselves. They passed through Jalco from time to time along our street, silent and shy, dressed in embroidered cotton clothes and wearing flat-brimmed hats decorated with feathers" (43).

18. Galarza's epigraph quotes from *The Education of Henry Adams*, emphasizing the educational aspect of Young Ernie's acculturation in the United States. This expectation is reversed, however, by the fact that the quote emphasizes autobiographical narration as a symbolic, rather than mimetic, narrative form.

19. My thanks to Tania Triana for this connection.

20. A point that is underscored by Young Ernie's uncle Don Gustavo's comment, "Coronel is smart. *Zopilotes* are very chicken. They will fight among themselves, but

if it's alive they won't even fight a fly" (32). I should also note that Gustavo calls the *zopilotes* "chicken," again highlighting the gendered nature of Galarza's rhetoric.

21. El Pipila (a.k.a. Juan José de los Reyes Martínez) was an indigenous miner from San Miguel de Allende. He distinguished himself in battle at Guanajuato when he helped take the Granaditas Corn Exchange by strapping a flagstone to his back to deflect gunfire. So armored, El Pipila set fire to the door of the exchange, allowing his compañeros to overrun the building.

22. Young Ernie explains, "The story of that tune [José] told me many times: the Empress Carlota who went completely daffy because she was unable to persuade President Benito Juárez to pardon her husband, the Emperor Maximilian, who was shot by a firing squad" (134).

23. Emperor Maximilian was installed as Mexican monarch in April of 1864 by the combined forces of Napoleon III, the Habsburg family, and monarchists in Mexico. His rule was highly unpopular in Mexico and abroad. Maximilian was overthrown in 1867 by Benito Juarez, the first mestizo leader of Mexico. As José's song recounts, Maximilian was executed in June of 1867. For more on Maximilian and his reign, see Jasper Ridley's popular history *Maximilian and Juarez* (2002).

24. The ideological baggage that accompanies multiculturalism and cultural pluralism are problematic (to say the least) for communities of color. I use them to underscore the fact that people of color in the United States are so outside a system of "legitimate" representation that the only forms of encounter available to someone like Miss Ryan are the problematic models of assimilation, multiculturalism, or cultural pluralism.

25. Jesús's older brother, Joaquín, was also an important activist and writer. See Winston James's discussion of Joaquín Colón (1998, 224–26). See also Joaquín Colón's history of the Puerto Rican colonia in New York, *Pioneros puertorriqueños en Nueva York* (2001).

26. Colón did complete his high school education in New York City in June of 1922. See "Jesús is Graduating Tonight" in *The Way It Was and Other Writings*.

27. See *A Puerto Rican in New York*, especially "Stowaway," "On the Docks it Was Cold," and "Easy Job, Good Wages."

28. *El lector* was a hired worker who read to cigar workers during their repetitive work. The tradition of *el lector* began in Cuba in the 1860s, spreading quickly to Puerto Rico and other parts of the Caribbean. When Cuban and Puerto Rican cigar makers began to immigrate to cigar centers in Tampa, Key West, and New York during the late nineteenth and the early twentieth centuries, they brought with them the tradition of *el lector*. *Lectores* were often respected and educated members of the community who were conversant in political philosophy and contemporary literature. Importantly, *el lector* was hired by cigar workers rather than factory owners. They thus catered the reading to workers' interests. As Bernardo Vega recalls, reading lists were often generated by a committee of cigarmakers (1984, 21–22). *El*

lector usually sat on an elevated platform, reading from political and literary texts throughout the day. Colón describes a typical day's readings: "In the morning, the reader used to read the daily paper and some working class weeklies or monthlies that were published or received from abroad. In the afternoon he would read from a novel by Zola, Balzac, Hugo, or from a book by Kropotkin, Malatesta or Karl Marx. Famous speeches like Castelar's or Spanish classical novels like Cervantes's *Don Quixote* were also read aloud by *'El lector'*" (1982, 11). For more on the tradition of *el lector*, see James (1998, 214–16), Quintero-Rivera (1983), and Pérez (1995). See also Bernardo Vega's chapter "The Customs and Traditions of the *Tabaqueros* and What It Was Like to Work in a Cigar Factory in New York City."

29. As Angel Quintero Rivera (1983) notes, *tabaqueros* were fundamental to the organization of the Socialist Party in Puerto Rico. Not coincidentally, the party was founded in Cayey, Colón's hometown, in 1915. Edna Acosta-Belén and Virginia Sánchez Korrol (1993, 22) point out that Colón, who was just fourteen, immediately joined the Federación Libre de Trabajadores and its political organ the Puerto Rican Socialist Party that same year.

30. The *Daily Worker* ceased daily publication in 1957. From 1958 to 1968 it became a weekend paper called *The Worker*. In 1961, a Tuesday edition titled *The Midweek Worker* was added. It also ran until 1968. In 1968, the party resumed a daily publication, this time titled the *Daily World* and renamed in 1986 the *People's Daily World*. In 1991, the party again ceased publication of a daily paper, producing instead *The People's Weekly World*. *The People's Weekly World* continues to run in both print and online versions.

31. The Jefferson School of Social Science was a Marxist adult-education school sponsored by the CPUSA. At its high point, the school enrolled over five thousand students. In 1956, the Subversion Activities Control board forced the closure of the school. For more on the Jefferson School, see the *Guide to the Jefferson School of Social Sciences (New York, N.Y.) Records and Indexes 1931–1958*, http://dlib.nyu.edu/findingaids/html/tamwag/jefferson.html.

32. In 1953, Colón ran for city council in New York, running for state assembly a year later. In 1969, he was the Communist Party candidate for New York City comptroller. For an interesting discussion of Colón's 1969 bid for city comptroller, see Silvio Torres-Saillant's (2003) discussion of the campaign.

33. For example, I conducted database searches of the EBSCO, MLA International Bibliography, ChicanoDatabase, Handbook of Latin American Studies, HAPI, Google Scholar, and Caribbean Abstracts databases in August of 2010. The search resulted in two dissertations, four book chapters, and a handful of journal articles that deal primarily with Colón and his work.

34. There is much to admire in James's *Holding Aloft the Banner of Ethiopia*, not the least of which is his fine historical perspective on antiblack racism both within and outside Puerto Rican colonias in Manhattan and Brooklyn during the early

twentieth century (223–28). I do not agree, however, with James's false dichotomy between Schomburg as a *race man* and Colón as a *class man*. While James is correct to point to Colón's views on race as evolving over time, his argument renders him little more than a straw man to Schomburg's fervent alignment with Marcus Garvey and early black nationalisms. As Adalaine Holton (2007) points out, James makes several reductionist statements, including his suggestions that Colón was "out of his depth when it came to the madness of race in America," and "it was as if his (Colón's) mind was too cultivated and civilized, his instincts too decent, generous, and human for him to have plumbed the stinking depths of American racism" (James 1998, 222). Leaving aside the fact that both statements contradict James's argument earlier in the chapter regarding the evolution of Colón's antiracist politics, understanding Colón as "too refined" to comprehend race ignores the antiracist positions he consistently enumerates in his writing. For more on Colón's view of race, see "Little Things are Big," "Maceo," and "The Mother, the Daughter, Myself, and All of Us" in *A Puerto Rican in New York*. See also "The Head on the Statue of Liberty," "The Two United States" (originally published as "Los otros Estados Unidos" in Colón's column in *Pueblos Hispanos*), "Little Rock," "The Negro in Puerto Rican History," "The Negro in Puerto Rico Today" in *The Way It Was and Other Writings*, and his letter to Paul Robeson (undated; The Jesús Colón Papers; 1983–01box 2; folder 6; Archives of the Puerto Rican Diaspora, Centro de Estudios Puertorriqueños Archives, Hunter College, CUNY).

35. Colón appeared before the House Un-American Activities Committee (HUAC) on November 16, 1959. He was summoned again in 1963. The summons was canceled on May 1, 1963, just five days before he was to appear. See "Statement by Jesús Colón to the Walter Committee on Un-American Activities" in *The Way it Was and Other Writings* and the Western Union telegram cancelling his summons (May 1, 1963; The Jesús Colón Papers; 1983–01; box 2; folder 3; Archives of the Puerto Rican Diaspora, Centro de Estudios Puertorriqueños Archives, Hunter College, CUNY).

36. For more on the Puerto Rican Student Union (PRSU), see Andrés Torres's introduction and Basilio Serrano's *"¡Rifle, Cañon, y Escopeta!: A Chronicle of the Puerto Rican Student Union"* in *The Puerto Rican Movement: Voices from the Diaspora* (1998).

37. As Colón notes, "There is hardly a nation that is not represented in the various statues that decorate the parks, museums, libraries, streets and avenues of this city. Every nationality save the Puerto Ricans has a statue" (135).

38. Thanks again to Tania Triana for this insight.

2. Crazy for the Nation

1. Even though he is a proponent of independence for Puerto Rico and a prison rights activist, Thomas was not aligned with any particular movement group. As

Michael Hames-García observes, however, writers like Thomas and Miguel Piñero "see their identities as prisoners (or as ex-cons) as having profound social and political implications, rather than as just an individual condition" (2004, 143).

2. While I use the 1989 Vintage editions for my comments about *The Revolt of the Cockroach People* and my subsequent references to Acosta's first novel, *The Autobiography of a Brown Buffalo*, the novels were originally published in 1973 and 1972. My comments consider the novels within the historical and social context of the late 1960s and early 1970s.

3. This is not to suggest that there weren't established Latina/o populations in cities prior to World War II. The Puerto Rican colonia in New York dates to the mid-nineteenth century. Likewise, the Mexican and Chicana/o enclaves in Los Angeles have historical roots that date to the late eighteenth century.

4. Title I of the Housing Act of 1949 (also called the Urban Renewal Program) provided for the destruction of inner-city neighborhoods in favor of roughly 800,000 new housing units nationwide. Coupled with federal urban redevelopment plans like Title III of the Housing Act of 1954, these policies disproportionately affected people of color. By the 1970s roughly 100,000 African Americans were displaced in New York City alone. All told, the urban redevelopment plans of the 1940s through the 1970s resulted in the demolition of 600,000 housing units, displacing 2 million tenants. For more on urban redevelopment see Judd and Kantor (2001).

5. Numerous historians and cultural critics have documented the importance of the zoot-suiter for contemporary Chicana/o and Latina/o communities. See, for example, Acuña (2007, 197–219) and Gutiérrez (1995, 123–25). For more recent studies of zoot suit culture, see Alvarez (2008) and Ramírez (2009).

6. Many Latina/o artists have cited the *vato loco* as a descendent of the pachuco. See Edward James Olmos's depiction of Santana as the son of pachucos in the film *American Me* (1992), Ron Arias's representation of Mario in *The Road to Tamazunchale* (1997), and the Hernández brothers' Speedy Ortiz in the *Love and Rockets* graphic novels. See also Malcolm X's reminiscence of his life as a zoot-suiter in *The Autobiography of Malcolm X* (1964).

7. In his position paper "Racial Exclusion," Acosta suggests that "*Machismo*, that instinctual and mystical source of manhood, honor and pride that alone justifies all behavior" (1996, 284) serves as the foundation for *vato loco* subjectivity.

8. All biographical information comes from Piri Thomas, *The World of Piri Thomas: Poet, Writer, Storyteller*, the official Piri Thomas web page (http://www.cheverote.com/piri.html).

9. http://www.cheverote.com.

10. http://www.cheverote.com/texts/theworldofpt.html.

11. Ibid.

12. According to a recent editorial in *The New York Times* (2008), nearly one in one hundred U.S. citizens is currently incarcerated. Alarmingly, one in nine black

men and one in thirty-six Latina/os are serving prison time. The total prison population in the United States has reached 1.6 million, "surpassing all other countries for which there are reliable figures." The National Center on Institutions and Alternatives reports that nonwhites account for over 70 percent of the increased prison population, with Latinos experiencing an incarceration rate 3.7 percent higher than whites. A 2002 Human Rights Watch report shows that between 4 and 8 percent of the *total* Latino adult male population is currently incarcerated in four states.

13. I use Piri to distinguish between author and protagonist in *Down These Mean Streets*.

14. As Frances Negrón-Muntaner explains, "A symptom that *West Side Story* remains a constitutive site for AmeRícan ethno-national identification is the fact that although the film is neither the first nor last portrayal of Puerto Ricans as criminal men and 'fiery' women, hardly any *boricua* cultural critic, activist, or screen actor can refrain from stating their own very special relationship to *West Side Story*" (2004, 58–59). Clearly, I am not immune to this impulse.

15. For example, in "How to be a Negro Without Really Trying," Piri experiences job discrimination when he applies for employment with the ironically named Mr. Christian. Mr. Christian employs the "white" applicants, while rejecting the "blacks," including Piri. Similarly, Piri's difficulty in procuring housing parallels literary representations by African American authors like Anne Petry (1946), Richard Wright (1945), and James Baldwin (1953).

16. Despite the fact that a recent mitochondrial DNA study showed that a majority of Puerto Ricans have some genetic component of indigenous blood, the phenotypic expression of these traits are rarely visible in the population. For more on the study, see Kearns (1999).

17. The scene also underscores sociology's imbrication as a discipline with assimilation and white supremacy. For more, see Horsman (1981), Gossett (1997), and Lipsitz (1998, 2001).

18. Thomas is explicit about engaging these authors in an essay on his web page: "I wrote about the conditions of life in the barrio back then, but in spite of books like *Down These Mean Streets* and *Manchild in the Promised Land* (by Claude Brown) and *The Wretched Of The Earth* (by Frantz Fanon), alas, the same conditions still exist for the poor today" (http://cheverote.com/texts/introduction.html).

19. This theme continues in the chapter "Sex in the Can." When propositioned by a man named Claude, Piri swears, "I ain't gonna break. One time. That's all I have to do it. Just one time and it's gone time. I'll be screwing faggots as fast as I can get them. I'm not gonna get institutionalized. I don't want to lose my hatred of this damn place" (263).

20. This idea returns more violently when Piri "passes" for Puerto Rican with a white prostitute in Jim Crow Texas. Aided by a Chicano comrade, Piri has sex with

the woman, subsequently telling her, "I just want you to know [. . .] that you got fucked by a nigger, *by a black man!*" (189).

21. Shimberlee Jirón-King (2008) makes a compelling case that the Gonzo journalism style was collaboratively created by Thompson and Acosta through a series of political and literary projects, including Acosta's two novels and Thompson's (1996) *Fear and Loathing in Las Vegas* and *Fear and Loathing: On the Campaign Trail '72*.

22. Acosta ran for Sheriff under the Raza Unida Party banner. Although his 107,000 votes didn't present a serious challenge to eventual winner Sheriff Peter Pitchess, he placed second in the voting—ahead of Everett Holladay, then Monterey Park chief of police.

23. Genaro Padilla (1984), for example, considers the author's work as an elaboration of "collective" autobiography, whereby Zeta discovers himself through his self-identification as Chicano. Similarly, Ramón Saldívar (1990) argues that Acosta's novels "fashion out of the instability and fragmentation of social life a utopian vision of collective action" (74). More recently, Michael Hames-García (2004) advocates understanding Acosta's novels as a part of a carnivalesque tradition that satirizes essentialist notions of identity and political action within the Chicana/o movement.

24. I will refer to Zeta as the protagonist of the novel in contradistinction to Acosta as author.

25. It is, however, important to recall that, as Rosaura Sánchez (1995) reminds us, there are important distinctions between upper-class California ranchers and working-class Chicana/os in contemporary settings.

26. It is also important to consider the novel's general lampooning of nonviolent protests. At the demonstration over the arrest of the St. Basil's Twenty-One, Zeta and other protestors engage in a hunger strike of sorts. Yet in contrast to Chávez's solitary and somber hunger strike, the gathering has the flavor of an outdoor festival, complete with musical entertainment and problematic sexual escapades (Acosta 1989b, 78–88).

27. Chávez's 1968 hunger strike was initiated to draw national attention to the ongoing grape strike that began in 1965. The hunger strike ran for twenty-five days, during which Chávez organized the national boycott on grapes. By 1970, the UFW settled on a new contract with grape growers that included health care benefits and increased wages.

28. The culminating incident in the novel is the bombing of the hall of justice after Zeta wins the Corky González murder trial. The final bombing underscores a progressive move from nonviolence to mediated violence (in the bombing of the Safeway store after the Robert Fernández inquest) to the unmitigated use of violence as a tactic for overturning the prevailing social order (Acosta 1989b, 254–58).

29. For example, *El Plan de Santa Barbara* privileges higher education as a primary site of struggle.

30. As the first *vato* Zeta meets, Gilbert represents the epitome of the *vato loco*. While Zeta comes to adopt Gilbert's *vato* subjectivity, he initially suspects Gilbert's politics. This conflict is figured as Zeta's estrangement from an "authentic" Chicano identity. Zeta's subsequent embrace of Gilbert as one of his key interlocutors symbolizes his evolution to a *vato loco* (i.e., authentic) subjectivity.

31. Decrying the Church's refusal to support the UFW grape boycott and the building of the $4 million St. Basil's Cathedral, Católicos por la Raza staged a series of protests, beginning on December 7, 1969, and culminating on Christmas Eve. The Christmas Eve protest escalated when protestors tried to interrupt the service at St. Basil's. As Acosta documents in *Revolt*, the Christmas Eve protestors were met by LAPD officers disguised as ushers. The officers were supported by uniformed police, who arrived for "mop-up" operations after plainclothes police had already beaten and maced fifteen, arresting seven.

32. For example, when Zeta drives to Jean Fisher's home in Watts, he notes that "the faded buildings are covered with slogans and grafitti [*sic*] the same as in Tooner Flats. It is an older war zone. The debris, the burnt buildings, the vacant lots, the For Sale signs are testimony to that early battle of the sixties" (Acosta 1989b, 164). While the comparison between the graffiti in Watts and Tooner Flats hint at common experiences of racialization and economic discrimination, Acosta's suggestion that Watts composes an "early battle of the sixties" is also important. By suggesting that it is one in a series of battles, the 1965 Watts uprising is figured as an ideological and political precursor of the Chicana/o movement.

33. It is also significant that Zeta presides over the autopsy performed to determine the inquest. As he attempts to ascertain "the truth," Zeta essentially directs the mutilation and disarticulation of Fernández's body. This portrayal suggests that even as one attempts to hold the state accountable, one is doomed to reinscribe violence and silence. As Zeta notes in the final lines of the chapter, "For the rest of my born days, I will suffer the knowledge of your death and your second death" (104).

3. Remaking the Insurgent Vision

1. Azaldúa describes the process through which individuals come to practice *la facultad*: "Those who are pushed out of the tribe for being different are likely to become more sensitized (when not brutalized into insensitivity). Those who do not feel psychologically or physically safe in the world are more apt to develop this sense. Those who are pounced on the most have it the strongest—the female, the homosexuals of all races, the darkskinned, the outcast, the persecuted, the marginalized, the foreign" (60).

2. Anzaldúa goes further by suggesting that contemporary machismo is a function of racism: "The modern meaning of the word 'machismo,' as well as the concept, is actually an Anglo invention. For men like my father, being 'macho' meant being

strong enough to protect and support my mother and us, yet being able to show love. Today's macho has doubts about his ability to feed and protect his family. His '*machismo*' is an adaptation to oppression and poverty and low self-esteem" (2007, 105).

3. See also point 10 of the Young Lords 13-Point Platform: "Under capitalism, our women have been oppressed by both the society and our own men. The doctrine of machismo has been used by our men to take out their frustrations against their wives, sisters, mothers, and children. Our men must support their women in their fight for economic and social equality, and must recognize that our women are equals in every way within the revolutionary ranks" (Young Lords Party, 1993).

4. Dolores Huerta cofounded the United Farm Workers Union with César Chávez. Paula Crisostomo was an architect of the Chicano "blowouts" that led more than 20,000 Chicana/o students to walk out of their classes in March of 1968. Esperanza Martell and Elizabeth Figueroa helped found El Comité/Movimiento de Izquierda Nacional Puertorriqueño (MINP).

5. Despite his relative acceptance into the canon of Chicano literature since Juan Bruce-Novoa's 1988 essay, "Homosexuality and the Chicano Novel," Rechy has pointed to the problematic position his work occupies within Chicana/o studies: "Since as far back as 1959, I was writing about 'Mexican-Americans,' and identifying myself as such, in the *Nation, Evergreen Review, Saturday Review*. In virtually all my novels, the protagonist's mother is Mexican, like mine. Still, I've known the question to be asked, whether or not I'm a 'real Chicano writer.' Why? Because I wrote also about homosexuality?" (1995, 113).

6. A notable exception is Amalia Gómez, the protagonist of Rechy's 1991 novel *The Miraculous Day of Amalia Gómez*.

7. As the narrator/Jim notes in the opening chapter of *The Sexual Outlaw*, "Jim—he calls himself that sometimes, sometimes Jerry, sometimes John" (23).

8. When speaking of his relationship to street hustling, the narrator/Jim says "even when I had good jobs, I was on the streets recurrently, pulled back as if by a powerful lover. *Even when* City of Night *was riding the best-seller lists*. I've seen copies of my books in the houses of people who have picked me up anonymously" (153; emphasis mine).

9. See for example Anaya's *Heart of Aztlán* (1976) and Valdez's *Zoot Suit* (1992).

10. José Saldívar is particularly interested in the resonance of Aztec warriors with the Chicana/o movement in *The Miraculous Day of Amalia Gómez*: "If 'Aztlán es una fabula,' it is partly so because its Chicano youth philosophy glorifying Aztec warriors while at the same time excluding women is itself a deception" (1997, 117).

11. As the narrator/Jim notes, "There would be commendable honesty in the S&M world if someone would admit: 'I want to be hurt and humiliated because I hate myself.' The hypocrisy comes when one calls it love. I find the inflicting of pain or the inviting of pain repugnant. I love the rush of being submitted to sexually—but that's different from inflicting pain" (68).

12. Rodríguez's argument in *Brown* centers on how recognizing race is a disservice to people of color because it separates them from mainstream culture. This reading ignores the historical exclusion of people of color and the centering of a white European subject as the primary "ingredient" to the "melting pot."

13. Unlike Rechy, Rodríguez disidentifies with both his sexual and ethnic identities. For example, Rodríguez refers to himself as "sexually secretive," barely acknowledging his homosexuality (2002, 14).

14. When asked in an interview how she feels she can "*adelantar la causa*" (advance the cause), Ortiz Cofer responds, "I feel very strongly that I am contributing in the only way I know how to contribute. If I were a musician and cared for my country, I would write music that exemplified that. I would not be a soldier, I would be a musician. I am a writer, I am not a political activist. When I wrote about those lives lived in poverty, those lives lived in naïveté and fear in Paterson, what I was doing was presenting a picture of the difficulties of Puerto Rican life in that city" (Acosta-Bélen 1993, 85–86).

15. For example, there is a long history of migration from the island to colonias in Tampa, Chicago, Paterson, Boston, Hawaii, and Hartford. For more on migration to centers outside of New York, see Clara Rodríguez's *Puerto Ricans: Born in the U.S.A.* (1989) and Edna Acosta-Bélen and Carlos E. Santiago's *Puerto Ricans in the United States: A Contemporary Portrait* (2006).

16. It is important that Ortiz Cofer does not reject the Nuyorican school: "The Nuyorican writers have nourished me in the sense that it is good to know that they are completing the mosaic of Puerto Rican literature in the United States. There is not just one reality to being a Puerto Rican writer. I am putting together a different view" (1992, 45)

17. As Bridget Kevane (2003) notes, Operation Bootstrap and the policies of development and industrialization that led to the dissolution of rural life on the island during the late 1940s and early 1950s provide part of the historical backdrop for the novel. Guzmán's immigration via an illegal labor recruiter has historical resonance with the lottery system that provided cheap labor for businesses in the United States, while also exporting "surplus population" from the island. Illegal labor recruiters often preyed on men like Guzmán, who came from dire economic circumstances but did not "win" immigration via the lottery. Indeed, there were two major strategies on the part of both the U.S. and island governments to control population on the island. One was immigration (as symbolized by Guzmán's interaction with the labor recruiter), the other was the sterilization of island women. For more on sterilization, see Laura Briggs's *Reproducing Empire: Race, Sex, Science, and U.S. Imperialism in Puerto Rico* (2003).

18. *Santería* is a syncretic religious practice that combines aspects of Catholicism with West African spiritual traditions. Largely practiced in Puerto Rico, Cuba, and the Dominican Republic, *Santería* is similar to other syncretic

traditions like Voodoo, Brazilian Candomblé, and Obeah. For readers unfamiliar with *Santería*, see Mercedes Cros Sandoval's *Worldview, the Orichas, and Santería: Africa to Cuba and Beyond* (2006).

19. In the epilogue, Marisol notes, "I concluded that the only way to understand a life is to write it as a story, to fill in the blanks left by circumstance, lapses of memory, and failed communication" (290).

20. As Marisol explains, "In my mind I had made his life story mine. I had kept track of him through my mother's stories, Mamá Cielo's letters, and all those late-night conversations I had stolen from my parents when they thought I was sleeping in my room. I had filled the gaps with my imagination until Guzmán had shown up at our door; then I had become his secret biographer, drawing excitement from all he represented to me" (282).

21. According to Angela Jorge (1995), *Mesa Blanca* in Puerto Rico is based on the writings of Allen Kardec, one of the "fathers of modern spiritism" (110). *Mesa Blanca* promotes a belief in the existence of spirits and in the ability of the living to communicate with the dead" (110). Interestingly, Jorge dates the development of *Mesa Blanca* to New York State, from which it was exported to Puerto Rico in the mid-19th century.

22. See, for example, Cisneros's *Caramelo* (2002a), Alvarez's *In the Time of the Butterflies* (1994) and *In the Name of Salomé* (2000), García's *Dreaming in Cuban* (1992), and Castillo's *So Far from God* (1993).

23. Marisol is particularly critical of Ramona's inability to adapt to Paterson: "On the streets of Paterson my mother seemed an alien and a refugee, and as I grew to identify with the elements she feared, I dreaded walking with her, a human billboard advertising her paranoia in a foreign language" (174). Marisol is also critical of her mother's docility, noting that she often conforms to her father Rafael's wishes even while he is at sea.

4. I Can't Be Me without My People

1. Rafael Leonidas Trujillo y Molina ruled the Dominican Republic from 1931 until his assassination in 1961. For more on the Trujillo regime, see Ignacio López-Calvo's *God and Trujillo: Literary and Cultural Representations of the Dominican Republic* (2005) and Lauren Derby's *The Dictator's Seduction: Politics and the Popular Imagination in the Era of Trujillo* (2009). For fictional accounts, see Mario Vargas Llosa's *The Feast of the Goat* (2001), Edwidge Danticat's *The Farming of Bones* (1998), and Junot Díaz's *The Brief Wondrous Life of Oscar Wao* (2007).

2. While several critics (Brown 2000; Stefanko 1996; McCallum 2000) have authored generative articles on genre blending in Alvarez's fiction, none have connected this narrative style with alternative historiography. Likewise, no genre

exists in a "pure" form, making the blending of genres that Alvarez deploys complex and multiply determined.

3. For more on historical trauma see Santner (1990), Felman and Laub (1992), and LaCapra (2001).

4. Mitchell (1999) and Martínez (1998) present compelling arguments on history in Alvarez's work. Again, my argument focuses on how Alvarez reimagines history to work through historical trauma.

5. See McCracken (1999), Brown (2000), and Johnson (2005).

6. Aida Cartagena Portalatín was a poet, essayist, and novelist born in 1918 in Moca, Dominican Republic. She was a member of the *poesía sorprendida* movement, a surrealist poetic style. Cartagena Portalatín was the author of seven poetry editions, a collection of short stories, and several scholarly anthologies. She is best known for her 1969 novel *Escalera para Electra*. Cartagena Portalatín died in 1994.

7. Derby suggests that the spectacle of sexual conquest was a primary way the regime exerted its power and elicited complicity from the public: "Trujillo's power and charisma were based on the consumption of women (and their status) through sexual conquest as well as the domination of enemies of state, and on the near mythological fear and resultant aura he acquired through eliminating men. Whereas Trujillo's insatiable sexual cupidity brought ignominy, it also brought respect and was a key element in his legitimacy as a caudillo-turned-statesman, respeto being a term which conjoins masculinity, authority, and legitimacy" (2009, 111).

8. In the wake of Trujillo, a series of regimes came to power through legal elections, coups, and countercoups. Among the presidents who held power were Trujillo's former vice-president, Joaquin Balaguer (1961–62), Rafael Bonnelly (1962–63), Juan Bosch (1963), a triumvirate headed by Donald Reid Cabral (1963–65), and Francisco Caamaño (1965). While Trujillo effectively closed the island, virtually prohibiting immigration of any kind, the Dominican Republic was opened by subsequent dictators, especially Balaguer. In 1965, Lyndon Johnson green-lighted Operation Power Pack, an invasion of the island designed to restore order. The invasion overturned the constitutionalist forces attempting to return the left-leaning Bosch (the only legally elected president of the period) to power, installing Balaguer. While Balaguer was somewhat more progressive than Trujillo, he essentially continued the dictator's policies. The invasion of 1965 and Balaguer's subsequent liberalization of immigration policies did, however, initiate the first substantial wave of Dominican migration to the United States. While Alvarez and her family were already in the United States by the mid-1960s, the census of 1980 showed between 150,000 and 200,000 Dominicans migrating to the United States during the 1960s. Immigration again soared in the 1980s, bringing half a million Dominicans to the United States, with more emigrating to Spain, Puerto Rico, and other countries.

9. For a few examples, see C. L. R. James's *The Black Jacobins* (1989), Aimé Césaire's *Discourse on Colonialism* (2001), and Frantz Fanon's *Black Skin, White Masks* (1968).

10. Trujillo instituted policies designed to "whiten" the race, including encouraging immigration from Spain. His most infamous action was the genocide of Haitians living in the Dominican Republic. On October 2, 1937, Trujillo ordered the execution of all Haitians. While the final death toll will never be known, estimates range between fifteen thousand and fifty thousand Haitians massacred by Trujillo's forces.

11. For example, in *¡Yo!*, the García's second daughter, Sandi, has a baby via a Dominican sperm donor. Even though the García's mother, Laura, assures them that "Dr. Puello screened the sperm," the family exhibits a high degree of racial anxiety at the baby's "dark olive" complexion and "kinky hair." Carlos García even suggests that the baby is "suntanned" (16). Despite the obvious racial anxiety, we don't learn much about racial politics on the island, except through these veiled references. More important, the scene is symptomatic of the persistent elision of race in Alvarez's novels.

12. This point is underscored by the representations of other U.S. Dominican authors like Junot Díaz (1996, 2007) and Angie Cruz (2002, 2006), who place heavier emphasis on working-class characters and themes.

13. I use the term postmodern in the sense that Hutcheon (1989) outlines. Postmodernism rejects rigid genre distinctions, emphasizing pastiche, parody, bricolage, irony, and playfulness. Hutcheon argues that irony, play, and pastiche are political strategies that question master narratives of history and aesthetics. I also point to Lyotard's (1985) arguments that postmodernism questions stability and totality, as well as Néstor García Canclini's (1995) suggestion that postmodernism critiques modernism.

14. Citing a survey she conducted in one of her classes, McCracken writes, "after students had read *How the García Girls Lost Their Accents*, only six respondents knew the name of the dictator in power in the Dominican Republic during the events in Alvarez's book; thirty-seven students were unable to answer this question. Several students named Fidel Castro as the dictator in power at the time, and some answered that the setting was Puerto Rico or Cuba" (210, n. 6).

15. As Laub recalls, during a meeting of historians who questioned the veracity of a woman's testimony about the Auschwitz uprising,

A psychoanalyst [Laub] who had been one of the interviewers of this woman, profoundly disagreed. "The woman was testifying," he insisted, "not to the number of the chimneys blown up, but to something else, more radical, more crucial: the reality of an unimaginable occurrence. One chimney blown up in Auschwitz was as incredible as four. The number mattered less than the fact of the occurrence. The event itself was almost inconceivable. The woman testified to an event that broke the all compelling frame of Auschwitz, where Jewish armed revolts just did not happen, and had no place. She testified to the breakage of a framework. That was historical truth" (60).

16. When asked by Goodman about the autobiographical aspects of her first novel, Alvarez replies, "That's the way they always catch me! I say, no, but it's fiction! (laughing) They say, 'well did you have three sisters?' Well, yeah, I have three sisters. 'Well did you come from the Dominican Republic?' Well, yes, I came from the Dominican Republic" (1997a). See also her comments about the publication of her first novel in the essay "Family Matters" (1998).

17. I am not suggesting Spanish as a delimiter of Latina/o identity—a view that imagines Latina/os only as immigrants. In fact, many English-dominant Latina/os (including myself) are vital community members. The use of Spanish in this scene functions as a local signifier of Yo's dislocation rather than as a broad designation of Latina/o social trends. For more on the relationship between language and panethnic, Latina/o identity, see Shorris (1992), Oboler (1995), Benmayor and Flores (1997), Aparicio (1999), Gonzáles (2000), and Caminero-Santangelo (2007).

18. We should not underestimate threats to Mexicans and Puerto Ricans in the United States. Especially since the militarization of the border after 9/11, the increased surveillance of the Clinton and Bush era, and the racial profiling of "immigration reform" initiatives like SB 1070 in Arizona, undocumented immigration has been driven into the dangerous desert and mountain areas of the interior Southwest. Likewise, inner-city crime, drug abuse, racism, and housing shortages are real concerns for Puerto Ricans and other Latina/o groups in the United States. However, the political persecution that blocked free access to the homeland in Alvarez's case is more akin to the prohibitions many Central American and Cuban immigrants experienced during the last third of the twentieth century.

19. No less than eleven different governments vied for control of the Dominican Republic between 1843 and 1856.

20. UNICEF, *At a Glance: Dominican Republic*, March 2, 2010, http://www.unicef.org/infobycountry/domrepublic_statistics.html#79.

21. Alvarez describes Dedé's "zero" moment in almost prelapsarian terms: "She remembers a clear moonlit night before the future began. They are sitting in the cool darkness under the anacahuita tree in the front yard, in the rockers telling stories, drinking guanábana juice. Good for the nerves, Mamá always says" (8).

22. Alvarez replicates this narrative closure in "Chasing the Butterflies" when she details an experience she and her husband have while visiting the site of the sisters' murder. Alvarez and her husband meet caretakers for Trujillo's former mansion where the sisters are presumed to have been killed. After a rough account of the murder, the caretakers offer to take Alvarez to meet with one of "the old people who heard the crash" (208). Alvarez refuses, noting that "my heart was too full in this grim place. The night was falling. The overgrown garden, the brick

buildings, the padlocked doors, the mossy stones that rang with our footsteps were ominous. I said we had to go" (208).

23. I use the term melancholia in the sense Freud outlines in "Mourning and Melancholia" (1978). Freud distinguishes between affectively processing trauma (mourning) and reinscribing limit events (melancholia). He advocates that therapists assist trauma victims by engaging in appropriate forms of mourning.

24. I refer to the character in the novel as Camila to distinguish her from the historical figure Henríquez-Ureña.

25. Between 1844 and 1864, General Pedro Santana Familias and Buenaventura Báez Méndez vied for control of the Dominican Republic after the overthrow of French colonial authority. After their struggle for power led to the reannexation of the Dominican Republic by Spain, the nation was rife with political struggle between the conservative Red party and the Blues, who were centered in the southern regions of the country.

Conclusion

1. ABC News reports that an estimated 58 percent of U.S. citizens felt race relations had improved as a result of President Obama's election. While an ABC News / *Washington Post* survey in January of 2010 showed this number declined to 41 percent, U.S. media outlets continue to laud the postracial society.

2. My thanks to the anonymous reviewer at the University of Minnesota Press for this observation.

3. For a few examples of the move toward transnationalism within Latina/o, Chicana/o, and Puerto Rican studies see Jorge Duany's *The Puerto Rican Nation on the Move* (2002), Juan Flores's *The Diaspora Strikes Back: Caribeño Tales of Learning and Turning* (2009), Paula M. L. Moya and Ramón Saldívar's "Fictions of the Trans-American Imaginary" (2003), and Kirsten Silva Gruesz's *Ambassadors of Culture: The Transamerican Origins of Latino Writing* (2002).

4. Even in the field of American studies—perhaps historically the quintessential field of national studies—there has been a move toward the transnational. The advent of the *Journal of Transnational American Studies* edited by former American Studies Association president Shelley Fisher-Fishkin and the themes of the 2002 and 2007 American Studies Association annual meetings, The Local and the Global & Recovery Project/Redefining "Nuestra América" and América Aquí: Transhemispheric Visions and Community Connections, respectively, attest to these recent trends.

5. Saldívar explains that "African Americans Zadie Smith, Colson Whitehead, and Touré; Asian Americans Karen Tei Yamashita and Sesshu Foster; Native American Sherman Alexie; Latina and Latino writers Marta Acosta, Michelle Serros, Yxta Maya Murray, Salvador Plascencia, and Junot Díaz" (1997, 37, n.1) all utilize the postracial novel.

6. Thanks to George Lipsitz for this observation.

7. In addition to its modernist and postmodernist narrative strategies, the novel has been read as semiautobiographical. Like Celaya, Cisneros is the only sister in a seven-child family. Also like her protagonist, Cisneros made frequent summer trips to Mexico City to visit her paternal grandmother. Cisneros notes these autobiographical resonances in a 2002 interview. When asked about the disclaimer at the beginning of the novel, Cisneros says, "I actually wanted to admit that characters were based on real people. But I wanted to also say and be truthful that it's based on real people but it isn't autobiography. Many books that you read, they have those disclaimers that say that, 'None of the events and none of the people are based on real life and so on . . .' Well, I don't believe that. I think that as human beings many people touch us, especially people we love the most and we can't help but do character sketches when we go to our art. I felt that I was taking some real filaments of my life, some real memories, but I was embroidering from that and departing from that and leaping" (Cisneros, 2002c).

8. See Steinbeck's *Travels with Charlie in Search of America* (2002) and Kerouac's *On the Road* (1999). For more on ethnic American writers' reconfigurations of the road trip, see Marci L. Carrasquillo's discussion of *Caramelo* and other Chicana/o and ethnic American texts in her dissertation, "The Perfect Freedom: Travel and Mobility in Ethnic American Literature" (2006).

9. In an interview with Ray Suarez, Cisneros comments on this aspect of the novel. Speaking of the Reyeses' back-and-forth movement, she says, "something about growing up in Chicago that many Latino communities, or Anglo communities, aren't aware of is that how [sic] they consider Mexico as a commuter suburb, you know, that back and forth from the Midwest to Mexico" (Cisneros, 2002b).

10. Eleuterio's immigration to Mexico isn't unilateral either. He returns to Spain for a time when he finds out that Regina is pregnant. For more, see chapter 34, "How Narciso Falls into Disrepute Due to Sins of the Dangler."

11. One of many examples of Soledad's racism occurs when she dismisses Candelaria after her near drowning in Acapulco: "Get me out of this inferno of Indians, it smells worse than a pigsty" (79). A little later, Soledad chastises Zoila for her improper Spanish and indigenous appearance, saying, "you sound like you escaped from the ranch. And to make matters even more sad, you're as dark as a slave" (85). In addition to relating the indio to place (pigsty), social position through the body (level of phenotypic indigeneity), and speech patterns, Soledad also aligns indios with class: they are virtually always laborers in *Caramelo*. This relation of indios with lower-class standing may account for Soledad's inability to connect with working-class Mexicans in Chicago. Thanks to Marci Carrasquillo for this observation.

12. The relationship between Mars and Inocencio is a fascinating meditation on tensions between Chicana/o and Mexican national communities in the United

States. While Inocencio describes Mars's Spanish as sounding as if it "came from another planet," he does recognize Mars as a "Mexican from the other side" (280). To Inocencio's protest of $50 Mars loans him, Mars replies, "it's cause we're *raza ése*," "because we're *raza*, [. . .] Know what I'm talking about? Because we're *familia*. And *familia*, like it or not, for richer or poorer, *familia* always gots to stick together, bro" (280–81).

Bibliography

Acosta, Oscar "Zeta." 1989a. *The Autobiography of a Brown Buffalo*. New York: Vintage Books.
———. 1989b. *The Revolt of the Cockroach People*. New York: Vintage Books.
———. 1996. "Autobiographical Essay." In *Oscar "Zeta" Acosta: The Uncollected Works*, ed. Ilan Stavans. Houston, Tex.: Arte Público.
Acosta-Belén, Edna, and Virginia Sánchez Korrol. 1993. "The World of Jesús Colón." In *The Way It Was and Other Writings*, ed. Edna Acosta-Belén and Virginia Sánchez Korrol. Houston, Tex.: Arte Público.
Acosta-Belén, Edna. 1993. A MELUS Interview: Judith Ortiz Cofer. *MELUS* 18 no. 3: 83-97.
Acosta-Belén, Edna, and Carlos E. Santiago. 2006. *Puerto Ricans in the United States: A Contemporary Portrait*. Boulder, Colo.: Lynne Reinner Publishers.
Acuña, Rodolfo. 2007. *Occupied America: History of Chicanos*. 6th ed. New York: Pearson Longman.
Alarcón, Norma. 1983. "Chicana's Feminist Literature: A Re-Vision through Malintzin/or Malintzin: Putting Flesh Back on the Object." In *This Bridge Called My Back*, ed. Cherríe Moraga and Gloria Anzaldúa. New York: Kitchen Table Books.
———. 1999. "Chicana Feminism: In the Tracks of 'The' Native Woman." In *Between Woman and Nation: Nationalisms, Transnational Feminisms, and the State*, ed. Norma Alarcón, Caren Kaplan, and Minoo Moallem. Durham, N.C.: Duke University Press.
Aldama, Frederick Luis. 2005. *Brown on Brown: Chicano/a Representations of Gender, Sexuality, and Ethnicity*. Austin: University of Texas Press.
Althusser, Louis. 2001. *Lenin and Philosophy and Other Essays*. Trans. Ben Brewster. New York: Monthly Review Press.
Alvarez, Julia. 1991. *How the García Girls Lost Their Accents*. Chapel Hill, N.C.: Algonquin Books of Chapel Hill.
———. 1994. *In the Time of the Butterflies*. Chapel Hill, N.C.: Algonquin Books of Chapel Hill.
———. 1997a. Interview with Amy Goodman, *Democracy Now!*, September 10. Pacifica Radio Network.
———. 1997b. *¡Yo!* Chapel Hill, N.C.: Algonquin Books of Chapel Hill.
———. 1998. *Something to Declare*. New York: Plume.

———. 2000. *In the Name of Salomé*. Chapel Hill, N.C.: Algonquin Books of Chapel Hill.
Alvarez, Luis. 2008. *The Power of the Zoot: Youth Culture and Resistance During World War II*. Berkeley: University of California Press.
Anaya, Rudolfo. 1976. *Heart of Aztlán*. Berkeley, Calif.: Justa Publications.
Anderson, Benedict. 2005. *Under Three Flags: Anarchism and the Anti-Colonial Imaginary*. London: Verso.
———. 2007. *Imagined Communities: Reflections on the Origins and Spread of Nationalism*. Revised ed. London: Verso.
Anderson, Linda. 2001. *Autobiography*. London: Routledge.
Anzaldúa, Gloria. 2007. *Borderlands/La Frontera: The New Mestiza*. 3rd ed. San Francisco, Calif.: Aunt Lute Books.
Aparicio, Frances. 1999. Reading the "Latino" in Latino Studies: Toward Reimagining Our Academic Location. *Discourse* 21, no. 3: 3–18.
Aparicio, Frances, and Susana Chavez-Silverman, eds. 1997. *Tropicalizations: Transcultural Representations of Latinidad*. Hanover: University Press of New England.
Aponte-Parés, Luis, and Jorge B. Merced. 1998. "Paginas Omitidas: The Gay and Lesbian Presence." In *The Puerto Rican Movement: Voices from the Diaspora*, ed. Andrés Torres and José E. Velázquez. Philadelphia, Pa.: Temple University Press.
Arias, Arturo, ed. 2001. *The Rigoberta Menchú Controversy*. Minneapolis: University of Minnesota Press.
Arias, Ron. 1997. *The Road to Tamazunchale*. Tempe, Ariz.: Bilingual Review Press.
Bakhtin, Mikhail, and Michael Holquist. 1981. *The Dialogic Imagination: Four Essays*. Trans. Caryl Emerson and Michael Holquist and ed. Michael Holquist. Austin: University of Texas Press.
Baldwin, James. 1953. *Go Tell It on the Mountain*. New York: Grosset and Dunlap.
Bart, Philip, Arthur Zipser, Theodore Bassett, and William W. Weinstone, eds. 1979. *Highlights of a Fighting History: Sixty Years of the Communist Party, U.S.A.* New York: International Publishers.
Beverly, John. 1993. *Against Literature*. Minneapolis: University of Minnesota Press.
———. 2004. *Testimonio: On the Politics of Truth*. Minneapolis: University of Minnesota Press.
Briggs, Laura. 2002. *Reproducing Empire*. Berkeley: University of California Press.
Brown, Isabel Zakrzewski. 2000. Historiographic Metafiction in *In the Time of the Butterflies*. *South Atlantic Review: The Publication of the South Atlantic Modern Language Association* 64, no. 2: 98–112.
Bruce-Novoa, Juan. 1988. "Homosexuality and the Chicano Novel." In *European Perspectives on Hispanic Literature of the United States*, ed. Geneviève Fabre. Houston, Tex.: Arte Público.

———. 1992. Judith Ortiz Cofer's Rituals of Movement. *The Americas Review* 19, no. 3–4: 88–99.
Buhle, Paul. 1987. *Marxism in the USA: Remapping the History of the American Left*. London: Verso.
Caminero-Santangelo, Marta. 2007. *On Latinidad: U.S. Latino Literature and the Construction of Ethnicity*. Gainesville: University of Florida Press.
Carrasquillo, Marci L. 2006. "The Perfect Freedom": Travel and Mobility in Contemporary Ethnic American Literature" (PhD diss., University of Oregon).
Castillo, Ana. 1993. *So Far From God*. New York: W. W. Norton.
Césaire, Aimé. 2001. *Discourse on Colonialism*. Trans. Joan Pinham. New York: Monthly Review Press.
Chabram-Dernersesian, Angie. 1992. "I Throw Punches for My Race, But I Don't Want to Be a Man: Writing Us—Chica-nos (Girl, Us)/Chicanas—into the Movement Script." In *Cultural Studies*, ed. Lawrence Grossberg, Cary Nelson, and Paula Treichler. New York: Routledge.
Chávez, Ernesto. 2002. *"Mi raza primero!" (My people first!): Nationalism, Identity, and Insurgency in the Chicano Movement in Los Angeles, 1966–1978*. Berkeley: University of California Press.
Chávez, Linda. 1991. *Out of the Barrio: Toward a New Politics of Hispanic Assimilation*. New York: Basic Books.
Cisneros, Sandra. 1984. *The House on Mango Street*. New York: Vintage Books.
———. 2002a. *Caramelo, or, Puro Cuento: A Novel*. New York: Alfred A. Knopf.
———. 2002b. Interview with Ray Suarez. Available from http://www.pbs.org/newshour/conversation/july-dec02/cisneros
———. 2002c. Interview with Robert Birnbaum. Available from http://www.identitytheory.com/people/birnbaum76.html.
Cohen, Lizabeth. 1990. *Making a New Deal: Industrial Workers in Chicago, 1919–1939*. New York: Cambridge University Press.
Colón, Jesús. 1982. *A Puerto Rican in New York*. New York, NY: International Publishers.
———. 1983–2001. The Jesús Colón Papers, Archives of the Puerto Rican Diaspora, Centro de Estudios Puertorriqueños, Hunter College, CUNY. Courtesy Benigno Giboyeaux.
———. 1992. *The Way It Was and Other Writings*, ed. Edna Acosta-Belén and Virginia Sánchez Korrol. Houston, Tex.: Arte Público.
———. 2001. *Lo que el pueblo me dice . . . : Crónicas de la colonia puertorriqueña en Nueva York*, ed. Edwin Karli Padilla Aponte. Houston, Tex.: Arte Público.
Colón, Joaquín. 2001. *Pioneros puertorriqueños en Nueva York*. Houston, Tex.: Arte Público.
Cruz, Angie. 2002. *Soledad*. New York: Simon and Schuster.
———. 2006. *Let It Rain Coffee*. New York: Simon and Schuster.

Dalleo, Raphael, and Elena Machado Sáez. 2007. *The Latino/a Canon and the Emergence of Post-Sixties Literature*. New York: Palgrave Macmillan.

Danticat, Edwidge. 1998. *The Farming of Bones*. New York: Soho Press.

Dávila, Arlene. 1997. *Sponsored Identities: Cultural Politics in Puerto Rico*. Philadelphia, Pa.: Temple University Press.

———. 2001. *Latinos, Inc.: The Marketing and Making of a People*. Berkeley: University of California Press.

Davis, Charles T. 1979. "From Experience to Eloquence: Richard Wright's Black Boy as Art." In *Chant of Saints: A Gathering of Afro-American Literature, Art, and Scholarship*, ed. Michael S. Shapiro and Robert B. Shapiro. Urbana, Ill: University of Illinois Press.

Decker, Jeffrey Louis. 1997. *Made in America: Self-Styled Success from Horatio Alger to Oprah Winfrey*. Minneapolis: University of Minnesota Press.

Deleuze, Gilles, and Félix Guattari. 1986. What Is a Minor Literature?. In *Kafka: Toward a Minor Literature*. Trans. Dana Polan. Minneapolis: University of Minnesota Press.

Delgado, Linda C. 2005. "Jesús Colón and the Making of a New York City Community." In *The Puerto Rican Diaspora: Historical Perspectives*, ed. Carmen Teresa Whalen and Victor Vázquez Hernández. Philadelphia, Pa.: Temple University Press.

De Man, Paul. 1979. Autobiography as De-facement. *Modern Language Notes* 94, no. 5: 919–30.

Denning, Michael. 1998. *The Cultural Front: The Laboring of American Culture in the Twentieth Century*. London: Verso.

Derby, Lauren. 2009. *The Dictator's Seduction: Politics and the Popular Imagination in the Era of Trujillo*. Durham, N.C.: Duke University Press.

Díaz, Junot. 1996. *Drown*. New York: Riverhead Books.

———. 2007. *The Brief Wondrous Life of Oscar Wao*. New York: Riverhead Books.

Duany, Jorge. 2002. *The Puerto Rican Nation on the Move*. Chapel Hill: University of North Carolina Press.

Espinoza, Leslie G. 1998. "Latino/a Identity and Multi-Identity: Community and Culture." In *The Latino/a Condition*, ed. Richard Delgado and Jean Stefancic. New York: New York University Press.

Fanon, Frantz. 1963. *The Wretched of the Earth*. New York: Grove Press.

———. 1968. *Black Skin, White Masks*. New York: Grove Press.

Felman, Shoshana, and Dori Laub. 1992. *Testimony: Crisis of Witnessing in Literature, Psychoanalysis and History*. New York: Routledge, Chapman and Hall, Inc.

Ferguson, Roderick. 2004. *Aberrations in Black: Toward a Queer of Color Critique*. Minneapolis: University of Minnesota Press.

Fischer, Michael M. J. 1986. "Ethnicity and the Post-Modern Arts of Memory." In

Writing Culture, ed. James Clifford and George Marcus. Berkeley: University of California Press.

Flores, Juan. 1982. Foreword in *A Puerto Rican in New York and Other Sketches*. Houston, Tex.: Arte Público.

———. 1997. "The Latino Imaginary: Dimensions of Community and Identity." In *Tropicalizations: Transcultural Representations of Latinidad*, ed. Francis Aparicio and Susana Chávez-Silverman. Hanover, N.H.: Dartmouth College Press.

———. 2009. *The Diaspora Strikes Back: Caribeño Tales of Learning and Turning*. New York: Routledge.

Flores, William, and Rina Benmayor. 1997. *Latino Cultural Citizenship*. Boston: Beacon Press.

Freud, Sigmund. 1978. Mourning and Melancholia. In *General Psychological Theory: Papers on Metapsychology*, ed. Phillip Rieff. New York: Collier Books.

Friedman, Susan Stanford. 1998. "Women's Autobiographical Selves: Theory and Practice." In *Women, Autobiography, Theory: A Reader*, ed. Sidonie Smith and Julia Watson. Madison: University of Wisconsin Press.

Galarza, Ernesto. 1964. *Merchants of Labor: The Mexican Bracero Story*. Santa Barbara, Calif.: McNally and Loftin.

———. 1970. *Spiders in the House, Workers in the Field*. Notre Dame, Ind.: University of Notre Dame Press.

———. 1971. *Barrio Boy*. Notre Dame, Ind.: University of Notre Dame Press.

———. 1977a. *Farm Workers and Agri-business in California, 1947–1960*. Notre Dame, Ind.: University of Notre Dame Press.

———. 1977b. *Tragedy at Chualar: El crucero de las treinta y dos cruces*. Santa Barbara, Calif.: McNally and Loftin.

García, Cristina. 1992. *Dreaming in Cuban*. New York: Knopf.

García Canclini, Néstor. 1995. *Hybrid Cultures: Strategies for Entering and Leaving Modernity*. Trans. Sylvia L. López. Minneapolis: University of Minnesota Press.

Gates, Henry Louis. 1988. *The Signifying Monkey: A Theory of Afro-American Literary Criticism*. Oxford: Oxford University Press.

Gatto, Katherine. 2000. Mambo, Merengue, Salsa: The Dynamics of Self Construction in Latina Autobiographical Narrative. *West Virginia University Philological Papers* 46: 84–90.

González, Juan. 2000. *Harvest of Empire*. New York: Viking.

Gossett, Thomas F. 1997. *Race: The History of an Idea in America*. New Edition. New York: Oxford University Press.

Gramsci, Antonio. 1985. "Justification of Autobiography." In *Selections from Cultural Writings*, ed. David Forgacs and Geoffrey Nowell-Smith. Cambridge, Mass.: Harvard University Press.

Gruesz, Kirsten Silva. 2002. *Ambassadors of Culture: The Transamerican Origins of Latino Writing*. Princeton, N.J.: Princeton University Press.

Gutiérrez, David. 1995. *Walls and Mirrors: Mexican Americans, Mexican Immigrants, and the Politics of Ethnicity*. Berkeley: University of California Press.
Gutiérrez-Jones, Carl. 1995. *Rethinking the Borderlands: Between Chicano Culture and Legal Discourse*. Berkeley: University of California Press.
Gutiérrez y Muhs, Gabriela. 2006. Sandra Cisneros and Her Trade of the Free Word. *Rocky Mountain Review of Language and Literature* 60, no. 2: 23–36.
Hall, Stuart. 1996. "New Ethnicities." In *Stuart Hall: Critical Dialogues in Cultural Studies*, ed. David Morley and Kuan-Hsing Chen. London: Routledge.
Hames-García, Michael. 2004. *Fugitive Thought: Prison Movements, Race, and the Meaning of Justice*. Minneapolis: University of Minnesota Press.
Heredia, Juanita. 2007. Voyages South and North: The Politics of Transnational Gender Identity in *Caramelo* and *American Chica*. *Latino Studies* 5: 340–57.
Hobsbawm, E. J. 1992. *Nations and Nationalism Since 1780: Programme, Myth, Reality*. 2nd ed. Cambridge: Cambridge University Press.
Holton, Adalaine. 2007. "Because He Spoke Spanish": The Politics of Print Community in the Writings of Jesús Colón. Paper presented at the Annual Meeting of the American Studies Association, Philadelphia, Pa.
Horno-Delgado, Asunción, Eliana Ortega, Nina M. Scott, Nancy Saporta Sternbach, ed. 1989. *Breaking Boundaries: Latina Writing and Critical Readings*. Amherst: University of Massachusetts Press.
Horsman, Reginald. 1981. *Race and Manifest Destiny: The Origins of American Racial Anglo-Saxonism*. Cambridge, Mass.: Harvard University Press.
Human Rights Watch Press Backgrounder. 2002. "Race and Incarceration in the United States." Accessed April 3, 2011. http://www.hrw.org/legacy/backgrounder/usa/race.
Hutcheon, Linda. 1989. *The Politics of Postmodernism*. London: Routledge.
Iglesias, César Andreu. 1984. Introduction to *Memoirs of Bernardo Vega: A Contribution to the History of the Puerto Rican Community in New York*, trans. Juan Flores, ed. César Andreu Iglesias. New York: Monthly Review Press.
James, C. L. R. 1989. *The Black Jacobins*. New York: Vintage Books.
James, Winston. 1998. *Holding Aloft the Banner of Ethiopia: Caribbean Radicalism in Early Twentieth-Century America*. London: Verso.
Jameson, Fredric. 1991. *Postmodernism, or, The Cultural Logic of Late Capitalism*. Durham, N.C.: Duke University Press.
Jirón-King, Shimberlee. 2008. Thompson's and Acosta's Collaborative Creation of the Gonzo Narrative Style. *Comparative Literature and Culture* 10, no. 1: 2–11.
Johnson, Kelli Lyon. 2005. *Julia Alvarez: Writing a New Place on the Map*. Albuquerque: University of New Mexico Press.
Johnson González, Bill. 2006. The Politics of Translation in Sandra Cisneros's *Caramelo*. *Differences: A Journal of Feminist Cultural Studies* 17, no. 5: 3–19.

Jorge, Angela. 1995. Mesa Blanca: A Puerto Rican Healing Tradition. In *Spirit Versus Scalpel: Traditional Healing and Modern Psychotherapy*, editors Leonore Loeb Adler and B. Runi Mukherji. Westport, Ct: Bergin & Garvey.

Judd, Dennis R., and Paul Kantor, eds. 2001. *The Politics of Urban America: A Reader*. New York: Longman Press.

Kanellas, Nicholas. 1989. *Biographical Dictionary of Hispanic Literature in the United States*. New York: Greenwood Press.

Kearns, Richard. 1999. Messages from the Taíno Restoration and Truth Reclamation / We Never Disappeared. Accessed April 3, 2011. http://www.centrelink.org/index.html.

Kerouac, Jack. 1999. *On the Road*. New York: Penguin.

Kevane, Bridget. 2003. *Latino Literature in America*. Westport, Conn.: Greenwood Press.

Knadler, Stephen. 2005. Blanca from the Block: Whiteness and the Transnational Latina Body. *Genders* 41: 37 paragraphs.

LaCapra, Dominick. 2001. *Writing History, Writing Trauma*. Baltimore, Md.: Johns Hopkins University Press.

Latina Feminist Group. 2001. *Telling to Live: Latina Feminist Testimonios*. Durham, N.C.: Duke University Press.

Lejeune, Philippe. 1989. *On Autobiography*. Minneapolis: University of Minnesota Press.

Libretti, Tim. 2004. Sexual Outlaws and Class Struggle: Rethinking History and Class Consciousness from a Queer Perspective. *College English* 67, no. 2: 154–71.

Lifshey, Adam. 2008. Indeterminacy and the Subversive in Representations of the Trujillato. *Hispanic Review* 76, no. 4: 435–57.

Lipsitz, George. 1990. *Time Passages*. Minneapolis: University of Minnesota Press.

———. 1998. *The Possessive Investment in Whiteness: How White People Profit from Identity Politics*. Philadelphia, Pa.: Temple University Press.

———. 2001. *American Studies in a Moment of Danger*. Minneapolis: University of Minnesota Press.

Lloyd, David. 1997. "Nationalisms against the State." In *The Politics of Culture in the Shadow of Capitalism*, ed. Lisa Lowe and David Lloyd. Durham, N.C.: Duke University Press.

Locke, John. 1988. *Two Treatises of Government*, ed. Peter Laslett. New York: Cambridge University Press.

López-Calvo, Ignacio. 2005. *God and Trujillo: Literary and Cultural Representations of the Dominican Republic*. Gainesville: University Press of Florida.

López-Springfield, Consuelo, ed. 1997. *Daughters of Caliban: Caribbean Women in the Twentieth Century*. Bloomington: Indiana University Press.

Lowenstein, Adam. 2005. *Shocking Representation*. New York: Columbia University Press.

Luis, William. 1998. Black Latinos Speak: The Politics of Race in Piri Thomas's *Down These Mean Streets*. *Indiana Journal of Hispanic Literatures* Spring, no. 12: 27–50.

Lyotard, Jean-François. 1985. *The Postmodern Condition: A Report on Knowledge*. Minneapolis: University of Minnesota Press.

Macpherson, C. B. 1964. *The Political Theory of Possessive Individualism: Hobbes to Locke*. Oxford: Clarendon.

Malcolm X. 1964. *The Autobiography of Malcolm X*. New York: Ballantine.

Márquez, Antonio C. 1990. Self & Culture: Autobiography as Cultural Narrative. *Discurso: Revista de Estudios Iberoamericanos* 7, no. 1: 51–66.

Marshall, Joanna Barszewska. 2008. "Translating Home in the Work of Judith Ortiz Cofer." In *Writing Off the Hyphen: New Critical Perspectives on the Literature of the Puerto Rican Diaspora*, ed. José L. Torres-Padilla and Carmen Haydee Rivera. Seattle: University of Washington Press.

Martell, Esperanza. 1998. "In the Belly of the Beast": Beyond Survival. In *The Puerto Rican Movement*, ed. Andrés Torres and José E. Velázquez. Philadelphia, Pa.: Temple University Press.

Martínez, Elizabeth Coonrod. 1998. Recovering a Space for History between Imperialism and Patriarchy: Julia Alvarez's *In the Time of the Butterflies*. *Thamyris* 5, no. 2: 263–79.

Matos Rodríguez, Felix, and Pedro Juan Hernández. 2001. *Pioneros: Puerto Ricans in New York City 1892–1948*. Charleston, S.C.: Arcadia Publishing.

McCallum, Shara. 2000. Reclaiming Julia Alvarez: *In the Time of the Butterflies*. *Women's Studies: An Interdisciplinary Journal* 29, no. 1: 93–117.

McCracken, Ellen. 1999. *New Latina Narrative: The Feminine Space of Postmodern Ethnicity*. Tucson: University of Arizona Press.

Méndez, Serafin, Gail Cueto, and Neysa Rodriguez Deynes, eds. 2003. *Notable Caribbeans and Caribbean Americans*. Westport, Conn.: Greenwood Press.

Mignolo, Walter. 2000. *Local Histories, Global Designs: Coloniality, Subaltern Knowledges, and Border Thinking*. Princeton, N.J.: Princeton University Press.

Mills, Charles. 1997. *The Racial Contract*. Ithaca, N.Y.: Cornell University Press.

———. 1998. *Blackness Visible: Essays on Philosophy and Race*. Ithaca, N.Y.: Cornell University Press.

Mitchell, David T. 1999. "The Accent of 'Loss': Cultural Crossings as Context in Julia Alvarez's *How the Garcia Girls Lost Their Accents*." In *Beyond the Binary: Reconstructing Cultural Identity in a Multicultural Context*, ed. Timothy B. Powell. New Brunswick, N.J.: Rutgers University Press.

Moore, Burton. 2003. *Love & Riot: Oscar Zeta Acosta and the Great Mexican American Revolt*, ed. Andrea Allesandra Cabello. Mountain View, Calif.: Floricanto Press.

Moraga, Cherrie, and Gloria Anzaldúa, eds. 1983. *This Bridge Called My Back: Writings by Radical Women of Color*. 2nd ed. New York: Kitchen Table Books.

Mosse, George L. 1985. *Nationalism and Sexuality: Respectability and Abnormal Sexuality in Modern Europe.* New York: Howard Fertig.
Moya, Paula. 2002. *Learning from Experience: Minority Identities, Multicultural Struggles.* Berkeley: University of California Press.
Moya, Paula M. L., and Ramón Saldívar. 2003. Fictions of the Trans-American Imaginary. *Modern Fiction Studies* 49, no. 1: 1–18.
Muñoz, José. 1999. *Disidentifications: Queers of Color and the Performance of Politics.* Minneapolis: University of Minnesota Press.
Négron-Muntaner, Frances. 2004. *Boricua Pop: Puerto Ricans and the Latinization of American Culture.* New York: New York University Press.
Negrón-Muntaner, Frances, ed. 2007. *None of the Above: Puerto Ricans in the Global Era.* New York: Palgrave Macmillan.
Negrón-Muntaner, Frances, and Ramón Grosfoguel, eds. 1998. *Puerto Rican Jam: Rethinking Colonialism and Nationalism.* 2nd ed. Minneapolis: University of Minnesota Press.
New York Times. 2008. Prison Nation. *New York Times*, March 10.
Noble, David W. 2002. *Death of a Nation: American Culture and the End of Exceptionalism.* Minneapolis: University of Minnesota Press.
Oboler, Suzanne. 1995. *Ethnic Labels, Latino Lives: Identity and the Politics of (Re)Presentation in the United States.* Minneapolis: University of Minnesota Press.
Olmos, Edward James. 1992. *American Me.* Hollywood, Calif.: Universal Studios.
Olney, James. 1972. *Metaphors of the Self: The Meaning of Autobiography.* Princeton, N.J.: Princeton University Press.
Omi, Michael, and Howard Winant. 1994. *Racial Formation in the United States: From the 1960s to the 1990s.* 2nd ed. New York: Routledge.
Organisation for Economic Co-operation and Development. 2008. *Reviews of National Policies for Education: Dominican Republic.* Paris: OECD.
Ortiz Cofer, Judith. 1989. *The Line of the Sun.* Athens: University of Georgia Press.
———. 1990. *Silent Dancing: A Partial Remembrance of a Puerto Rican Childhood.* Houston, Tex.: Arte Público.
———. 1992. Puerto Rican Literature in Georgia?: An Interview with Judith Ortiz Cofer. *The Kenyon Review* 14, no. 4: 43–50.
———. 1994. The Infinite Variety of the Puerto Rican Reality: An Interview with Judith Ortiz Cofer. *Callaloo: A Journal of African American and African Arts and Letters* 17, no. 3: 730–42.
———. 2000. *Woman in Front of the Sun: On Becoming a Writer.* Athens: University of Georgia Press.
Padilla, Genaro. 1984. The Self as Cultural Metaphor in Acosta's *Autobiography of a Brown Buffalo. Journal of General Education* 43, no. 2: 242–58.
———. 1993. *My History, Not Yours: The Formation of Mexican American Autobiography.* Madison: University of Wisconsin Press.

Paredes, Américo. 1998. *With His Pistol in His Hand*. Austin: University of Texas Press.
Paredes, Raymund. 1981. Mexican American Authors and the American Dream. *Journal of the Society for the Study of the Multi-Ethnic Literature of the United States (MELUS)* 8, no. 4: 71–80.
———. 1995. "Los Angeles from the Barrio: Oscar Zeta Acosta's *The Revolt of the Cockroach People*." In *Los Angeles in Fiction*, ed. David Fine. Albuquerque: University of New Mexico Press.
Patterson, Orlando. 1982. *Slavery and Social Death*. Cambridge, Mass.: Harvard University Press.
Pérez, Louis. 1995. *Essays on Cuban History*. Gainesville: University of Florida Press.
Perez-Torres, Rafael. 1994. "The Ambiguous Outlaw: John Rechy and Complicitous Homotextuality." In *Fictions of Masculinity: Crossing Cultures, Crossing Sexualities*, ed. Peter F. Murphy. New York: New York University Press.
———. 2006. *Mestizaje: Critical Uses of Race in Chicano Culture*. Minneapolis: University of Minnesota Press.
Petry, Ann. 1946. *The Street*. Boston, Mass.: Houghton Mifflin.
Phelan, James. 2006. "Rhetoric, Politics, and Ethics in Sandra Cisneros's *Caramelo*." In *What Democracy Looks Like: A New Critical Realism for a Post-Seattle World*, ed. Amy Schrager Lang. New Brunswick, N.J.: Rutgers University Press.
Plascencia, Salvador. 2005. *The People of Paper*. New York: Harvest.
Puri, Shalini. 2004. *The Caribbean Postcolonial: Social Equality, Post-Nationalisms, and Cultural Hybridity*. New York: Palgrave Macmillan.
Quijano, Aníbal. 2000. Coloniality of Power, Eurocentrism, and Latin America. *Nepantla: Views from the South* 1, no. 3: 533–80.
Quintero Rivera, Angel G. 1983. Socialist and Cigarmaker: Artisan's Proletarianization in the Making of the Puerto Rican Working Class. *Latin American Perspectives* 10, no. 2/3: 19–38.
Ramírez, Catherine Sue. 2009. *The Woman in the Zoot Suit: Gender, Nationalism, and the Cultural Politics of Memory*. Durham, N.C.: Duke University Press.
Rampersad, Arnold. 2007. *Ralph Ellison: A Biography*. New York: Alfred A. Knopf.
Rechy, John. 1963. *City of Night*. New York: Grove Press.
———. 1967. *Numbers*. New York: Grove Press.
———. 1970. *This Day's Death*. New York: Grove Press.
———. 1977. *The Sexual Outlaw: A Documentary*. New York: Grove Weidenfeld.
———. 1991. *The Miraculous Day of Amalia Gomez*. New York: Arcade Publishing.
———. 1995. Interview: John Rechy. *Diacritics* 25, no. 1: 113–25.
———. 2003. John Rechy at Home. *The Gay and Lesbian Review* 10, no. 4: 24.
Reid-Pharr, Robert. 1997. "Tearing the Goat's Flesh: Homosexuality, Abjection, and the Production of a Late Twentieth-Century Black Masculinity." In *Novel Gazing: Queer Readings in Fiction*, ed. Eve Kosofsky Sedgwick. Durham, N.C.: Duke University Press.

Ridley, Jasper. 2001. *Maximilian and Juarez*. London: Phoenix Press.
Rivera, Carmen Vivien. 1998. "Our Movement: One Woman's Story." In *The Puerto Rican Movement*, ed. Andrés Torres and José E. Velázquez. Philadelphia, Pa.: Temple University Press.
Rodríguez, Clara. 1989. *Puerto Ricans: Born in the U.S.A*. Boston, Mass.: Unwin Hyman.
Rodríguez, Juana María. 2003. *Queer Latinidad: Identity Practices, Discursive Spaces*. New York: New York University Press.
Rodríguez, Richard. 1982. *Hunger of Memory: The Education of Richard Rodriguez*. Boston, Mass.: David R. Godine.
———. 2002. *Brown: The Last Discovery of America*. New York: Penguin.
Rosaldo, Renato. 1987. Politics, Patriarchs, and Laughter. *Cultural Critique* 6: 65–86.
Saldívar, José David. 1997. *Border Matters: Remapping American Cultural Studies*. Berkeley: University of California Press.
Saldívar, Ramón. 1990. *Chicano Narrative: The Dialectics of Difference*. Madison: University of Wisconsin Press.
———. 2009. "Race and Narrative Theory in Postrace America: Ethnic Literature and the Post-postmodern Turn." Paper presented to the Department of English, University of Oregon, May 7.
Saldívar-Hull, Sonia. 2000. *Feminism on the Border: Chicana Gender Politics and Literature*. Berkeley: University of California Press.
Sánchez, Marta. 2005. *"Shakin up" Race and Gender: Intercultural Connections in Puerto Rican, African American, and Chicano Narratives and Culture (1965–1995)*. Austin: University of Texas Press.
Sánchez, Rosaura. 1995. *Telling Identities: The Californio Testimonios*. Minneapolis: University of Minnesota Press.
Sánchez González, Lisa. 2001. *Boricua Literature: A Literary History of the Puerto Rican Diaspora*. New York: New York University Press.
Sánchez Korrol, Virginia E. 1983. *From Colonia to Community: The History of Puerto Ricans in New York City*. Berkeley: University of California Press.
Sandoval, Chela. 2000. *Methodology of the Oppressed*. Minneapolis: University of Minnesota Press.
Sandoval, Mercedes Cros. 2006. *Worldview, the Orichas, and Santería: Africa to Cuba and Beyond*. Gainesville: University Press of Florida.
Santiago, Esmeralda. 1994. *When I Was Puerto Rican*. New York: Vintage Books.
Santner, Eric. 1990. *Stranded Objects: Mourning, Memory, and Film in Postwar Germany*. Ithaca, N.Y.: Cornell University Press.
Serrano, Basilio. 1998. "¡Rifle, Cañón, y Escopeta!: A Chronicle of the Puerto Rican Student Union." In *The Puerto Rican Movement*, ed. Andrés Torres and José E. Velázquez. Philadelphia, Pa.: Temple University Press.
Shorris, Earl. 1992. *Latinos: A Biography of the People*. New York: W. W. Norton.

Sklodowska, Elzbieta. 1996. "Spanish American Testimonial Novel: Some Afterthoughts." In *The Real Thing: Testimonial Discourse and Latin America*, ed. George M. Gugelberger. Durham, N.C.: Duke University Press.
Smethurst, James. 1995. The Figure of the *Vato Loco* and the Representation of Ethnicity in the Narratives of Oscar Z. Acosta. *MELUS* 20, no. 2: 119–32.
Smith, Sidonie, and Julia Watson. 2001. *Reading Autobiography: A Guide for Interpreting Life Narratives*. Minneapolis: University of Minnesota Press.
Socolovsky, Maya. 2009. Telling Stories of Transgression: Judith Ortiz Cofer's *The Line of the Sun*. *MELUS* 34, no. 1: 95–116.
Sommer, Doris. 1991. *Foundational Fictions: The National Romances of Latin America*. Berkeley: University of California Press.
———. 1996. "No Secrets." In *The Real Thing: Testimonial Discourse and Latin America*, ed. George M. Gugelberger. Durham, N.C.: Duke University Press.
———. 2004. *Bilingual Aesthetics: A New Sentimental Education*. Durham, N.C.: Duke University Press.
Stanchich, Maritza. 2010. "Insular Interventions: Jesús Colón Unmasks Racial Harmonizing and Populist Uplift Discourses in Puerto Rico." In *Hispanic Caribbean Literature of Migration: Narratives of Displacement*, ed. Vanessa Pérez Rosario. New York: Palgrave Macmillan.
Stavans, Ilan, ed. 1995. *Bandido: Oscar "Zeta" Acosta and the Chicano Experience*. New York: Icon Editions.
———, ed. 1996. *Oscar "Zeta" Acosta: The Uncollected Works*. Houston, Tex.: Arte Público.
———. 2001. *The Hispanic Condition: The Power of a People*. 2nd ed. New York: Rayo.
Stefanko, Jacqueline. 1996. New Ways of Telling: Latinas' Narratives of Exile and Return. *Frontiers: A Journal of Women's Studies* 17, no. 2: 50–69.
Steinbeck, John. 2002. *Travels with Charlie in Search of America*. New York: Penguin.
Suárez, Lucia M. 2004. Julia Alvarez and the Anxiety of Latina Representation. *Meridians: Feminism, Race, Transnationalism* 5, no. 1: 117–45.
Thomas, Piri. 1967. *Down These Mean Streets*. New York: Vintage Books.
Thompson, Hunter S. 1983. *Fear and Loathing on the Campaign Trail '72*. New York: Warner.
———. 1996. *Fear and Loathing in Las Vegas and Other American Stories*. New York: Modern Library.
Torres, Andrés. 1998. "Introduction: Political Radicalism in the Diaspora—The Puerto Rican Experience." In *The Puerto Rican Movement: Voices from the Diaspora*, ed. Andrés Torres and José E. Velázquez. Philadelphia, Pa.: Temple University Press.

Torres, Andrés, and José E. Velázquez, eds. 1998. *The Puerto Rican Movement: Voices from the Diaspora*. Philadelphia, Pa.: Temple University Press.
Torres, Lourdes. 1991. The Construction of the Self in U.S. Latina Autobiographies. In *Third World Women and The Politics of Feminism*, eds. Chandra Talpade Mohanty, Ann Russo, and Lourdes Torres. Bloomington: University of Indiana Press.
Torres-Saillant, Silvio. 2003. Inventing the Race: Latinos and the Ethnoracial Pentagon. *Latino Studies* 1, no. 1: 123–51.
Valdez, Luis. 1992. *Zoot Suit and Other Plays*. Houston, Tex.: Arte Público.
Vargas Llosa, Mario. 2001. *The Feast of the Goat*. Trans. Edith Grossman. New York: Farrar, Straus, Giroux.
Vasconcelos, José. 1997. *The Cosmic Race: A Bilingual Edition*. Trans. Didier T. Jaén. Baltimore, Md.: Johns Hopkins University Press.
Vega, Bernardo. 1984. *Memoirs of Bernardo Vega: A Contribution to the History of the Puerto Rican Community in New York*. Trans. Juan Flores, ed. César Andreu Iglesias. New York: Monthly Review Press.
Waldron, John V. 2008. Solving Guzman's Problem: "An Other" Narrative of La Gran Familia Puertorriquena in Judith Ortiz Cofer's *The Line of the Sun*. *Bilingual Review* 29, no. 1: 49–65.
Walters, Wendy W. 2005. *At Home in Diaspora: Black International Writing*. Minneapolis: University of Minnesota Press.
Wright, Richard. 1945. *Black Boy: A Record of Childhood and Youth*. New York: World.
Young Lords Party. 1993. Young Lords Party 13-Point Program and Platform. Accessed April 3, 2011. http://www2.iath.virginia.edu/sixties.

Index

acculturation. See assimilation/ acculturation
Acosta, Oscar "Zeta": and Gonzo journalism, 83, 86–87, 206n21; life of, 82–84, 197n21, 206n22; works: "Autobiographical Essay," 92, 97; *The Autobiography of a Brown Buffalo*, 83, 84; "Racial Exclusion," 204n7. See also *The Revolt of the Cockroach People*
Acosta-Belén, Edna, 51, 52, 57, 202n29
Adams, Henry, 7, 8, 200n18
African Americans. See intergroup coalitions; Puerto Rican/African American triangulation
Alarcón, Norma, 19, 43
Albizu-Campos, Pedro, 4
Aldama, Frederick, 107, 109, 113–14
Algarín, Miguel, 68
Alianza Obrera Puertorriqueña (Puerto Rico), 51
alternative gender roles. See gender oppression disruption
Alvarez, Julia, 137, 147, 159; works: "Chasing the Butterflies," 144, 146–47, 158, 213–14n22; "Doña Aida, With Your Permission," 137–38; "A Genetics of Justice," 145–46; *How the García Girls Lost Their Accents*, 135, 147–52, 153–54, 212n14, 213n16; *In the Name of Salomé*, 135, 139, 141, 163–68, 214n24; *¡Yo!*, 135, 152–56, 212n11. See also Alvarez's writings; *In the Time of the Butterflies*
Alvarez's writings, 135–69; and class, 139–40, 150, 212n12; collectivization of historical trauma in, 151–52; critics on, 137, 144, 210–11n2; diaspora in, 137, 138, 139, 148–49; disruption of racial/ethnic binaries in, 14; female-centered past in, 127–28; geographic ruptures in, 149–50; hemispheric nationalism in, 167–68; and historical truth, 142, 143, 144, 154, 157, 212n14; home in, 185; inheritors in, 164; insurgent nationalism in, 5, 20; melancholia in, 163, 214n23; memory in, 160, 161–62; personal-historical identification in, 164–68; and race/ethnicity, 139, 150–51, 212n11; silence in, 136–37, 138, 148, 161, 213–14n22; storytelling in, 153–56, 166; witnessing in, 160–61, 164, 213n21. See also genre in Alvarez's writings
American Dream, 37
American Labor Party, 51
American studies, 214n4
Anaya, Rudolfo, 109
Anderson, Benedict, 24, 30, 33, 39, 172, 188
Anderson, Linda, 8

231

Anzaldúa, Gloria: on Aztec eagle/serpent symbols, 43; and Aztec warrior icon, 110; on borderlands, 17, 196n14; on brownness, 114; on *la facultad*, 101–2, 207n1; on insurgent nationalism, 17, 19; on machismo, 102–3, 207–8n2
Aparicio, Frances, 19, 20, 21
Aponte-Parés, Luis, 103–4
Arana, Marie, 179
armed struggle. *See* violence
assimilation/acculturation: in *Barrio Boy*, 37, 38, 46, 47–49, 200n10, 201n24; and pachuco (zoot suit) culture, 63
Ateneo Obrero Hispano (Puerto Rico), 51
At Home in Diaspora (Walters), 118
Augustine, Saint, 65
"Autobiographical Essay" (Acosta), 92, 97
autobiography: canonical traditions, 7, 8, 25, 200n18; Gramsci on, 9–11. *See also* first-person personal narrative
The Autobiography of a Brown Buffalo (Acosta), 83, 84
The Autobiography of Benjamin Franklin, 7, 8, 25
Aztec eagle/serpent symbols, 43
Aztec warrior icon, 110, 208n10

Báez Méndez, Buenaventura, 214n25
Bakhtin, Mikhail, 177
Balaguer, Joaquin, 211n8
Barrio Boy (Galarza), 29–33, 36–50, 59–60; acculturation/assimilation in, 37, 38, 46, 47–49, 200n10, 201n24; capitalism in, 38–39, 43, 200nn12, 14, 15; colonialism in, 40–41, 200n17; critics on, 37–38; education in, 44–49, 200n18; epigraph of, 200n18; gender oppression in, 43, 201n20; history in, 41, 44; intergroup coalitions in, 49; nationalism in, 39–40; oppositional consciousness in, 41–45, 49–50, 200–201n20; political action in, 11, 24, 29–30; protagonist of, 200n11
Belpre, Pura, 69
Bender, Stephen, 113
Benmayor, Rina, 22
Beverly, John, 11, 12, 158
Biltmore Six (*California v. Montez*), 83
black nationalism, 76–77, 205n18
Black Panthers, 77, 91
Bolivar, Simón, 57, 58, 167
Bonnelly, Rafael, 211n8
borderlands, 17, 37–38, 196n14
Bosch, Juan, 211n8
Bracero Initiative, 30, 32, 36, 198n4
Bravo, Francisco, 87, 88
bridge consciousness, 108, 120
The Brief Wondrous Life of Oscar Woo (Díaz), 174, 177
Briggs, Laura, 195n5
Brown, Claude, 65, 76, 77, 78, 205n18
Brown, Isabel Zakrzewski, 144, 158
Brown Berets, 14, 23, 25, 30, 83
brownness, 114–15, 116, 209n12
Bruce-Novoa, Juan, 122, 208n5
Burgos-Debray, Elizabeth, 11

Caamaño, Francisco, 211n8
California v. Montez (Biltmore Six), 83
Californios, 8, 98, 196n9, 206n25
Caló, 63
Caminero-Santangelo, Marta, 69–70, 71–72
canonical autobiographical traditions, 7, 8, 25, 200n18

capitalism: in *Barrio Boy*, 38–39, 43, 200nn12, 14, 15; Dominican Republic, 162–63; embeddedness in U.S. culture, 200n13; and liberal individualism, 38–39; in *The Line of the Sun*, 132; and transnationalism, 173–74

Caramelo (Cisneros), 174, 177–89, 181–89; Chicana/o/Mexican relations in, 215–16n12; critics on, 179–80; and first-person personal narrative, 215n7; home in, 185–86, 189; imagined community in, 188–89; insurgent nationalism in, 187–88; matrixed subjectivity in, 175; movement in, 181–83, 186, 188; narrative strategies in, 181–82; plot in, 177–79; racism in, 183–84, 215n11; rebozo symbol in, 185; Spanish language in, 179–80

carnivalesque, 206n23
Carr, Vicky, 91
Cartagena Portalatín, Aida, 137–38, 211n6
Casa de Puerto Rico, 51
Casillo, Charles, 109
Castillo, Ana, 128
Castillo, Debra, 106–7
Católicos por la Raza, 83, 197n21, 207n31
Chabram-Dernersesian, Angie, 14, 33, 64
"Chasing the Butterflies" (Alvarez), 144, 146–47, 158, 213–14n22
Chávez, César, 89–90, 206nn26, 27
Chávez, Ernesto, 94
Chávez, Linda, 13
Chávez-Silverman, Susana, 19
Chicana/o identity. *See Barrio Boy*; Chicana/o movement; Cisneros,

Sandra; *The Revolt of the Cockroach People*; *The Sexual Outlaw*
Chicana/o movement: and Acosta, 83–84; and Aztec warrior icon, 208n10; and education, 90–91, 92, 206n29; gender oppression in, 14–15, 17, 43; homophobia in, 111; and national-transnational triangulation, 187–88; state infiltration of, 94; and *vato loco*/gangster figure, 84–85; and Watts Riots, 207n32. *See also* insurgent nationalism

CIO (Congress of Industrial Organizations), 29, 198n1. *See also* CIO-era roots of insurgent nationalism

CIO-era roots of insurgent nationalism, 29–35, 198n1; and ethnic Americanism, 34–35, 37, 199n6; and Latina/o community changes, 30, 198n4; and Popular Front, 30, 31–32, 33–34, 44; and violent struggle, 31. See also *Barrio Boy*; *A Puerto Rican in New York*

Cisneros, Sandra, 5, 127, 176, 179–80; *The House on Mango Street*, 181. See also *Caramelo*

City of Night (Rechy), 105
class: and Alvarez's writings, 139–40, 150, 212n12; and intergroup coalitions, 113; and national-transnational triangulation, 215n11; and organic intellectuals, 199n7
Cleaver, Eldridge, 65, 76, 77, 78
Cliff, Michelle, 118
Cohen, Lizabeth, 31
COINTELPRO (Counter Intelligence Program), 94
Cold War, 30, 31
collective subjectivity. *See* matrixed subjectivity

Colón, Jesús: autobiography career timing, 196n8; critics on, 52, 202–3nn33, 34; and Galarza, 198n3; life of, 31, 35, 50–51, 52, 197n21, 201–2nn26, 28, 32, 203n35; on public art, 55–56, 203n37; and Puerto Rican/African American triangulation, 68; and socialism, 69; works: *Lo que el pueblo me dice: Cronicas de la colonia puertorriqueña en Nueva York*, 52; *The Way It Was and Other Writings*, 52. See also *A Puerto Rican in New York*

Colón, Joaquín, 201n25

colonialism: in *Barrio Boy*, 40–41, 200n17; Dominican Republic, 165; and Latina/o identity, 22; and minor literature, 37; and Puerto Rican/African American triangulation, 72. See also U.S. hegemony

El Comité/Movimiento de Izquierda Nacional Puertorriqueño (MINP), 21, 208n4

Communist Party USA (CPUSA): Colón's membership in, 32, 51, 52, 197n21, 202n32; and intergroup coalitions, 34; Jefferson School of Social Science, 51, 202n31; publications, 51, 202n30; and race/ethnicity, 198–99n5

Congress of Industrial Organizations (CIO), 29, 198n1. See also CIO-era roots of insurgent nationalism

Council of La Raza, 36

Counter Intelligence Program (COINTELPRO), 94

Criminal Conspiracy Section (LAPD), 94

criminality: and individualism/collective consciousness tension, 66–67; and oppositional consciousness, 78; and redemption narrative, 65. See also prison experience; *vato loco*/gangster figure

criminalization of racial minorities, 16, 67–68, 204–5n12

Crisostomo, Paula, 103, 208n4

Crouch, Stanley, 107

Cruz, Angie, 212n12

Cuba, 168

Cueto, Gail, 157

cultural creation. See cultural production

Cultural Front, 24

cultural nationalism. See insurgent nationalism

cultural production: and insurgent nationalism, 54; and political action, 10, 32; in *A Puerto Rican in New York*, 54, 58–59; and social relations, 7

cultural remittances, 119, 132, 197n22

The Daily Worker, 51, 202n30

The Daily World, 51, 202n30

Dalleo, Raphael, 5, 6, 137, 158, 161, 195–96n7

Dávila, Arlene, 20, 33, 74, 120

Davis, Charles T., 26, 27

Decker, Jeffrey Louis, 25

Deleuze, Gilles, 3

Delgado, Linda, 52

DeLillo, Don, 140

de Man, Paul, 13

Denning, Michael, 24, 29, 32, 33–34, 198n1

Derby, Lauren, 135, 138, 139, 211n7

de Silva, Andy, 88

diaspora: in Alvarez's writings, 137, 138, 139, 148–49; and first-person personal narrative, 137; and historical trauma, 141–42, 149, 163; and

The Line of the Sun, 117–20, 124–25, 131–32, 133; and Nuyorican movement, 131–32; and oppositional consciousness, 119; and transgression, 118, 122–23, 124–25

Díaz, Junot, 1, 135, 176, 195n6, 212n12; *The Brief Wondrous Life of Oscar Woo*, 174, 177

dichotomous categorical identity, 14. *See also* racial/ethnic binary identities

DiGiorgio fruit strike (1947), 35, 36

Dominican Republic: independence struggle, 163, 164, 214n25; migration from, 149, 211n8, 213n18; political divisions within, 149–50, 213n19; post-Trujillo politics, 139, 150, 162–63, 211n8; and U.S. hegemony, 139, 151, 152, 211n8. *See also* Alvarez's writings; historical trauma; Trujillo regime

"Doña Aida, With Your Permission" (Alvarez), 137–38

Down These Mean Streets (Thomas), 1–2, 65–82; antiblack racism in, 72–73, 74, 205n15; critics on, 65–66, 68–70; disruption of racial/ethnic binaries in, 14; distance from Puerto Rico in, 2, 195n3; as first-person personal narrative, 70–71; gender oppression/homophobia in, 78–82, 205–6nn19, 20; genre in, 26; indigeneity in, 70; individualism/collective consciousness tension in, 16, 64–65, 66–68, 70–71; insurgent nationalism in, 65, 78, 82; matrixed subjectivity in, 66, 71; mixed-race identity in, 75–76; nationality in, 71–72, 76; Nuyorican movement in, 2, 65, 68; oppositional consciousness

in, 22, 69, 74–75, 76–77; play in, 1–2, 195n2; protagonist of, 195n1, 205n13; as redemption narrative, 65; and *testimonio*, 12; and U.S. hegemony, 4

"the dozens," 2, 195n2

Duany, Jorge, 117–18, 119, 197n22

East LA Thirteen (*People v. Castro*), 83, 88

education: and assimilation/acculturation, 46–49; and oppositional consciousness, 42, 44–46, 200n18; and political action, 90–91, 92, 206n29; and racism, 46–49, 201n24

The Education of Henry Adams (Adams), 7, 8, 200n18

Ellison, Ralph, 198n5

Emerson, Ralph Waldo, 8

Enlightenment, 173

Espinoza, Leslie, 14, 196n13

ethnic Americanism, 34–35, 37, 199n6

exceptional identities, 9–10, 86

la facultad, 101–2, 207n1

family life: and home, 185–86; and homophobia, 112; and racism, 73–74

Fanon, Frantz, 76, 205n18

Farm Workers and Agri-business in California, 1947–1960 (Galarza), 36

Fear and Loathing in Las Vegas (Thompson), 206n21

Fear and Loathing on the Campaign Trail (Thompson), 206n21

Federación Libre de Trabajadores (Puerto Rico), 51, 202n29

Felman, Shoshana, 142, 144, 151, 160

feminism, 14–15. *See also* gender oppression disruption

Ferguson, Roderick, 19

Figueroa, Elizabeth, 103, 208n4

first-person personal narrative, 4–5, 189–90; career timing of, 7, 196n8; and diaspora, 137; and excluded people, 26, 197–98n23; and genre, 13; Gramsci on, 9–11; and historical truth, 25–27; importance of, 5, 195n6; and liberal individualism, 6–7; and matrixed subjectivity, 7, 8–9; and new millennial authors, 174–75, 195n6; varieties of, 12–13. *See also specific texts*
Fischer, Michael M. J., 23, 78
Flores, Juan, 19, 20, 52, 66, 119, 197n22
Flores, William, 22
Fourteenth of July Movement, 139, 156, 159
Franklin, Benjamin, 7, 8, 25
Freud, Sigmund, 160, 214n23
Friedman, Susan Stanford, 6–7

Galarza, Ernesto: autobiography career timing, 196n8; and Aztec warrior icon, 110; and Colón, 198n3; life of, 35–36, 197n21, 200n16; works: *Farm Workers and Agri-business in California, 1947–1960*, 36; *Merchants of Labor*, 36; *Spiders in the House, Workers in the Field*, 36; *Tragedy at Chualar: El crucero de las treinta y dos cruces*, 36. *See also Barrio Boy*
gangster figure. *See vato loco*/gangster figure
García, Cristina, 127
García Canclini, Néstor, 140, 212n13
Gates, Henry Louis, 195n2
Gatto, Katherine, 8
gay liberation movements, 104–5, 113, 114
gender oppression: in *Barrio Boy*, 43, 201n20; and borderlands, 196n14; in *Caramelo*, 178; in Chicana/o movement, 14–15, 17, 43; and disruption of racial/ethnic binaries, 69; in *Down These Mean Streets*, 78–82, 205–6n20; and generative contradictions, 15; and homophobia, 103, 107, 129; and Puerto Rican/African American triangulation, 82, 205–6n20; and racism, 102–3, 207–8n2; in *The Revolt of the Cockroach People*, 86, 96–97; and *vato loco*/gangster figure, 63, 64, 86, 97, 204n7. *See also* gender oppression disruption; insurgent nationalism and gender oppression
gender oppression disruption, 125–31; and *la facultad*, 102; and female-centered past, 127–28; and insurgent nationalism, 124; and intergender coalitions, 128–29; and intersecting identities, 117; and nonnormative masculinity, 125–28; and queer identity, 129–30; and transgressive female characters, 131, 210n23. *See also* gender oppression
generative contradictions, 14–17. *See also specific texts*
"A Genetics of Justice" (Alvarez), 145–46
genre, 12–13; in *Down These Mean Streets*, 26; and historical truth, 25–27; historiographic metafiction, 26, 143–44, 153; in *The Line of the Sun*, 26; in *A Puerto Rican in New York*, 11–12, 53; in *The Revolt of the Cockroach People*, 25–26; in *The Sexual Outlaw*, 105–6, 112; *testimonio*, 11–12, 158. *See also* genre in Alvarez's writings
genre in Alvarez's writings, 135, 136, 140–47, 152; and constructed nature of history, 146–47; critics on, 137, 144, 210–11n2; first-person personal narrative, 5, 137–38, 141–42, 145, 147, 213n16; historiographic metafiction, 143–44, 153; narrative

strategies, 141–42, 157–60; and postmodernism, 140–41, 143; and *testimonio*, 11, 158; as therapeutic tool, 144–45, 146
globalization, 19, 173, 179. *See also* transnationalism
Gonzaléz, Juan, 20, 57, 66
Gonzo journalism, 83, 86–87, 206n21
Goodman, Amy, 145, 213n16
Gramsci, Antonio, 9–11, 51, 196n10, 199n7
The Grapes of Wrath (Steinbeck), 113
Gruesz, Kirsten Silva, 22
Guattari, Félix, 37
Gusdorf, Georges, 6
Gutiérrez, David, 62
Gutiérrez-Jones, Carl, 17, 43, 83, 103
Gutiérrez y Muhs, Gabriela, 179, 180

hacienda system, 40
Hall, Stuart, 16
Hames-García, Michael, 78, 79, 83, 96–97, 203–4n1, 206n23
hegemonic subjectivity, estrangement from, 8, 14, 96
hemispheric nationalism, 167–68
Henríquez-Ureña, Camila, 163, 214n24
Heredia, Juanita, 171, 179, 180
heteronormativity. *See* homophobia
Himes, Chester, 118
historical trauma: collectivization of, 151–52; denial of, 138–39, 146; and diaspora, 141–42, 149, 163; and genre as therapeutic tool, 144–45, 146; and geographic ruptures, 151; and historical truth, 142, 143, 144, 154, 212–13n15; and matrixed subjectivity, 8; and memory, 160, 161–62; and narrative strategies, 141–42; and silence, 136–37, 138, 143, 148, 161, 213–14n22; and storytelling, 153–56; and witnessing, 160–61

historiographic metafiction, 26, 143–44, 153
history, 41, 44. *See also* Alvarez's writings; historical trauma
Hobsbawm, Eric J., 17, 33
Holding Aloft the Banner of Ethiopia (James), 202–3n34
Holton, Adalaine, 203n34
home: and diaspora, 118, 119, 122–23, 132, 133; and national-transnational triangulation, 178–79, 185–86, 189. *See also* family life
homophobia: and disruption of racial/ethnic binaries, 69; in *Down These Mean Streets*, 78–82, 205n19; and gender oppression, 103, 107, 129; and generative contradictions, 15; and insurgent nationalism, 19, 103–5, 106; and intergroup coalitions, 113; and machismo, 106; and oppositional consciousness, 110–11; in *The Revolt of the Cockroach People*, 96–97; and *vato loco*/gangster figure, 64, 97; and violence, 79–81, 130
Horno-Delgado, Asunción, 19
Hostos, Eugenio María de, 58, 167
House Committee on Un-American Activities (HUAC), 31, 35, 52
The House on Mango Street (Cisneros), 181
Housing Act (1954), 204n4
How the García Girls Lost Their Accents (Alvarez), 147–52, 153–54, 212n14, 213n16
HUAC (House Committee on Un-American Activities), 31, 35, 52, 203n35
Huerta, Dolores, 103, 208n4
Hutcheon, Linda, 26, 27, 140, 143, 144, 197–98n23, 212n13
hybridity, 69, 172, 173, 174

ideology: and generative contradictions, 15; and *vato loco*/gangster figure, 63–64, 96
"If" (Kipling), 56–57
Iglesias, César Andreu, 56
imagined community, 16, 18, 39, 101, 133, 171, 188–89
immigration: and Latina/o identity, 22, 197n20; and racism, 183–84, 213n18. *See also* migration
indigeneity, 70, 74, 184, 205n16, 215n11
individualism. *See* individualism/collective consciousness tension; liberal individualism
individualism/collective consciousness tension: and criminality, 66–67; in *Down These Mean Streets*, 16, 64–65, 66–68, 70–71; as generative contradiction, 15–16; in *The Sexual Outlaw*, 113–14; and *vato loco*/gangster figure, 16, 64–65, 93–94
insurgent nationalism, 17–20, 25; and cultural production, 54; definition, 33, 196–97n16; in *Down These Mean Streets*, 65, 78, 82; and globalization, 19; and homophobia, 19, 103–5, 106; and national-transnational triangulation, 187–88; and post-sixties literature, 5–6; and *A Puerto Rican in New York*, 52, 54–57; and transnationalism, 18–19, 25, 172, 173–74. *See also* Chicana/o movement; CIO-era roots of insurgent nationalism; insurgent nationalism and gender oppression
insurgent nationalism and gender oppression, 17, 19, 33; and borderlands, 196n14; in *Down These Mean Streets*, 78, 82; and gay liberation movements, 104–5; and

Latina/Chicana feminisms, 14–15; official platforms, 103, 208n3; Ortiz Cofer on, 124; and racism, 102–3, 207–8n2
intergroup coalitions: in *Barrio Boy*, 49; CIO-era, 34; and class, 113; and homophobia, 113; in *The Line of the Sun*, 128–29; in *A Puerto Rican in New York*, 57–58; in *The Revolt of the Cockroach People*, 21, 92–93, 207n32; in *The Sexual Outlaw*, 21–22, 106–7, 112. *See also* Puerto Rican/African American triangulation
International Day for the Elimination of Violence against Women, 145
International Longshoreman's Association (ILA), 199n6
International Workers Order, 51
intersecting identities, 2–3, 14; and intergroup coalitions, 107; in *The Line of the Sun*, 116–17, 119; and oppositional consciousness, 115–16; in *The Sexual Outlaw*, 107, 109, 115–16. *See also* matrixed subjectivity; Puerto Rican/African American triangulation
In the Name of Salomé (Alvarez), 135, 139, 141, 163–68, 214n24
In the Time of the Butterflies (Alvarez), 135, 156–63; class in, 139–40; first-person personal narrative in, 141–42, 145; genre in, 26, 157–58; inheritor in, 164; postmodernism in, 141; post-Trujillo era in, 162–63; and *testimonios*, 158; witnessing in, 160–61, 213n21
Islas, Arturo, 105

James, Winston, 50, 52, 202–3n34
Jameson, Fredric, 140
Jefferson, Thomas, 200n13

Jefferson School of Social Science, 51, 202n31
Jirón-King, Shimberlee, 86–87, 206n21
Johnson, Kelli Lyon, 138
Johnson González, Bill, 179–80
Jones Act, 62
Jorge, Angela, 210n21
Joyce, James, 114
Juarez, Benito, 201n23
Justicia, 51

Kanellas, Nicholas, 198n3
Kardec, Allen, 210n21
Kevane, Bridget, 209n17
Kipling, Rudyard, 56–57
Knadler, Stephen, 139, 163, 166

Lara, Augustín, 179
La Raza Unida Unity Conference, 36
Latina Feminist Group, 14, 33, 64, 101, 102
Latina/o community changes: and CIO-era roots of insurgent nationalism, 30, 198n4; urbanization, 62, 88, 204n3
Latina/o identity, 20–23; and cultural citizenship, 22–23; diversity within, 20–21, 197n19; and immigration, 22, 197n20; and intergroup coalitions, 21–22; and language, 120, 148, 179–80, 213n17
Latino cultural citizenship, 22–23. See also intergroup coalitions
Laub, Dori, 142, 144, 151, 160, 212–13n15
League of United Latin American Citizens (LULAC), 89
el lector, 50–51, 201–2n28
Lejeune, Philippe, 13
Liberación, 51
liberal individualism: and capitalism, 38–39; and first-person personal narrative, 6–7; and racism, 56, 66, 94; rejection of, 2, 56–57. See also individualism/collective consciousness tension; matrixed subjectivity
Libretti, Tim, 105
Lifshey, Adam, 141
La Liga Puertorriqueña e Hispana, 51
The Line of the Sun (Ortiz Cofer), 116, 120–33; critics on, 122–24; and diaspora, 117–20, 124–25, 131–32, 133; *la facultad* in, 101–2; gender oppression in, 124; genre in, 26; insurgent nationalism in, 20; intergender coalitions in, 128–29; intersecting identities in, 116–17, 119; narrative in, 121–22, 128, 210nn19, 20; nonnormative masculinity in, 125–28, 133; plot in, 120–22; political action in, 11, 121; queer identity in, 129–30; transgressive female characters in, 130–33, 210n23
Lipsitz, George, 7, 31, 54, 140
Little Steel Strike (1937), 35, 199n6
Lloyd, David, 33, 61, 196n16
Locke, John, 200n13
López-Springfield, Consuelo, 64
Lo que el pueblo me dice: Cronicas de la colonia puertorriqueña en Nueva York (Colón), 52
Lora, Federíco, 21
Lowenstein, Adam, 136
Luis, William, 68–69, 70, 74
LULAC (League of United Latin American Citizens), 89
Lyotard, Jean-François, 212n13

Maceo Grajales, Antonio, 57, 58
Machado Sáez, Elena, 5, 6, 137, 158, 161, 195–96n7
machismo, 102–3, 106, 207–8n2. See also gender oppression

Macpherson, C. B., 200n13
Madero, Francisco I., 199n8
Madero Revolt, 35, 40, 45, 48, 199n8
Mainstream, 51
Malcolm X, 65, 76, 77, 78
MALDEF (Mexican American Legal Defense and Education Fund), 36, 89
La Malinche, 43
Márquez, Antonio C., 30
Marshall, Joanna Barszewska, 122–23
Martell, Esperanza, 103, 208n4
Martí, José, 50, 57, 167, 168
Marxism, 163, 197n16
masculinism. *See* gender oppression; homophobia
matrixed subjectivity, 2, 6–8; in *Barrio Boy*, 38; in *Down These Mean Streets*, 66, 71; and first-person personal narrative, 7, 8–9; Gramsci on, 9–10; and new millennial authors, 175; and oppositional consciousness, 8; in *A Puerto Rican in New York*, 53–54, 57–58, 59
Maximilian (emperor of Mexico), 45, 201nn22, 23
McCarthyism, and Colón, 31, 35, 52
McCracken, Ellen, 141, 142, 212n14
melancholia, 163, 214n23
memory, 160, 161–62
Menchú, Rigoberta, 11
Méndez, Serafín, 157
Merced, Jorge B., 103–4
Merchants of Labor (Galarza), 36
Mesa Blanca, 122, 210n21. *See also* spiritism
mestizaje, 85, 173, 187, 188
Mexican American Legal Defense and Education Fund (MALDEF), 36, 89
Mexican Civil War, 45
Mexican Revolution (1910–20), 44–45, 49, 198n4

Mignolo, Walter, 20, 140
migration: in *Caramelo*, 178; from Dominican Republic, 149, 211n8, 213n18; and national-transnational triangulation, 183, 215n10. *See also* Puerto Rican migration
Mills, Charles, 13–14, 29, 73, 200n13
minor literature, 37–38
MINP (El Comité/Movimiento de Izquierda Nacional Puertorriqueño), 21, 208n4
Mirabal sisters, 144–45, 156–57
The Miraculous Day of Amalia Gómez (Rechy), 110, 113–14, 208nn6, 10
misogyny. *See* gender oppression
modernism, 114
Moore, Burton, 83, 90
Moraga, Cherríe, 105
Mosse, George, 104
Moya, Paula, 19
Muhammad, Elijah, 77
multifaceted subjectivity. *See* matrixed subjectivity
multivocality, 144–45
Muñoz, José, 15, 19
Muñoz Marín, Luis, 195n5

National Farm Labor Union (NFLU), 36
National Farm Workers Union, 197n21
nationalism: in *Barrio Boy*, 39–40; CIO-era, 33–34; and diaspora, 117–20, 138; hemispheric, 167–68; and homophobia, 104; and imagined community, 16, 18, 39, 101, 133, 171, 188–89; and intergroup coalitions, 57; new millennium, 171–74; and political action, 33–35; and postnationalism, 18, 172. *See also* insurgent nationalism; national-transnational triangulation

nationality: and movement, 183, 215n9; and Puerto Rican/African American triangulation, 71–72, 76
national-transnational triangulation, 177–89; and Chicana/o movement, 187–88; and class, 215n11; and home, 178–79, 185–86, 189; and imagined community, 188–89; and *mestizaje*, 187, 188; and migration, 183, 215n10; and movement, 181–83, 186, 188; and plot of *Caramelo*, 177–79; and racism, 183–84, 215n11; and rebozo symbol, 185
Nation of Islam, 76–77, 78
Negrón-Muntaner, Frances, 19, 53, 197n22, 205n14
Neruda, Pablo, 58
New Left, 105
new millennial authors, 171–72, 174–77, 195n6. See also *Caramelo*
New School Puerto Rican literature, 69
Noble, David W., 173–74
nonviolent resistance, 89–90, 206nn26–28
Numbers (Rechy), 105
Nuyorican movement: and Colón, 52; and diaspora, 131–32; in *Down These Mean Streets*, 2, 65, 68; and Ortiz Cofer, 120, 209n16

Oboler, Suzanne, 20
Ocasio, Rafael, 119–20
Old School Puerto Rican literature, 69
Olney, James, 6
Omi, Michael, 23
Operation Bootstrap, 4, 30, 62, 195n5, 198n4, 209n17
oppositional consciousness: and Aztec warrior icon, 110, 208n10; in *Barrio Boy*, 41–45, 49–50, 200–201n20; and criminality, 78; and Cultural Front, 24; and diaspora, 119; in *Down These Mean Streets*, 22, 69, 74–75, 76–77; and education, 42, 44–46, 200n18; and first-person personal narrative, 8; and gay culture, 111–12, 208n11; and intersecting identities, 115–16; and matrixed subjectivity, 8; and new millennial authors, 176; Ortiz Cofer on, 209n14; and prison experience, 67–68, 76–77, 204n1; and Puerto Rican/African American triangulation, 2, 22, 69, 74–75, 76–77; in *The Sexual Outlaw*, 109, 110–12, 115–16; and transgression, 124; and *vato loco*/gangster figure, 85–86, 87–88, 89–90, 91–92. See also political action
organic intellectuals, 35, 51, 199n7
Ortiz Cofer, Judith: on diaspora, 119–20; and home, 185; and insurgent nationalism, 5; life of, 117; on oppositional consciousness, 209n14; works: *Silent Dancing: A Partial Remembrance of a Puerto Rican Childhood*, 117; *Woman in Front of the Sun: On Becoming a Writer*, 117, 120. See also *The Line of the Sun*
outlaw figure. See sexual outlaw figure; transgression; *vato loco*/gangster figure

pachuco (zoot suit) culture, 63, 204n6
Padilla, Genaro, 8, 83, 84, 196n9, 206n23
Paredes, Américo, 62, 109
Paredes, Raymund, 37, 83, 84, 85
patriarchy. See gender oppression
Patterson, Orlando, 23
Peaches, Peter, 87, 88
Peirce, Charles Sanders, 3–4
The People of Paper (Plascencia), 174, 177

The People's Weekly World, 202n30
People v. Castro (East LA Thirteen), 83, 88
Pérez-Torres, Rafael, 85, 86, 106, 108, 109, 140
Phelan, James, 185–86
Piñero, Miguel, 68, 204n1
El Pipila, 44, 201n21
El Plan de Santa Barbara, 206n29
Plascencia, Salvador, 176, 195n6; *The People of Paper*, 174, 177
play, 2, 195n2
political action, 23–25; Acosta, 83–84, 197n21; in *Barrio Boy*, 11, 24, 29–30; Colón, 51, 197n21, 202n32; and education, 90–91, 92, 206n29; Galarza, 36, 197n21; Gramsci on, 9–10, 11, 196n10; and intergroup coalitions, 21; in *The Line of the Sun*, 11, 121; and nationalism, 33–35; nonviolent resistance, 89–90, 206nn26–28; and state violence, 95–96; and *testimonio*, 11; Thomas, 203–4n1; and *vato loco*/gangster figure, 84–85, 92; violent struggle, 12, 31, 89–90, 110, 206n28. *See also* Chicana/o movement; insurgent nationalism; oppositional consciousness
political autobiography, 12
pop culture, 179
Popular Front, 30, 31–32, 33–34, 44
postmodernism, 69, 140–41, 143, 212n13
postnationalism, 18, 172
postracial era/literature, 171, 175–77, 214n1
post-sixties literature, 5, 195–96n7
prison experience, 67–68, 76–77, 204n1. *See also* criminality; criminalization of racial minorities
property. *See* capitalism

proto-Borderlands consciousness, 37–38
PRSU (Puerto Rican Student Union), 54
PSP (Puerto Rican Socialist Party), 103, 202n29
public art, 55–56, 203n37
Los Pueblos Hispanos, 51
Puerto Rican/African American triangulation, 1–2, 65; and colonialism, 72; and distance from Puerto Rico, 2, 195n3; and family life, 73–74; and gender oppression, 82, 205–6n20; and hybridity, 69; and indigeneity, 70, 74, 205n16; and nationality, 71–72, 76; and oppositional consciousness, 2, 22, 69, 74–75, 76–77; and phenotype, 75; and play, 1–2, 195n2; and political action, 69; and racial/ethnic binary identities, 69; and racism, 2, 68–69, 72–73, 74, 205n15; and *vato loco*/gangster figure, 78. *See also* intergroup coalitions
Puerto Rican identity: and criminalization, 67; and racism, 66; and transnationalism, 197n22; and urbanization, 62, 204n3; and *West Side Story*, 205n14. See also *Down These Mean Streets*; *The Line of the Sun*; Puerto Rican/African American triangulation; *A Puerto Rican in New York*
A Puerto Rican in New York (Colón), 29–33, 52–60; cultural production in, 54, 58–59; disruption of racial/ethnic binaries in, 14; foreword to, 52; genre in, 11–12, 53; and insurgent nationalism, 29, 52, 54–57; intergroup coalitions in, 57–58; matrixed subjectivity in, 53–54,

57–58, 59; political action in, 24; on public art, 55–56, 203n37; rejection of liberal individualism in, 56–57

Puerto Rican migration: and diaspora, 117–18, 119, 120; history of, 195n5, 198n4, 209n15; and illegal labor recruiters, 121, 209n17; and racism, 62–63, 66

Puerto Rican Socialist Party (PSP), 103, 202n29

Puerto Rican Student Union (PRSU), 54

Puerto Rico, 2, 4, 195n5, 209n17. *See also* Puerto Rican identity

Puri, Shalini, 18–19, 171, 172–73, 174

Pynchon, Thomas, 140

queer identity: critique of, 111–12, 208n11; and gay liberation movements, 104, 113, 114; and gender oppression disruption, 129–30; and marginalization, 112–14; and violence, 130. *See also* homophobia; *The Sexual Outlaw*

Quijano, Anibal, 140

Quinn, Anthony, 91

Quintero Rivera, Angel G., 50, 202n29

race/ethnicity: and Alvarez's writings, 139, 150–51, 212n11; and Communist Party USA, 198–99n5; in *Down These Mean Streets*, 68–71; and sexual outlaw figure, 114–15; and Trujillo regime, 139, 150, 212n10. *See also* racial/ethnic binary identities; racism

racial/ethnic binary identities, 195n4, 196n13; in *Down These Mean Streets*, 69, 71–72; and gender oppression, 69; and nationality, 72; and Puerto Rican/African American triangulation, 69; and racism, 13–14; and *vato loco*/gangster figure, 67–68

"Racial Exclusion" (Acosta), 204n7

racial stereotypes, 1–2, 53, 56, 66, 205n14

racism: Colón on, 203n34; criminalization of racial minorities, 16, 67–68, 204–5n12; and education, 46–49, 201n24; and family life, 73–74; and gender oppression, 102–3, 207–8n2; and generative contradictions, 15; and immigration, 183–84, 213n18; and intergroup coalitions, 21, 113; and Latina/o urbanization, 62–63, 66, 88; and liberal individualism, 56, 66, 94; and national-transnational triangulation, 183–84, 215n11; new millennial situation, 171, 214n1; and postracial era, 171, 175, 214n1; and Puerto Rican/African American triangulation, 2, 68–69, 72–73, 74, 205n15; and racial/ethnic binary identities, 13–14; racial stereotypes, 1–2, 53, 56, 66, 205n14; and sociology discipline, 75, 205n17; and urban redevelopment, 63, 204n4; urban/rural distinctions, 88

Ramparsad, Arnold, 198n5

Raza Unida Party, 25, 30, 197n21, 206n22

Rechy, John: and alienation, 109, 208n6; critics on, 208n5; and *testimonio*, 11, 12; works: *City of Night*, 105; *The Miraculous Day of Amalia Gómez*, 110, 113–14, 208nn6, 10; *Numbers*, 105; *This Day's Death*, 105. *See also The Sexual Outlaw*

Reddin, Thomas, 87
redemption narrative, 65
Reid Cabral, Donald, 211n8
Reid-Pharr, Robert, 79, 80
representing relations, 3–4
The Revolt of the Cockroach People (Acosta), 83–98; critics on, 83, 84–85, 96–97, 206n23; definitions of *vato loco* figure in, 86–87; as first-person personal narrative, 83–84, 94; gender oppression/homophobia in, 86, 96–97; generative contradictions in, 15, 196n15; genre in, 25–26; Gilbert as epitome of *vato loco* figure, 207n30; individualism/collective consciousness tension in, 16, 64–65, 93–94; intergroup coalitions in, 21, 92–93, 207n32; nonviolent resistance in, 89–90, 206nn26, 28; oppositional consciousness in, 85–86, 87–88, 89–90, 91–92; protagonist of, 206n24; state violence in, 94–96, 207n33; St. Basil's protest in, 91, 93, 207n31; and *testimonio*, 12; urban/rural distinctions in, 88–89, 206n25
revolutionary consciousness. *See* oppositional consciousness
Reyes, Celaya, 175
Rivera, Carmen Vivian, 103
Rivera, Diego, 58
Rodríguez, Juana María, 19
Rodríguez, Richard, 13, 38, 114, 209nn12, 13
Rodriguez Deynes, Neysa, 157
Rosaldo, Renato, 37–38
Rushdie, Salman, 140

sadomasochism (S&M), 111–12, 208n11
Saldívar, José, 107–8, 109, 120, 208n10
Saldívar, Ramón, 9, 38, 44, 83, 175–76, 195n6, 206n23
Saldívar-Hull, Sonia, 1, 17, 33, 64, 103
Sánchez, Marta, 26, 69–70, 79
Sánchez, Rosaura, 206n25
Sánchez González, Lisa, 5, 33, 64, 69, 70, 123, 124, 127
Sánchez Korrol, Virginia, 51, 52, 57, 195n5, 202n29
Sandoval, Chela, 17, 19, 20, 64, 140
San Francisco General Strike (1934), 34–35, 199n6
Santana Familias, Pedro, 214n25
Santería, 121, 122, 209–10n18. *See also* spiritism
Schomburg, Arturo, 50, 52, 57, 69, 203n34
self-reliance ideology. *See* liberal individualism
semiotics, 3–4
sexism. *See* gender oppression
sexual oppression. *See* homophobia
The Sexual Outlaw (Rechy), 105–16; Aztec warrior icon in, 109–10; critics on, 107–8; dualism in, 108–9; *la facultad* in, 101–2; as first-person personal narrative, 109, 208nn7, 8; generative contradictions in, 15, 105, 196n15; genre in, 105–6, 112; individualism/collective consciousness tension in, 113–14; insurgent nationalism in, 20, 106; intergroup coalitions in, 21–22, 106–7, 112; intersecting identities in, 109, 115–16; marginalization in, 112–14; oppositional consciousness in, 109, 110–12, 115–16; political action in, 11; protagonist of, 106; race/ethnicity in, 114–15
sexual outlaw figure, 106; as Aztec warrior, 109–10; definition, 196n15;

and generative contradictions, 15, 16; and oppositional consciousness, 109, 110–11, 112; and race/ethnicity, 114–15
Shorris, Earl, 20
Silent Dancing: A Partial Remembrance of a Puerto Rican Childhood (Ortiz Cofer), 117
Sklodowska, Elzbieta, 11
S&M (sadomasochism), 111–12, 208n11
Smethurst, James, 64, 84–85, 90
Smith, Sidonie, 6–7
socialism, 39, 69, 200n12
Sociedad Fraternal Cervantes, 51
Socolovsky, Maya, 123–24
solidarity. *See* intergroup coalitions
Sommer, Doris, 10, 11, 128, 167, 196n10
Southern Tenant Farmers Union (STFU), 35, 36. *See also* National Farm Labor Union
Spanish language, 46–47, 120, 148, 179–80, 213n17
Spiders in the House, Workers in the Field (Galarza), 36
spiritism, 121, 122, 131, 209–10nn18, 21
Stanchich, Maritza, 52
state violence, 94–96, 207n33
Stavans, Ilan, 83
St. Basil's protest (1969), 91, 93, 207n31
Steinbeck, John, 113
STFU (Southern Tenant Farmers Union), 35, 36. *See also* National Farm Labor Union
storytelling, 153–56, 166
Suarez, Ray, 215n9
syncretism, 120, 132, 185, 209–10n18

tabaquero culture, 50–51, 201–2nn28, 29
testimonio, 11–12, 158
This Day's Death (Rechy), 105

Thomas, Piri: and criminality, 65, 66–67; life of, 65, 204n1; "The World of Piri Thomas: Poet, Writer, a Voice for Unity," 66–67. *See also Down These Mean Streets*
Thompson, Hunter S., 83, 206n21
Toña la Negra, 179
Tongolele, 179
Torres, Lourdes, 7
Torres-Saillant, Silvio, 52
Tragedy at Chualar: El crucero de las treinta y dos cruces (Galarza), 36
transgression, 116, 117; in *Barrio Boy*, 37–38; in *Caramelo*, 180; critics on, 122–24; and diaspora, 118, 122–23, 124–25; and gender, 125–31; and narrative, 124; and oppositional consciousness, 124; and plot of *The Line of the Sun*, 120–21; and queer identity, 129–30; and spiritism, 122
transnationalism: and American studies, 214n4; and heritage culture, 179; and insurgent nationalism, 18–19, 25, 172, 173–74; and new millennial authors, 171–72; and pop culture, 179; and Puerto Rican identity, 197n22. *See also* national-transnational triangulation
travel narratives, 180
triangulation, 3–4. *See also* national-transnational triangulation; Puerto Rican/African American triangulation; *specific texts*
Trujillo, Ramfis, 139
Trujillo regime, 135, 210n1; and class, 139–40; Mirabal sisters, 144–45, 156–57; and race, 139, 150, 212n10; and sexual conquest, 139, 211n7. *See also* historical trauma
twenty-first century authors. *See* new millennial authors

UFW (United Farm Workers), 89
Ulysses (Joyce), 114
United Farm Workers (UFW), 89, 206n27, 207n31, 208n4
urban gangster figure. See *vato loco/gangster* figure
urban redevelopment, 63, 204n4
Urban Renewal Program, 204n4
Ureña, Salomé, 163
U.S. hegemony: and Dominican Republic, 139, 151, 152, 211n8; and education, 45; and ethnocentrism, 58–59; and Latina/o identity, 22; and Puerto Rican migration, 195n5, 198n4; and Puerto Rico, 2, 4, 195n5, 209n17. See also colonialism

Valdez, Luis, 109
Vasconcelos, José, 184
vato loco/gangster figure, 61–65, 67–68, 84–98; and Californios, 98; and criminalization of racial minorities, 16, 67–68; critics on, 84–85; definitions of, 86–87, 196n15; and gender oppression/homophobia, 63, 64, 86, 97, 204n7; and generative contradictions, 15, 16; Gilbert as epitome of, 207n30; and ideology, 63–64, 96; and individualism/collective consciousness tension, 16, 64–65, 93–94; and Latina/o community changes, 62–63; and mutability, 87; and nonviolent resistance, 89–90; and oppositional consciousness, 85–86, 87–88, 89–90, 91–92; and pachuco (zoot suit) culture, 63, 204n6; and political action, 84–85, 92; and Puerto Rican/African American triangulation, 78;

and state violence, 94–96; and urban/rural distinctions, 88–89; and violent struggle, 89–90, 206n28
Vega, Bernardo, 50, 51, 68, 69, 201n28
violence: and gender oppression, 79; and homophobia, 79–81, 130; and political action, 12, 31, 89–90, 110, 206n28; state, 94–96, 207n33
La Voz, 51

Waldron, John V., 126
Walters, Wendy, 118, 119
Watson, Julia, 6–7
Watts Riots (1965), 87, 207n32
The Way It Was and Other Writings (Colón), 52
West Side Story, 53, 56, 66, 71, 205n14
Williams, William Carlos, 69
Winant, Howard, 23
witnessing, 160–61, 213n21. See also historical trauma
Woman in Front of the Sun: On Becoming a Writer (Ortiz Cofer), 117, 120
The Worker, 51, 202n30
"The World of Jesus Colón" (Acosta-Belén and Sánchez Korrol), 52
"The World of Piri Thomas: Poet, Writer, a Voice for Unity" (Thomas), 66–67
Wright, Richard, 118, 198n5

¡Yo! (Alvarez), 135, 152–56, 212n11
Yorty, Sam, 87, 88
Younger, Evelle, 87, 88
Young Lords, 14, 23, 54, 197n22, 208n3

Zapata, Emiliano, 40
zoot suit (pachuco) culture, 63, 204n6
Zoot Suit Riots, 30

DAVID J. VÁZQUEZ is assistant professor of English at the University of Oregon. *Triangulations* is his first book.

www.ingramcontent.com/pod-product-compliance
Lightning Source LLC
Chambersburg PA
CBHW031807220426
43662CB00007B/558